Gui Ren

Extraordinary Stories of Ordinary People

Erin O'Neil

Printed in the United States of America
10 9 8 7 6 5 4 3 2 1

ISBN 978-1-7333380-0-4

Library of Congress Control Number: 2019910412

The stories in this work are from the experiences of the author and represent only one perspective. Certain names and identifying characteristics have been changed or omitted out of respect for the individuals involved.

Fishtail Publishing LLC
www.OnMyList.org

Cover Design Consulting by Eric & Christina Irvin

Dedicated to You

| To a life of epic adventure, unconditional love, & meaningful connections |

To Mary —
And to the people, places,
and experiences that make
us who we are.
Here's to adventure!

and experiences that make

Gui Ren

/ Gui Rɛn /

Gui Ren is a written Chinese phrase that encompasses the synchronicity of people entering your life with purposeful timing to help guide you through difficult challenges.

Introduction

This is the story of a journey that took 34,613 miles, 27 flights, 9 trains, 4 visas, 29 passport stamps, and 183 days. It was a journey of 10 countries, 15 cities, and 1 post-graduate dream gone wrong. This book is about travel, but it is not a travel book. Yes, the word 'plane' is mentioned 36 times, and, yes, I talk an awful lot about language barriers and cultural immersion. But this book is about people. It's about the stories we tell, the stories we learn, and the stories we leave behind. It's about my *Gui Ren*, the people who synchronistically appeared on my path to guide me through some of the most challenging moments in my life. It's about the people with whom I connected regardless of ethnic background, social class, professional title, skin color, or even native language. *Gui Ren* is about the authentic relationships we establish with others when we remember that, underneath it all, we are one thing: human.

This story did not start in Asia. No, like any good story there was time spent on plot construction and character development. There was 22 years worth of preparation for this adventure in the form of education, career planning, and relationships. I grew up in the suburbs of Columbus, Ohio, but that was not the only city that shaped the individual I was destined to become. Throughout high school and college I had opportunities to travel and explore that began to feed my wanderlust and taste for adventure. It was in Concepción, Chile in 2010 that I first discovered the phenomenal connections achieved through travel, and in Toulouse, France I learned how thrilling it can be to step outside your comfort zones. During a collegiate semester-long study abroad program in Western Europe, I gained experience in navigating a foreign city alone and letting the tides of life take me on spontaneous adventures.

Over the 22 years I spent unknowingly preparing for what Asia would bring into my life in 2017, I developed a hunger for new challenges, unfamiliar lands, and conversations with people from all over the world. I had a thirst for life-changing experiences that forced me to question my perceptions and try something new. But the person I was before I moved to Asia was not quite the same person that returned six months later. Stories are about adapting, learning, and transitioning. So this story would simply be incomplete without knowing the individual I was before leaving my hometown in Columbus in pursuit of travel, adventure, and connection. Let's start at the beginning.

My mom always knew that she wanted to be a nurse, my grandmother was destined to be an educator, and my best friend from high school knew she would one day work in veterinary medicine. When I was little, I wanted to be an astronaut who danced on the moon. My aspirations were literally out of this world and it didn't end with childhood. When I was in middle school I had plans to become a lawyer to represent the underserved. During my freshman year of high school I had my heart set on New York University and Broadway. By junior year, marketing and business had caught my attention. After a year at Butler University in Indianapolis, I switched from international relations to journalism. And by the time I graduated, I had a degree in digital media production. Maintaining course was not exactly my calling. I am what some might refer to as a

'Multipotentialite;' that is, someone with many interests and creative pursuits. I do whatever my heart calls me to do and my Type-A personality helps carry me to the finish line.

So as I sat in a coffee shop the winter before graduating from college, I stared at several job postings on my computer. Marketing director, event coordinator, videographer and editor, travel agent, and content creator; all conceivable paths, but none of them sparked anything. I knew that I would be capable of taking on any opportunity I wanted, but none of the current contenders tugged at my heart. I sat there pining over my blank five-year plan and suddenly came to recognize one common thread in each of my variable interests: a desire to create meaning in the everyday moments. Whether it was designing a memorable moment for a client on their big day, introducing the world to a new perspective through creative video, or sending someone to their dream destination across the globe, I wanted to find and create that spark. I wanted something meaningful, something that would leave greater impact than a standard 9-5, something that existed somewhere outside the boundaries of the job descriptions that stared back at me from my computer screen.

During the first semester of my junior year at Butler University, I discovered the *National Geographic* Digital Storytelling Fellowship. Winners of the grant receive funding to conduct in-depth research in up to three different countries while producing stories of global change through multimedia publications. Without any other plan for graduation, and desiring future work in any field related to my degree in digital media production, I figured this would be an impressive start to my post-graduate career. It would mean actively pursuing three of my passions: travel, storytelling, and creating that spark. I listed out a variety of topics that would interest me and ultimately came to rest on developing an application to study environmental sustainability and its effect on happiness around the world. Like I said, my interests have no limitations.

My plan was to conduct studies in three dissimilar countries around the globe on a scale of most sustainable to the least. Among potential contenders were Sweden, Denmark, China, and India. So, at the very beginning of my second semester, when I stumbled upon a university-led program that would take a group of Butler students to Shanghai, China for a six-week internship in the industry of their choosing, I immediately applied. I knew it would not only be an exciting adventure, but would also demonstrate a committed interest to the *National Geographic* review board. Upon being accepted into the Butler University study abroad program, I requested an internship within the field of environmentalism and social responsibility.

That summer, I spent six weeks in Shanghai, China working for an entrepreneur who had started a business in corporate responsibility and environmental consulting. Utilizing my academic studies in digital media, I provided the company with video production services, audiovisual equipment support, infographic design, and photography. I assisted in developing what would be the first episodes in a series of interviews with sustainability leaders from all over the world. We spoke with businessmen and women, innovators, incubators, and young leaders of tomorrow about their efforts in reducing waste and creating positive change within the scope of environmental sustainability. I not only gained knowledge about corporate responsibility and business management, but also meaningful insight into creating, building, and maintaining a business and life filled with purpose. As I listened to successful entrepreneurs tell of their grit and determination, and as they exuded genuine passion with every sentence they spoke, I began to crave a unique path of my own. I wanted their spark and originality. I just didn't know how to get it.

While in China I had the fortunate opportunity of getting to know one of my distant cousins and his wife. Dagan and Bree had settled in Shanghai for a few years after having traveled all over the world for career opportunities with DreamWorks Animation. Before ever having met them, I deeply admired their adventurous spirits. They were pursuing their career goals while taking thrilling vacations and managing to start a family amidst the chaos; their daughter was born in India and their son in China. Throughout the course of a few dinners and outings together in Shanghai, I gained worldly insight and career advice from two people I soon came to idolize.

During one particular dinner, Dagan and I discussed creativity and entrepreneurship. As I hemmed and hawed over my many potential career paths he openly encouraged me to take risks and seize opportunities while I'm still young. He reinforced with confidence that now was the time to put both myself and my ideas out there without a fear of failure. All I knew was that I wanted to tell stories that would inspire and impact positive change, but I hadn't yet found the spark.

Dagan set down his drink and leaned in. "What is your goal in telling these stories, Erin? Why do you want to do it?"

I stumbled over my thoughts. "I want to change people's lives."

He nodded, "Then you need to find a way to do it that is unlike any other method out there. You need to be bold."

We soon found ourselves diving into a deep conversation about storytelling, popular media, and social psychology. He brought up how, most often, successful international films have more spectacle than substance; more explosions, faster cars, hotter actors, flashier sets, and more dynamic soundtracks.

"Meaning is not made with spectacle," he said. "The most moving films are ones that don't require all the extra 'stuff' to engage an audience."

I considered how his observation directly reflected so many of society's challenges with consumerism. When material belongings are the definition of success, and the number of followers is more important than the content, who cares if you're a happy or developed individual?

Dagan continued by pointing out that storytellers need to identify what makes their content unique or interesting to the average viewer.

"Take *National Geographic* as an example," he started. "No one knew they needed such immersive looks into wildlife, history, and culture until Nat Geo introduced them to it. They made an otherwise inaccessible world accessible to all, and that alone created meaning."

People were riveted when *National Geographic* provided them an up-close and personal view of wild animals, not because they needed it, necessarily, but because it was new and invigorating.

Dagan continued, "I like watching documentaries because I'm constantly searching for the unexpected lion in *National Geographic*. I want to find the perspective or piece of information that hasn't yet been aired by any other storyteller or media outlet."

And then he said something I never expected. "Whatever you do, don't become a McDonald's." I looked at him blankly.

He continued, "McDonald's reaches millions worldwide, but with what substance? They aren't changing your life every time you walk through the door. They're selling you a quick fix for your immediate hunger."

Dagan took another sip of his drink. "Think about the times you've visited a smaller, family-owned restaurant. In that setting, they can create a more intimate environment and they have the opportunity to make your experience unique. They can leave a lasting impression."

He motioned for the waiter to bring the check as he finished his thought. "You just can't make a meaningful impact if you're a McDonald's."

Dagan encouraged me to identify my lion; to figure out what it is that is new or unique about my story or perspective that will capture an audience's attention. While there are billions of people worldwide buying into spectacle and entertainment, there are still those seeking mind-opening and personally meaningful content. I just had to figure out what my story was and how I was going to tell it....

At the end of my six-week internship, I was putting the final touches on a few video projects when my boss, whom I shall refer to as 'R,' told me that my contributions to his company were only just beginning. He said my work ethic and quality output was exactly what he needed on his team, and offered to pay for me to remain in Shanghai. It was difficult to decline the offer; I had located my dream job before I'd even earned my undergraduate degree. But the timing wasn't right and I was hardly prepared for an extended stay, so I returned home. As a compromise, I continued editing videos for R remotely as I finished my studies in the States. He received the edits he needed, and I continued to watch and learn from leaders around the world.

I never applied to the *National Geographic* Digital Storytelling Fellowship. I found myself overwhelmed with the topic and utterly directionless. The proposal was stressing me out, not because I couldn't handle the work but because it ultimately wasn't authentic to my passions. I realized that I wanted to pursue the topic of sustainability and happiness for the wrong reason: because it meant I could travel. It was interesting, I won't deny that, but committing to a nine-month research project I wasn't passionate about would have been much more daunting than buying a plane ticket. If travel was what I wanted, I was going to have to find it elsewhere.

I sat in a campus coffee shop on a particularly cold winter afternoon, sensing graduation looming just around the corner. I stared at the job postings open on my laptop and, in a moment of frustration for not having an answer or a clear path, decided to put my post-graduate job search on hold. I gave myself until March 1st of 2017 just to enjoy my senior year and focus on the cluster of video projects I had already started. In the months leading up to graduation, I produced a series of study abroad student spotlights for my capstone project and worked with the

Domestic Violence Network in Indianapolis to produce their 20th anniversary video. I continued to run camera for live sports productions on Butler's campus, and spent what little free time I had socializing with my friends. Little did I know that without much effort, and without any warning, my post-graduate opportunity of a lifetime was headed my way.

Home Sweet Shanghai

Fist Bumps & Airplane Food

Friends can help each other. A true friend is someone who lets you have total freedom to be yourself. That's what real love amounts to - letting a person be what he really is.

~ Jim Morrison ~

In February of 2017, just a few months before graduating from Butler University, I woke up to an unexpected email in my inbox:

"Hey Erin.

Wanted to run something by you. Call it a proposal.

Given the work we did last summer, and have done recently, I wanted to see if you were interested in coming back to Asia on a short term (post-graduate) project. The project being very simply to follow me around Asia as I do my thing, to support me interviewing people, and to build what I hope will be an amazing Youtube channel filled with inspirational stories and projects.

It would add a number of new stamps into your passport as I set up meetings, events, interview entrepreneurs, and rant my way through HK, Singapore, Bangkok, Jakarta, Taipei, and a few other places.

Expenses obviously covered. Equipment provided. Salary to be discussed. Awesome shit guaranteed.

Now. I know you know that I have whacky ideas, and I know that you probably have better offers, but if you are keen let me know. You are my first ask because I know that you will hustle like hell and will find the adventure fulfilling, which is what it requires.

So, hoping you are interested.. and if so, let's find a time to talk in the coming week or two.

Hope all is well,

R"

My eyes scanned to the bottom of the email as I simultaneously leapt for joy and became filled with a crippling anxiety. My heart didn't know whether to be thankful that my job search was over, or panicked at the thought of accepting an offer that would take me so far away from home. I'd always dreamed of traveling the world, meeting new people, and creating videos that would inspire and celebrate new perspectives and positive social change. But with the opportunity resting in my inbox, I was overcome with fear. *What if I fail? What if I get lost? What if I can't come home when my family needs me? What if I can't afford my student loans? What if I get sick? What if, what if, what if….*

But then Hayley, one of my best friends from college, brought my unproductive train of thought to a screeching halt when she asked, "First reaction, no thinking, where do you see yourself after graduation?"

And I heard myself say, "China."

My friends and family were incredibly supportive of my desire to move to Asia. They were all excited for the adventures, the stories, and the possibility of networking with just the right person to find my next big opportunity. But there was one person in particular who confidently reassured me that what I was about to do would change my life forever in more ways than one. I met Josh at a New Year's Eve party back home in Columbus, Ohio, just hours before the most exhilarating year of my life would begin. He was well-dressed, handsome, and had the kindest of eyes. He had been standing against the wall drinking punch from a red Solo Cup and listening as our mutual friends delved into a discussion about the social and mental implications of virtual reality being introduced to the consumer market. Oh, did I mention all my friends are huge nerds? As the debate was reaching its peak, I made a comment about how virtual reality is essentially an illusion because, regardless of how accurate a recreation, no two people can experience anything the same exact way. Our background, culture, experiences, and perspectives, make every individual's perception unique and inimitable. Josh smiled and leaned across the group, holding out his fist. As I hit my knuckles against his I could feel my face turn 37 shades of hot pink. It was love at first fist bump.

Josh and I talked nonstop for the next several months. Our friendship flourished despite living three hours apart; he remained back home in Columbus while I continued my education in Indianapolis. One weekend in March I went home to visit him and we spent an afternoon playing soccer in the park, eating ice cream, listening to Ed Sheeran, and watching the new "Beauty and the Beast". We played several of his virtual reality games, and he showed me his 3D printer and extensive collection of Rubiks cubes. He was a total nerd, but a cute one, and I was hooked. At two o'clock in the morning, after I still hadn't motivated myself to leave his house, we sat together talking, and I admitted my hesitancy about moving to Asia.

"Josh, I'm not sure if I should do it... I feel like I would be missing out on so much back home. Plus, after the job is over, I just have to restart my job search. I feel like I'm making a mistake."

Deep down I knew that I was making excuses. If I decided to move to China, the feelings I had developed for him would have to be set aside. No one in their right mind would start a brand new relationship in these circumstances. In my head, his response to my self-doubt would tell me precisely how he felt.

"You should go," he said. "It's such an amazing opportunity... Just imagine the adventures you'll have to share when you get back!"

I wasn't sure if this was his way of supporting my passion or telling me our romantic relationship had no future. Was there any chance that his words of encouragement were of affection, rather than disinterest?

A month later Josh visited me in Indianapolis, and after an evening walk through Butler University's campus we sat in my bedroom. I could sense the energy between us, and it both enthralled and terrified me.

Bubbling up from within my stomach were the words, "I think we're making a mistake."

He looked at me, puzzled. "What do you mean?"

"Josh, I like you, a lot. But I'm moving to China in two months. What are we doing?" I looked down at my hands.

He suddenly stood up and said, "I have a few things for you. Pick a number: 1, 2, or 3?"

I sat there stunned. Had my admission of fear meant nothing to him? "Ummmm, 2?"

He handed me a tall purple bottle shaped like a cat, with a cork sticking up at the top.

"I heard you like wine," he said, winking at me. Despite my confusion, I gushed happily over the unique shape of the bottle. At least I would have wine to help cope with whatever was coming next.

He looked at me eagerly, "Okay, 1 or 3?"

"1, I guess."

He handed me a Rubiks cube. "I figured you might be bored on the plane, and it's about time you learn how to solve one. But I got you one without stickers because I knew you'd just try to take them off." He looked at me sternly, "That's cheating, Erin." He already knew me so well.

There was only one gift left. I watched as he pulled from his backpack a beautiful ribbon-bound notebook decorated with the image of an antique map on the front. I opened the cover to find it filled with handmade paper. He sat on the bed beside me, handed me an ink pen and said, "This is for your trip. I can't wait to hear about all your adventures."

I looked at him with tears in my eyes.

He took one of my hands in his own. "Erin, I've waited my whole life for you. What's another six months?"

As I boarded the plane to Shanghai in June of 2017, I cast aside a clearly defined career path in favor of adventure and the pursuit of storytelling. There was no entry level position, nor series of promotions awaiting my future; just a short-term, six-month position without promise of long-term career benefits. There would be no 401k contributions or health insurance. I voluntarily put an ocean and 13 hours time difference between myself and a brand new relationship. I packed up six months of my life to relocate alone to a land of uncertainty where I couldn't utter so much as "Where is the bathroom?" in the local language. Yet fear was not something that crossed my mind. I was thrilled to take on the adventure alone, excited to explore Asia with a fresh perspective, and starry-eyed at the anticipation of networking with international leaders in business and corporate responsibility. In fact, I was so focused on a year filled with unforgettable experiences, that I almost missed a blatant sign from the universe telling me to give up, turn around, and go home.

I have a strange affinity for anything travel related: hotels, train tickets, suitcases, passport stamps, tiny shampoos, ginger ale (a beverage I only ever order from over 30,000 feet in the air), travel pillows, and airplane food. Yes, I'll admit, I actually enjoy airplane food. Certainly not because of the horrible indigestion or tasteless quality of the so-called, "chicken," but because I get to eat it while buckled into a plane seat watching a documentary I otherwise wouldn't have time for in my daily adult life. Not to mention I get to do both of these things while being transported halfway around the globe. Airplane food brings about a sort of nostalgia that only fellow crazy travel-addicts would likely understand. Nonetheless, I tend to savor the extra bit of me-time that involves a tiny media player strapped to the back of a headrest and eating rice with a plastic spork. Which is why, when my dinner was rudely interrupted by my seat mate not even an hour and a half into our flight, I was - to say the least - disturbed.

A fifteen-hour flight meant I was wearing sweatpants with green fuzzy socks, happily awaiting my first in-flight meal while a documentary about Warren Buffet drowned out the rest of the cabin around me. My petite seat companion and her young son had been watching cartoons since I sat down. I was only beginning to indulge in my microwave delicacy when she began laughing hysterically (and quite obnoxiously loud for a full grown adult) at a children's cartoon which, in my humble opinion and basic knowledge of cartoons, did not appear to be that funny. But I was on a journey of self-discovery that did not involve judging others for their enjoyment of modern enter-tainment. So I let it go.

A few moments later I could feel a cold set of eyes on the right side of my face. In my peripheral I could see my seat mate staring at me; her eyes widened in a fearsome glare that both begged for help and threatened my very existence. Naturally, I did what any awkward person like myself would do and smiled quietly, nodded hello, then returned to my documentary. De-spite my attempt at a cooperative friendship, however, she con-tinued to sit there and glare at me as I struggled to open my brownie with what were now trembling hands. Everyone says airplane desserts are a waste of time, but I wasn't yet convinced.

I kept my head square with the entertainment console as, in my peripheral, I saw her jab her finger in my direction and start speaking rapidly to her son in an Asian dialect. Despite having spent the last hour on the plane surrounded by native speakers, I had not yet managed to learn any of the language, and I had a feeling she wouldn't be willing to type her words into any of my translation apps. So I sat quietly in my seat, uninformed and perplexed. Her finger remained forcibly pointed at my chest as her voice grew louder. I silently scanned the other passengers around me as pairs of horrified eyeballs began to take me in: a young white female donning a cheap airplane headset, a pair of bright green fuzzy socks, and a bit of drool from the unwarranted temptation of her highly processed dessert. I began to panic.

Back when the flight attendant had served our meal, my seat mate could barely communicate with enough English to get out the words "rice" and "orange juice." Yet, somehow, in the amount of time it had taken the fear-induced sweat to thoroughly soak the armpits of my jacket, she had suddenly learned the English language.

My seat mate started spouting off to her son in broken English, "She scary. She want kill us. We kill her first. We have kill her first."

I turned slowly to face her, stunned. And then, without warning, she whipped her head around and stared so deeply into my soul I could feel the chicken and pasta coming right back up.

She gritted her teeth as we locked eyes, "You have die now."

I'd like to say I handled this like a total champ and eloquently expressed my concerns to the flight attendants while maintaining a low profile, but it didn't quite play out like that. I wiggled my way out from the seat as my tray table remained in its meal-time position, and wobbled my way to the nearest flight attendant where I began babbling incessantly. The unsuspecting and kind-eyed older gentleman was, to say the least, caught off guard. The sweat was now dripping down my back and my knees felt like they might give out altogether. The flight attendant approached my seat mate who suddenly started shouting about the giant knife in my bag with which I intended to kill everyone onboard. She also decided it was an opportune time to inform everyone in the near vicinity that she knew how to shoot a gun. Insert the tears of a billion mistakes... here.

My carry-on was carefully searched, a set of passenger restraints were brought out "just in case," and the airline crew discussed emergency landing. And, to top it all off, amidst a thorough search for the supposed giant knife, they instead removed the giant Build-a-Bear stuffed bunny I'd squished in my backpack last minute and handed her to me like you might comfort a four-year-old who had just awoken from a nightmare. They asked me where my parents were, and when I regretfully informed them that I was moving to China alone at the age of 22 I could feel their parental instincts screaming "Who in God's name would send this fragile child to live alone in a foreign country?!"

I was instructed not to return to my seat, or even reenter my assigned cabin, and was instead upgraded to an open first class cubicle - which was perhaps the only major plus of this incredibly traumatizing event. Oh, and they brought me many servings of ice cream without my even asking for it. Guess that's Air Canada for you, eh? I sobbed for three of the remaining thirteen hours in the air, and the rest I spent stuffy-nosed and red-eyed. I knew moving to Asia alone was a mistake. If this wasn't the universe's way of telling me to bail while there was still a chance, I didn't know what was. I had assumed the flight over would be the easiest step in moving overseas, but I was quickly realizing how wrong I had been. For the next handful of grueling hours I spent attempting to preoccupy myself with Bedazzle and I-Spy, a thousand thoughts raced through my head. *Who am I to believe that I'm ready for this? How the heck did I think I was going to move myself to Shanghai for six months and not destroy everything in my path? Do I seriously think I'm that special just because I got invited back to China after one measly six-week internship? Who needs a career anyway? I still might have time to find some cats and rent a small condo in Florida... We could just skip the icky parts in the middle and retire right now!*

What I didn't realize was that despite the hours of insufferable doubt and self-loathing, somewhere in my mind I knew I was right; I wasn't ready for this. I had no idea what I was doing. I was hopelessly flailing and hoping to catch a crack in the wall on my way down so I didn't become Humpty himself. But looking back, that fall was exactly what I needed. And all the tumbles that followed were necessary too. Sometimes, we have to lose to understand how to win. So when it became my turn to rise from my seat and head out into the unpredictable world that would now become my home, I picked myself up, collected my things, and walked off with as much confidence as I could pretend to embody. After all, on the other side of those interior plane walls was a world I knew I could figure out. Maybe not eloquently, and maybe not without the occasional stumble, but I could do it. So long as I never saw my seat mate again.

ATMs & Chocolate Cake

*I believe that everything happens for a reason. People change so
that you can learn to let go, things go wrong so that you appreciate
them when they're right, you believe lies so you eventually learn to
trust no one but yourself, and sometimes good things fall apart so
better things can fall together.*

~ Marilyn Monroe ~

Shanghai, China | June 2017

I don't have many fears when it comes to travel; I've spent a
fair share of time on sketchy busses that hug much too tightly to
the edge of winding mountain roads, I've bargained on cheap
hostels, eaten foods I couldn't identify, and wandered off to
places people often recommend never visiting alone. But if
there's one thing that I make every effort to avoid, it's foreign
police.

I had heard all the stories loud and clear: Chinese police offi-
cers forcing foreigners to pay fraudulent fees under the threat of
arrest; foreigners being blamed for an accident caused by someone else; tricky locals who scam international visitors by claim-
ing to law enforcement that they were robbed or injured. So as I
reluctantly entered the local police station in the Changning district of Shanghai, China, an anxiety began to creep up into my
throat.

WeChat, a name you'll see frequently throughout this book,
is a mobile survival tool for navigating China that works as if

Instagram, Facebook, GrubHub, eBay, Apartment Finder, Venmo, and text messaging all crawled into bed together. You can book hotels, purchase movie tickets, donate to charity, sell your stuff, and even run an entire social enterprise through this glorified mobile application. So it will come as no surprise that WeChat is how I found my apartment in Shanghai. In the months leading up to my arrival I browsed through several WeChat newsfeeds and agency accounts until I located an apartment that was within my budget and was reasonably close to where I would be working. I sent over a signed letter of intent, promising to take over the current tenant's lease upon arrival, and the apartment was mine. Oh, if only other adult things could be that easy.

What proved to be much more difficult was registering once I had arrived. China requires foreign visitors to register with the local police department every time they move or travel. If they don't do so within 24 hours of settling they are subject to fines, arrest, and - worst case scenario - deportation. My moves throughout the country were constantly tracked, so any time I traveled anywhere that required an overnight stay or a border crossing, I knew I would have to register. Before this particular trip, passport registration had been taken care of by the hotels I had stayed in with my study abroad group. Now, it was all up to me.

I took a deep breath as I crossed the threshold into the station. Two rows of blue seating were arranged back to back in the middle of the room. Fans were buzzing against the wall, a TV screen in the corner boasted rows of Chinese characters, and several locals fanned themselves while waiting their turn to speak with an officer. I had come prepared for registration with my apartment lease and passport, but couldn't read the signage to understand which officer I needed. I showed a particularly tired local my apartment lease and passport, and she waved me to the opposite side of the room. I sat down in one of the blue chairs and shifted back and forth, nervously rehearsing in my head several phrases in basic English to help explain what it was that I needed. Sweat began to pool under my knees and I wasn't sure if it was because of the humidity or the recent spike in blood pressure. I hadn't done anything wrong, nor was I attempting anything illegal, but the threat of not being able to communicate with a government official left me shaking. While I waited, I decided to translate a few things around the room to ensure I had a backup plan if verbal communication proved to be useless. I pointed my camera at the blue line on the floor that I assumed to mark the beginning of a line in which we were to wait. The nice thing about Google Translate was its ability to provide real-time translation as you pointed your camera at a word or phrase. The unfortunate reality was its reliability. I stifled a laugh as Google read back to me, "In a foreign noodle waiting." *Welp. There goes that plan.*

When it was finally my turn to sit down with the officer I stuffed my papers through an opening beneath the clear bulletproof barrier. She took one look at my stack of documents and said only one word, "Copy." *Huh?* She waived me away and turned to help someone else.

"Uh, wait, copy?" I leaned into the tiny holes in the barrier. "What copy?"

She scoffed and began pulling papers out of my stack and setting them in a different pile. "Copy. This. This. This."

I was wasting her time, she made that very clear. When she finished separating the stack, she shoved everything back through the slot beneath the window and pointed to the exterior wall of the station. "Copy." *At least I no longer have to worry about being able to communicate.*

There was only one storefront across the street, so I gathered my things and walked into what appeared to be a shop selling beer, wine, beer, liquor, beer, and more beer. Every imported beer and wine that existed was here in China. Belgian, German, French, Spanish, Irish, Mexican; you name it, the Beer Lady probably had it. But Beer Lady also had a giant machine that every foreigner nearby needed at one point or another: a copy machine. I handed over my stack of papers and she ran them through meticulously. As I pulled out my wallet to pay she said something that sounded vaguely like "two Kuai," Kuai being the colloquial (and much cooler) way of saying 'yuan,' which is a unit of Chinese currency. So when she handed over my copies I handed her two Kuai. Proud of myself for successfully completing a transaction in Mandarin, I started for the door. No sooner had I reached the exit when Beer Lady began to chase after me, yelling uninterpretable words in my direction. I spun quickly on my heels, my heart thumping through my chest, my eyes widened with fear. I had been so terrified of the police I forgot how scary shop owners could be when they yelled at me in a language I couldn't understand.

Since I hadn't yet learned Mandarin, I didn't realize she had said nine Kuai instead of two. I unknowingly tried to steal seven Kuai worth of this woman's livelihood. Embarrassed, I apologized profusely and pulled out several more coins. She politely laughed off my mistake but then insisted on teaching me how to count to ten and refused to let me leave until I could recite it on my own.

We stood with the cash register between us as she slowly repeated, "Yī, èr, sān, sì, wǔ, liù, qī, bā, jiǔ, shí."

She smiled as I spoke with her, doing my best to mimic her tones. She taught me the correct pronunciations and then showed me the accompanying hand movements for each number. I never forgot how to count to ten again. Back at the police station, I handed over my copies and, without exchanging a single word, received my registration papers and was sent on my way.

Among countless other things, China taught me valuable lessons in shame, courage, trust, perception, and communication. I learned that shame is merely a construct of our imagination; if a local can strut onto the metro in his matching pajama set, then you can set aside your fear of rejection and apply to a job for which you're under qualified. China is a place where crotchless pants are a recommended choice for toddlers, and men of all ages turn their shirts into crop tops on particularly hot days (although unfortunately this style has yet to be adopted by hunks with six packs and instead remains popular with beer gut nation). In China, courage is not considered an admirable quality but rather a requirement of survival. If you allow China to maul you over with a cart full of wooden dining chairs, then it will do so. Shanghai doesn't stop for anyone, not even an emergency medical vehicle with its sirens on. I wish I were kidding.

If you're falling behind, then behind you shall stay until you give yourself a kick in the pants, or a stranger tells you that crying on the outside is shameful and from here on out you should only cry on the inside. Shanghai also taught me how to trust others, as I handed over my dignity to shop owners so they could help me count my change, and relied on locals to point me in at least a reasonably right direction (I'd say this worked 73% of the time). I learned how to perceive adversity and discomfort as learning opportunities; if I hadn't, I wouldn't have survived for as long as I did. And don't even get me started on how I perfected the art of the charades communication style as I acted like a chicken in the middle of a grocery store and performed renditions of a clogged sink for my landlord. Invite me to your improv nights. I dare you.

But perhaps one of the most valuable lessons I learned was about impermanence. It's not just the people that are constantly moving, progressing, and innovating, but the buildings themselves seem to grow legs and quite literally up and leave whenever they get bored. So one day, when the structure that had once been my bank was suddenly laying in a crumpled heap on the sidewalk, it didn't exactly come as a surprise.

In order to load money onto my WeChat account so that I could pay for groceries, order take out, and pay my utilities, I had to open a Chinese bank account. After some careful research online I decided to go with ICBC, the Industrial and Commercial Bank of China. It seemed to be foreigner friendly and easy to navigate, so I grabbed my passport and headed for the bank. My first attempt was simply poor planning; I stopped by during the tellers' lunch break, so no one was around to help except a very sleepy security guard who absentmindedly handed me a blank application that I took home to fill out.

After several lengthy dates with Google Translate I walked back to the branch where I waited my turn behind several other hot and sweaty individuals. When I finally sat down in front of the glass barrier and handed my application through the slot, the teller took one look at it, shook her head, and tossed it onto her desk. She then disappeared behind a door and when she resurfaced slid me another blank application. My heart sank. *Did I fill it out incorrectly? Or was it the wrong application altogether?* I searched her eyes for answers but she sat down in her swivel chair, turned her shoulder to me, and pressed a button to summon the next person in line. Feeling like a rejected middle schooler at a dance, I shuffled away to a desk along the wall to try again. I sat there with my passport and Google Translate filling out box by box until it appeared I had done the same exact thing as before. I sighed, trying not to feel preemptively defeated, and got back in line.

The sweat dripped down my neck and into my shirt as the teller reviewed my application again and then sighed with irritation as she began to punch in my information. *One step further than before! Progress!* After what appeared to be several attempts in verifying my passport number, she handed back my application and shook her head. *Oh, what now?* I sat there staring at her while she waved her hands in front of her face, shaking her head, as she signaled for the next customer. But this time, I refused to move. I pulled out Google Translate.

"Is there a problem?" I typed into the phone and held what was likely a poor translation up to the glass. She pulled out a piece of paper and scribbled across the page impatiently. She shoved it up against the glass.

She had written my name, 'Erin O'Neil.' I nodded in confusion. She then peeled the paper from the barrier, crossed out the apostrophe, gave me an irritable look, and shook her head. She waved on the next customer as I smiled back at her.

Grabbing a pen from the desk I wrote my name down on the back of a stray receipt, 'Erin ONeil,' sans apostrophe. I showed her through the glass, and gave her a wide smile with a thumbs up. She looked at me with suspicion, but waved for me to hand over my passport and turned back to her computer. A few minutes later, once the punctuation had been removed from my last name, I was handed a shiny new ATM card and sent on my way. Just outside the branch I deposited a few hundred Kuai into the ATM, prouder than ever for standing my ground and having the confidence to resolve an issue despite significant language barriers. But perhaps I was all the more thrilled that I no longer needed a physical wallet to go on spontaneous ice cream binges; all I had to do was maintain my WeChat balance. The only downside was that, with WeChat, the Chinese government had record of every time someone ordered 12 Yang's dumplings all to themselves or took a cab for less than two blocks because they were being lazy. But I'm not talking about anyone in particular....

Once everything was set up it was quite easy to maintain my WeChat balance. I would stop by an ICBC ATM and use my Charles Schwab card to withdraw money from my American account. Using the same ATM I would then immediately deposit the cash into my Chinese account. (Pro-tip: Charles Schwab has no ATM fees, so if you're headed abroad, go Schwab). To make things easier, there was an ICBC branch right down the road from where I worked so I could easily deposit funds on my way back from lunch. With my financial strategy in place and a restored confidence in my ability to function as a local, everything felt like it was coming together. But, in normal Shanghai fashion, just as I'd established a routine, I headed for the ATM one day only to find my favorite branch shut down. And I'm not meaning shut down as in doors are chained and a sign reads, "CLOSED." I'm talking ATM machines ripped from the walls, windows busted out, frames detached, wires poking out from where the ceiling used to be, and debris all over the sidewalk. Shanghai can literally destroy buildings overnight.

Two short weeks after moving to Shanghai I, myself, began to face destruction. Before I boarded my flight to China, R confirmed that we had trips planned, equipment purchased, and we had even decided upon a method of payment. When I arrived for my first day at the office I didn't have a desk, an active email, the equipment I needed, nor anything to work on. R wasn't even in the country. But my spirits were high; I excitedly anticipated our first international adventure and I couldn't wait to get started on producing meaningful content. I felt a responsibility to get something done regardless of where in the world R was traveling, but I had no idea what I was supposed to be doing. Every so often R would send me content to edit, but the rest of the time I sat there waiting. I didn't mind the lack of direction, but what was beginning to worry me was the lack of travel itineraries. I mean, he had said trips were already confirmed. So where were the tickets? Within a week and a half of being in Shanghai, it became clear that not a single work trip had been booked and R showed no intentions of planning one.

Every day that I walked into the office my gut screamed a little louder, "This doesn't feel right." So I confided in a few of my long-term coworkers, several of whom had been there during my internship last summer. They knew my work ethic, understood my working relationship with R, and I trusted their opinions given their tenure. I asked for their guidance in communicating with R, and shared my concerns about the lack of travel plans. The responses I received were not the answers I wanted to hear:

"Be careful."

"He can't be trusted."

"I wouldn't be so sure of his intentions."

"He's changed."

Their words of wisdom left me feeling all the more terrified. *This surely can't be happening... Everything has been falling into place so flawlessly, how could it be that the sole reason I came back is the one thing turning my world upside down?* I was uneasy and alert. For the next several weeks I kept my head down and continued working hard, determined to prove them all wrong. When R came back from his trip I tended to his every need, fulfilling each of the projects he assigned with timeliness and attentiveness to detail. But my enthusiasm was not always met with reciprocity. R had a peculiar ability to treat you like his best friend one day, only to decide the next that you were the employee he never wanted to bring onto the team. It was an unpredictably hot and cold environment; I never knew what I was walking into when I opened the office door.

During my previous internship, R was fun, challenging, and personable. He was a respectable leader and a wonderful mentor who encouraged creativity and celebrated success. He had high expectations and our team produced quality work as a result. This time, R turned out to be the kind of person who spent two days telling me about a delicious, one-of-a-kind, chocolate cake, but when the time came and I'd already skipped breakfast (to save room, duh), gawked at the menu, and was drooling down the pastry case, he said, "Let's go somewhere else, I don't want to eat here." The list of broken promises grew longer each day I was there.

In the course of a year, he'd somehow transformed into someone who made nothing but empty promises, some arguably more important than cake. I was constantly misguided on assignments and criticized when I subsequently couldn't provide my best work. I couldn't sleep at night and the only reason I worked out was because I desperately needed to blow off steam. The anger boiled my blood and it felt as though if I sat still for too long I might burst. My passion for my work was dying, my creativity fleeing, and any remaining optimism was crumbling. I felt like a failure, a fraud who psyched up her friends and family back home for this incredible career opportunity only to turn around and reveal that it had been a complete scam. But I didn't quit. I had made a promise to R and I wasn't going to be the one to break it. I was determined to prove myself to him and to everyone else that I could do it; that I could make the most of what I had. Sometimes life isn't fair, not everything runs smoothly, and some people just don't understand how to lead a successful organization. But my job wasn't to fix him or his business; it was to produce the highest quality of work possible and innovate on his company's media output to better engage their audience and market their research. And goshdarnit, I was going to do just that.

My one shining light in the office was Augustine, a marketing intern from Singapore. She was the company's social media manager, daily video blog narrator, and unspoken office comedian. Her joyful eyes and contagious laughter regularly provided momentary relief from R's dreary work assignments and attitude. She had a bubbly spirit and engaging charisma that left us clutching our sides, wondering how such enormous spunk could occupy such a tiny figure. Most notable, perhaps, was her thick Singaporean accent that made even the most basic of discussion questions sound a little more interesting. In case you haven't yet been graced with the sound of a Singaporean native saying "Thumb drive," it sounds a lot like, "tum-drive," and is unforgettably adorable.

But perhaps all the more memorable was her unwavering positivity and authentic joy. She radiated an energy that never once gave me the impression that she was struggling in the same way I was; I thought I was alone in my frustration with R. That is, until a project we submitted together was published online. One of the most frustrating aspects of working for R was his tendency to edit your work right before taking it live and never informing you of the changes. It was dishonest and, frankly, offensive. On July 9th, less than a month into my position, Augustine noticed that a part of the original video I'd sent her wasn't in the final version that had been posted online. I clicked through the online version and confirmed that part of the weekly template was indeed missing from our final production.

"I had it in there…" I messaged her from across the office, watching from behind my laptop to see her reaction. "He must have edited it out."

I took a deep breath and admitted to her, "This job is very challenging for me…"

Just typing it felt as though a weight had been lifted. Augustine surprisingly empathized with my pain and told me that I was not alone; R also changed and deleted her work without telling her. She went on to tell me about past interns who couldn't even bear to put their name on their work because by the time it had been edited and published, it was no longer theirs. Which, by the way, rarely mattered, because R published most everything in his own name anyway. Behind most of the articles published under his name, were several unpaid or below minimum wage interns.

Augustine and I grew closer and she helped soothe my anger on particularly rough days. Even after she returned home to Singapore at the end of her internship in July, she was just a quick WeChat message away. One particular afternoon I asked her how she coped with R's sporadic behaviors.

She messaged me back, "I tell myself that this is his company, he can do whatever he wants. But I'll still keep creating. If he wants to delete it, so be it, at least I know I did my best." She recommended I develop a few side projects of my own to have another avenue in which to develop my talents and test out my potential. She told me not to take it personally when he said things like, "This is why I don't ask people to do things because I just end up awake all night fixing it," and, "You millennials are so needy it's no wonder I don't get anything done around here." I told her how frustrating it was to stand behind the camera at every presentation listening as he spoke to other business leaders about how to make employees feel more valued in the workplace. Augustine and I mutually agreed that while he was great at talking the talk, he was horrendous at walking the walk. As my first month in Shanghai came to a close, I took refuge in knowing I wasn't alone.

Despite knowing I had supporters - people who empathized with my pain - my heart broke into a million pieces as I stood before what was becoming a chain-on-the-door, windows blown out, wires falling from the sky, tragedy. Just like my bank, my dream job had been destroyed within a few weeks. I was angry, hurt, and hopeless. I felt as though I'd been exploited, taken advantage of, and regrettably misplaced. If this was just the beginning, what would the end look like? This was my first shot at a meaningful career and I was completely botching it. One month in and I knew my trip wouldn't end with friendly handshakes and a "Stay in touch." But if there's anything Shanghai had already taught me, it was that, just like my bank, I could be rebuilt elsewhere.

Gym Memberships
& Toothbrushes

The only way to make sense out of change is to plunge into it, move
with it, and join the dance.
~ Alan Watts ~

Shanghai, China | July 2017

At the start of every new beginning we make choices that effect our sequential experiences. We make decisions about our
social groups, jobs, attitude, attire, behaviors, values, and goals.
We decide what our story is and how we tell it. We create and
recreate ourselves as our lives ask us to. So as I started writing
my story in Shanghai, the newest chapter in my life's adventures, I searched for purpose and belonging. I sought out a solid
ground from which I could develop and grow.

One evening in July, just a month after I arrived in China, I
ventured out to the Shanghai Bund to film some footage at R's
request. The Bund is one of Shanghai's most recognizable and
bustling waterfront areas in the city, and is decorated with elements of Gothic, Baroque, and neoclassical architecture along its
mile-long stretch against the Huangpu River. Whether it's
watching the locals do their daily exercises, admiring the buzz
of excited tourists, or watching a sunset against the cityscape of
the financial district, you haven't seen Shanghai until you've
been to the Bund. With my camera bags and tripod in tote, I

found a perch across from the Oriental Pearl Tower, a TV and radio tower built with such unique architectural elements that it is now one of Shanghai's iconic symbols. The number of visitors grew in masses as the sun began to sink in the sky, so I embraced the opportunity to capture some energized footage. Standing up, I wrapped the DSLR camera strap around my neck and swung my hips slowly as if to mimic a camera stabilizer as it panned across the horizon. I probably resembled a very tired drunk, but hey, the shot looked great. When you have limited resources, you learn to make do.

By the time I had the footage I needed, the sun was shining the last of its pink hues on the windows of the buildings across the river. I looked around to find myself trapped by hundreds of people as the benches were packed with families watching the sunset. Although I had planned to duck out and head home before the skies darkened, I decided not to fight the masses and instead stick around to watch. As the night sky appeared and the cityscape lit up the financial district, I was approached by a local. He was young, likely a university student, with dark hair and a bashful smile. He pointed at my camera and asked what I was doing, so I showed him the videos I had taken. I introduced myself and began to ask him about himself, but it became very clear to me that English was not his strong suit.

He gestured towards my purse and said, "WeChat?"

I nodded and smiled at him, pulling out my phone. We added each other as contacts and he introduced himself via text. His name was Xie Lin Yue, but, for foreigners, he went by 'Mark'. We spent the next hour communicating via WeChat translate and incredibly simple English. WeChat's built-in translation feature was frequently helpful, but not always accurate.

It was then that he noticed my name on my WeChat profile. "Are you name Erin?"

"Yes. Erin. I do not have a Chinese name." I tend to avoid using contractions when speaking with foreigners.

He nodded at his phone screen and typed in response, "Okay good name. You can take a Chinese name."

Considering Erin is a very difficult name for native Mandarin speakers to pronounce, I thought this might be a good plan, "How do I take one?"

He glanced up at the sky before messaging me back, "What do you like about China?"

I considered his question for a moment. "I like Shanghai and the beautiful views. I like understanding different cultures and traveling." I hit send, hoping I hadn't used words that wouldn't translate well.

He sent back: "You prefer to compare Chinese names to westernization. You are called Haili in Chinese. What do you think? 海丽"

He looked up from his phone and repeated the characters to me out loud. It sounded a lot like he was saying, "Hayley."

I smiled, realizing he'd just assigned me the name of my best friend from college who helped me decide to move to China in the first place.

I messaged him back, "That is pretty. Is it compared to my name? Erin?" I thought maybe he had simply taken the syllables of my name and found similar characters in Mandarin.

"It means beautiful scenery of Shanghai."

I smiled. "That is perfect."

We continued texting each other as we walked back towards the metro. It was strange to be so focused on my phone, only because I was so interested in having a conversation with the person next to me. Often times I feel too reliant on technology, but without it, my conversation with Mark wouldn't have been possible. We stood together swaying in a metro car while he told me about his hometown and local cultural traditions; he sent photos of colorful parades and costumes. We talked about our families and traveling through China, and he shared with me some of his favorite American movies. I had a feeling that if communication hadn't been so difficult, we might have become very good friends.

When the train pulled into Hongqiao Road station I messaged him, "This is my stop." I stepped off the train as I waved goodbye, smiling at him as he leaned against the wall of the train. He nodded and pointed at his phone, a silent agreement to stay in touch. I arrived back at my apartment feeling more connected and confident with my new life in Shanghai. I finally felt a sense of belonging; a sort of renewed individuality. Sometimes a name can be a powerful thing.

My apartment in Shanghai was a palace compared to most. It featured a spacious living room already furnished by its previous tenants, a large fully-equipped kitchen, and a bathroom with a shower head that wasn't directly above the toilet. Apparently, that is common in Chinese apartments. I don't know about you, but if I ever have the need to use the toilet and shower at the same time, there's something seriously wrong. In my new home I had my own private bedroom that came pre-stocked with all the toiletries, towels, knick-knacks, and IKEA storage containers that the previous tenant had left behind. She even left a beginners Chinese textbook and a brand new yoga mat. It was sort of a blessing that her suitcases were only so big. The living room was furnished with two charcoal grey couches and a low black coffee table, and the dining area featured a stark white table with four plastic chairs. It was minimalistic, but spacious. Beneath the bay window in the dining room was a drying rack rarely devoid of freshly washed clothes and bedding. My new home wasn't lavish, but compared to most other residences in the city, it was comfortable, clean, and had all the amenities I needed.

When I took over the lease from the previous tenant, she had also offered to transfer her local gym membership into my name. She had already paid through the end of the year so it would have otherwise gone to waste. Having recently rekindled my relationship with regular exercise, and figuring I'd need a treadmill after pumping myself full of rice and dumplings every day, I agreed to take it off her hands. But unlike the tiny bottles of shampoo and purse-sized tissue packs, the gym membership was not complimentary. I paid half of the transfer fee and purchased the remaining months of her contract. It was no small payment, but worth the accessibility of continuing my healthy habits. Thus began my regular post-work visits to Rockies Fitness, a small gym located on the basement floor of a nearby mall that had all the basics: weights, machines, a yoga studio, training area, locker rooms, and showers. Or, at least, most of the basics; although they had plenty of toilet paper, they didn't have any kind of towels or hand dryers. If you planned on cleaning any kind of grime off your body post-workout or bathroom trip, you had to provide your own linens. Regardless of its minor flaws, Rockies was the perfect place to burn off steam after a long day of work.

One day I worked up the courage to take a group yoga class. I had been practicing yoga for several years, so I figured I could rely on my ability to recognize positions and flows, without necessarily understanding the instructor. After overcoming some incredible confusion about how to even register for the class, I finally made my way into the dimmed studio and laid down the yoga mat I had discovered in my apartment. Fortunately, this particular yoga instructor knew enough English to indicate when to, "look forward," "inhale," "exhale," "up," "plank," and "relax"; the primary phrases anyone really needs to recognize while upside down. But when I simply couldn't understand her instructions, she would come over, laugh a little, and then guide my body in the direction it needed to go. Once I finally got it figured out, she would then apply enough pressure to leave me permanently stuck in that position for days. I knew the Chinese culture was to succeed and achieve, but she had no idea how tight and sore my muscles were already from lifting weights the day before. And with phones being banned from the studio, there was no way I could tell her.

She quite literally pushed me to my limits, which is something I would have complained about had this been a class full of English speakers. But no matter how much my body fought back against her persuasive pushing, and regardless of how badly I wanted to speak up and say, "Usually I could do this but my biceps are still aching from yesterday," I couldn't stop her.

I couldn't make excuses, and she didn't want to hear them. Even if I had gotten the words out, she wouldn't have understood me. And much to my surprise, I achieved stretches and positions that day that I typically would have decided were much too difficult for my physical abilities. Because I couldn't communicate, it was impossible to make excuses, and she expected me to do my best regardless. Her confidence in my ability to bend combined with her persistence in seeing progress in her students, meant I became stronger (and far more flexible) than I'd ever thought possible in one class. I began to wonder if a lack of communication could teach me more than any conversation would.

I shared my four-bedroom Shanghai apartment with two young German men. I will never forget the way one of them introduced himself; by pointing out that while most of the world seems to think Americans are unintelligent egomaniacs who are politically screwing over an entire global population, he doesn't think all of them are so terrible and he was willing to give me a chance. It was truly flattering, really. After going on a mini-rant about American politics and Donald Trump, he invited me out to get drinks with him and our other roommate later that night. Much to my chagrin, I was in need of local friends, so I agreed. I will be honest that a part of me was apprehensive to be knowingly representing an entire nationality even if it was just over pizza and beer. But despite sporadically landing on topics of American politics and religion throughout the evening, we mostly discussed German business development and investments. About which I had zero opinions. Yes, snooze indeed. But I was managing to form relationships, albeit less than invigorating ones, with the only other two people in my every-day life, so I was content.

Both of my flatmates pretty much kept to themselves. I fell into a fairly comfortable routine and we all gained a respectful acknowledgment of each other's environment in the apartment. Except, of course, our shared bathroom. I guess excessive mold just doesn't bother some people... And whoever decided that the plumbing in China wasn't good enough to flush paper products and therefore required everything - I mean EVERY-THING - to go in the garbage cans next to the toilet, was not considering the fact that some of us have to live with men. So, shortly after I moved in, I began letting myself into the private bathroom of our unoccupied master bedroom where I could take a shower that wouldn't make me feel filthier than before I got in. And in the mornings I would brush my teeth while look-ing out over the city in the master bedroom's closed-in balcony. I had my own space and my own refuge for when the standoff to empty the waste basket of used toilet paper began. Every-thing was perfect.

And then Jenny showed up.

The previous tenant of my room had been best friends with the previous tenant of the master bedroom, but when they both left Shanghai, only one of them found a replacement. So it wasn't surprising to me that I one day received a WeChat mes-sage from the previous owner of the master bedroom asking if I wouldn't mind showing the apartment to a potential renter. I was certainly less than thrilled. I felt bad the tenant was still paying rent on a place she didn't live in, but I wasn't about to give up my unwritten rights to the master bathroom. It crossed my mind to pretend I never received her message due to my phone being crushed by a bus or dropped between the metro platforms, but my kindness got the better of me and I begrudgingly agreed to help. When the day came to show the prospective renter the apartment, I answered the door with only one thought, *I really hope she doesn't like it here.* My toothbrush and I very much enjoyed our routine and I was not about to let anyone take that away. I momentarily considered fabricating a roach infestation.

I pulled open the apartment door to find a young redhead standing tall in the doorway. Without much of an introduction, I welcomed her inside.

We stood in the hallway by the rows of shoes as she immediately began drilling me with questions: "How much are utilities?" "Are your flatmates noisy?" "How much space is in the fridge?" "Who's stuff is piled here in the living room and when will it be moved?"

It was as though she had been reciting the questions in her head the entire duration of her walk from the metro and they now came spilling out all at once. She was certainly someone whose first impression left me with the words, 'bold, ambitious, and totally fierce.' I showed her around the apartment and as our tour came to a conclusion we stood in the living room chatting about her work with InternMore, an international career development company. She told me more about her studies in Hong Kong and travels throughout Europe, and while we talked about her career aspirations I began to see her vivacious personality break through. Her charm perfectly complimented her audaciousness, and once I got past her protective layer of skepticism, I discovered a caring and loving individual. The red-headed go-getter was winning me over. And apparently the apartment had successfully won her, too.

Jenny moved in a few days later and unpacked her extensive collection of Haribo gummy bears and intricately patterned work shirts. She had a no-bullshit, outspoken attitude with dauntless energy. She made space in the kitchen where she saw fit, coordinated an equal division of shelf space in the fridge, and pushed aside some of the clutter in the living room we'd been avoiding for sake of tripping hazards. If there was something Jenny needed, she spoke up, and if there was something that needed accomplished, she took charge. She saw the world through hungry and courageous eyes, and it sparked within me a tenacity I hadn't known existed. I was intimidated, yet entranced. After one week of living with Jenny, sharing a bathroom with the boys didn't seem so horrible, because at least it meant I had a new companion next door.

One afternoon Jenny and I were standing in the kitchen together making stir fry, a meal I ate frequently due to the mere fact that it was healthy, cheap, and took very little time to make. She was telling me about her simple recipe for overnight oats when we got onto the topic of eating healthy in China.

"I feel like I'm going to explode every time I go out to eat here." I stuck out my stomach as far as I could in an attempt to look like I might soon give birth to a litter of baby dumplings.

"I know what you mean." Jenny fidgeted with the stovetop settings and stirred the chicken. "There are many places in Shanghai that have healthy options, like salads and soups, but they're not exactly cheap."

I continued cutting carrots while I considered my options. "I'm thinking about ordering protein powder to help fill me up during the day."

Jenny tilted her head, "Will you go to the grocery with me? You know so much about health foods and working out. I want to be fit!" She dropped the spatula in the pan as she lifted her arms, popped her hip, and flexed her biceps.

I looked at her sideways and pointed to the stovetop, "I hardly think eating stir fry every night for dinner qualifies me to be a health coach."

"Yeeeaaahhh but you're so fit and healthy, look at you, skinny mini."

I thanked her for the compliment but told her that the only real secret to my success was going to the gym. That way, even if I gained weight, it was less than if the only exercise I got was walking to the metro everyday. But my regular cardio routine was certainly no match for the amount of carbs I was consuming.

"Which gym do you go to?" She popped a stray carrot into her mouth.

"Rockies. It's on the bottom floor of a mall near the metro station."

She bolted out of the kitchen as she yelled, "Then let's go to the gym!"

A few seconds later she returned holding a Rockies Fitness envelope. "I found a membership in my room, we can go together!"

That's when I learned that the previous tenant of Jenny's master bedroom had also left behind her Rockies membership card. But when I suggested we reach out to see if Jenny could buy it from her, Jenny laughed.

"Why would I pay her? She already bought this, so she's thrown away the expense. She's not here to use it, so it makes no difference if I use it or if it sits on the desk. If she wanted me to pay her, she clearly does not know about supply and demand."

Jenny, I came to realize, was an economist by trade.

Without knowing for sure whether they'd even let her in, we filled our water bottles, threw on our tennis shoes, rode the elevator down from our 11th floor apartment and began searching for two orange Mobikes. Mobike was one of many bike share programs that were popular all over China and throughout many other countries in Asia. With one mobile application you could locate and unlock bikes that were parked all over the city. All you had to do was scan the QR code between the handlebars with your phone's camera, and the bike was yours. The cost was minimal and the convenience was irreplaceable. And no matter how hot it was, Mobike made commuting around the city a breeze. So Jenny and I biked together to Rockies and as we walked up to the counter I scanned my membership card and slipped through the turnstile. I then nonchalantly watched as Jenny threw her shoulders back, grinned at the women working at the front desk, threw her self-claimed membership card onto the scanner and waltzed through the turnstile right behind me. I couldn't decide whether to be impressed or upset by the fact that I had paid full price when I could have just practiced confidence for free.

I messaged my boyfriend, Josh, later that night and said, "I think Jenny and I will be friends."

Over the next month my daily routine adapted to include Jenny in what had previously been a list of boring adult errands. We began accompanying each other to the grocery store; did loads of laundry together; and even went out to get smoothie bowls when we had cash to spare. We cuddled up to watch movies on the weekends while occasionally chowing down on cheesecake from a nearby restaurant called Boxing Cat. There were bike rides, shopping trips, and Starbucks dates. There was even the afternoon we spent at an all-inclusive group outing that involved sand meditation, nutritional programming, a boxing class, and all-natural protein smoothies. If we were close to anything, it was an old married couple, and Jenny and I wouldn't have had it any other way.

Most importantly, Jenny and I kept each other accountable. We would trade off at the gym between lifting weights, running, or inventing training circuits. Working out by myself felt good, but having someone else there to help push me felt even better. Jenny helped keep me motivated and focused on the things I valued in my every day routine. Without meaning to or recognizing it, she provided a stability I otherwise might not have created myself. Even on the days I worked out without her because she had to stay late at work, or ate junk food for dinner because I didn't feel like cooking, I always came back to the healthy foods and exercise which Jenny expected from me. Jenny and I kept each other in check and created a stable foundation, and that made all the difference in making Shanghai a home.

Metro Maps & White Canes

Our willingness to own and engage with our vulnerability determines the depth of our courage and the clarity of our purpose; the level to which we protect ourselves from being vulnerable is a measure of our fear and disconnection.

~ Brené Brown ~

Hong Kong | July 29 - August 2, 2017

Growing up, I always seized opportunities to challenge myself; trying a new sport, beating the highest level of a video game, or seeing how long I could go without talking (my parents rather liked that one). One of the challenges I discovered was showering in the dark. I'm not quite sure how it started, but what began as a test of my memory and coordination soon became so enjoyable and rehearsed that I couldn't imagine showering any other way (that is, of course, until I started shaving). I would stand there in silence staring into the black abyss as the water ran over my body. After my parents yelled up the stairs to tell me my shower was already running too long, I would begin my routine. With enough practice, my hand began to land directly on the shampoo bottle, as if I'd been able to see in the dark all along. I'd feel a sense of accomplishment as I successfully completed each of my usual shower routines without being able to see. It was oddly reassuring that when my eyes were of no help, my mind and my body knew just what to do.

I eventually grew so familiar with my new practice that it no longer felt like a challenge. But every time I turned off the faucet and reached for my towel, I began to search for the light from beneath the bathroom door. I trusted myself within the confines of the shower curtain, but found myself helpless outside of its protection. The unpredictability and unfamiliarity of that particular darkness was a threat I couldn't yet trust my body to guide me through. I only now realize how poetic it was that my trust had limitations; the belief in my ability to succeed without eyesight was only within the confines of that shower curtain. Outside, the darkness proved much too significant a threat.

R finally came to the conclusion that if he didn't get me out of China, my visa would soon expire and he'd be in a lot of trouble. So he picked the easiest place for us to conduct interviews and allowed me to fly out two days early, alone. As I boarded the plane to Hong Kong I felt a renewed sense of passion and motivation. R was finally following through, another adventurous stamp would be added to my passport, and I would get to try out a few new challenges. I thought maybe, just maybe, things were turning around after all.

When my plane landed in Hong Kong I was met with the sudden realization that I was terrified of traveling alone, if not for any other reason than I just didn't want to be lonely. I was afraid of being intimidated to try new things, of becoming frustrated and overwhelmed and, above all, I was afraid of failing. The same thoughts that ran through my head when my plane landed in Shanghai just a month and a half earlier, now swarmed my brain. Having never been to Hong Kong, I didn't know what to expect. But before I left Shanghai my coworkers had reassured me that Hong Kong was like Britain and China had a baby country together; plenty of English and convenient public transportation, but still familiar to the culture in which I had been immersed. So whatever I was about to face, I knew I'd be able to handle it on my own.

I stepped out into the bright Hong Kong sun, GoPro in hand, determined to conquer the city. My hotel was fairly central but still required a short hike to the metro station. So I had confidently packed my purse with a map, snacks, sunscreen, and my camera, and left the lobby in pursuit of a subway sign with an arrow that pointed down a set of stairs disappearing beneath the ground. Twenty minutes and several underground tunnels to nowhere later, I begrudgingly realized that the subway sign I'd been following merely indicated a passageway beneath the main roads. I'd taken each of the tunnels in variable directions in multiple attempts to locate a train, but alas, there was no metro to be found. Not even a ticket booth or security gate.

I learned that, unlike other major cities I'd been to around the world, 'subway' and 'metro' were not interchangeable words. I'd spent the entire time zig-zagging underneath the highway and not getting any closer to a metro. But, when all is lost (and you're not that far from home), you just start over. So I defeatedly meandered back to the hotel and pulled a stereotypical tourist move as I lingered just outside the building to soak up some free WiFi. After confirming I had greatly misjudged the distance of the metro, and determining that I would indeed get much more sweaty with this walk, I once again took a confident leap and started again.

Fast forward 20 minutes when I found myself standing alone immersed in a busy underground railway system with little to no clue which ticket to purchase or how to navigate the tunnels. Just when I thought I understood basic public transportation... To make matters worse, Hong Kong was essentially a British Shanghai, so there was plenty of English to go around. This meant my ego was far more fragile; a language barrier was no longer an excuse. But I let my pride get the best of me and decided to stand there for a substantially awkward amount of time before finally working up the courage to ask for help. I hand-picked a friendly looking family of foreigners as they waited by a ticket window.

"Um, excuse me, do you speak English?" Looking back, I wish I would've used a less stereotypical 'I'm lost and am in desperate need of your assistance' line, but it did the trick and they wearily smiled back at me, nodding. As a naturally bubbly individual and a particularly nervous Chatty Kathy, I had picked two of the quietest souls in all of Asia. I had also somehow managed to find two of the tallest people in Hong Kong. Simône stood at least at a head taller than myself, while her son, Laurens - despite being four years younger than me - towered over both of us.

"Do you know how to get to Victoria's Peak?" I pointed to my map as though still assuming they couldn't speak English.

"Ah, we don't know. We're just waiting for my husband." I was infatuated as Simône spoke, her words hitting the air with a soft musical quality and a thick Dutch accent poking through each syllable.

"Where are you from?"

"The Netherlands," she replied.

My heart jumped, "Oh, I LOVE The Netherlands! I've been to Amsterdam and Rotterdam and something called Oostvaarder-splassen. It's a re-wilding sight in The Netherlands and it's so incredible. Where do you live?!" It was instantaneously clear to me that I was far too energetic for them first thing in the morning.

"We live about an hour outside of Amsterdam," Simône responded with a subdued simplicity. She explained that her husband is a pilot for KLM Royal Dutch Airlines so they were taking advantage of a short family vacation.

After what seemed like an eternity of awkward small talk, another particularly tall and thin individual appeared through the crowd. He blitzed past me, making a beeline for the ticket booth where he purchased several metro cards and then turned to find me staring up at him like I'd finally located my long lost father. I updated him on my current status of being hopelessly lost.

He introduced himself and shook my hand with the confidence of a successful CEO. "Wick, nice to meet you." He was much bolder and more outgoing than his counterparts; I sighed with relief as my excessive energy no longer seemed to drain the underground metro of its air.

"You're headed to Victoria's Peak?" Wick smiled at me as I nodded in response. He waved me along, "So are we, you are welcome to join us."

It crossed my mind that the last thing I wanted to do was impede on their family vacation, but at the forefront of my thoughts was the reality that saying goodbye and walking the same way might be just as awkward as crashing a family function. So I accepted his kind offer and jogged hurriedly behind them as they sauntered towards the trains, their long legs carrying them down the hallways twice as fast as my own. It dawned on me that perhaps I should have found shorter people to ask for help....

As we navigated towards the peak Wick explained that his family enjoys quite a bit of travel together. They've been all over the world, but Hong Kong is one of their favorite places because of the culture and bustling city life. Despite having only been in the city for less than three hours I could easily say I agreed. The city was just as all of my coworkers had said: like Shanghai turned British. The signs were peppered with Chinese characters and the street food reminiscent of traditional Chinese delicacies, but English was the primary written language and the streets were undeniably less cluttered with garbage and empty takeaway boxes. Familiar luxury brands like Chanel and Gucci occupied most storefronts, and finding someone who spoke English was surprisingly less difficult than I'd thought. Even the metro system featured the lovely tones of a British woman saying, "Please mind the gap." The closer we got to Victoria's Peak, the more confident I became that I could continue navigating the city on my own.

After breezing through the metro and sweating our way to the base of the peak, we stumbled upon what appeared to be the longest line for cable cars I've ever seen. People swarmed the ticket booths as the queue wrapped in and around the supporting columns of the highway above. We took one look and unanimously decided to take a taxi. Wick insisted that I take advantage of their fare and refused to let me sit in the backseat. The car whipped around the tightly wound roads as unique ethnic chanting beat rhythmically through the stereo. The tambourines and drum solos were culturally unidentifiable with what little exposure I had to Middle Eastern music.

"Oh, I love this song," Wick commented from the backseat where he sat crunched next to Simône and Laurens. I turned around to find him smirking and we all quietly giggled under our breath, hoping that the driver couldn't detect sarcasm.

The view from the peak was impressive, but certainly would have been more exciting had the fog not settled itself in a curtain just behind the first row of skyscrapers. We took several obligatory panoramic photos and watched down the mountainside as the cable car lifted itself slowly up to the peak. After taking some family pictures with my Dutch crew, they waved a hearty goodbye and went off to finish their vacation (sans strange American).

Later that afternoon after I'd found my way back down from the peak, I used my printout map of the city to navigate. Without cell phone service, I didn't have much else to rely on. In honoring a recommendation from a coworker, I found my way to Lan Kwai Fong where I discovered the crowds to be fairly subdued and uninteresting. It turns out that bar streets aren't exactly the life of the party at two o'clock in the afternoon. I decided to forgo the Happy Hour specials and meandered instead towards the waterfront where a ferry shuttled me across to the mainland. From my seat on the boat I watched as the sun began to sink behind the buildings. I could feel the cool sprays of water when the boat collided with the oncoming wake. On the shore there were large bustling crowds, vendors selling photography, and a tiny man dressed like Spiderman perched on top of an electrical box. I never said everything I witnessed while traveling was "normal." I had no idea where to go, and didn't have any specific plan, so I allowed myself to be corralled by the crowds until I found myself standing at the water's edge overlooking the bay. There, I was greeted by a local who called himself James.

I had noticed James observing me from the row of bleachers while I took video footage of the ferry returning to harbor.

He addressed me with reservation, "Where are you from?"

I smiled back at him. "I am from the United States. Where are you from?" I was careful to over-enunciate in case he wasn't fluent in English.

"I am from here. Hong Kong. Do you want me take a photo for you?" I handed him my phone and posed obediently in front of the sunset, smiling while he carefully evaluated the lighting and directed me to move a bit to the left. I noticed he captured photos from several different angles.

"Are you a photographer?" I knew the signs when I saw them.

"Yes, yes, I take many photo. Lots. I'll show you." He promptly handed my phone back to me and reclaimed his seat on the bleacher. I sat down beside him and he unlocked his phone, scrolling through stunning images of flowers, waterfalls, ponds, and blooming trees. He had taken most of them at Singapore's Gardens by the Bay. It was clear he had a knack for photography and a keen eye for natural beauty. He showed me a photo of which he was particularly proud, that while at first appeared as though it were edited in grayscale, he explained was in fact a kind of Silver Ragwort; a plant that is naturally grey in color.

We sat talking about cameras and photography until the sun had fully set. The buildings had begun to illuminate the bay with neon strands and spotlights. Hong Kong was known for its Symphony of Lights, a show hosted every night along the bay's cityscape. I had heard great reviews of the performance and was thrilled at the prospect of sharing that experience with someone else. James suggested we go for sushi before watching the light show together. So we headed off into the nearby mall to track down some dinner before it began. Now, I don't know what it is about eating with strangers, but whenever I do I seem to get pretty courageous in trying new foods. James ordered us fried chicken cartilage, baked eggplant, eel sushi, and… wait for it… squid. Yep, I ate squid. And loved it. What's the saying? When in Hong Kong? We finished our evening together watching the light show where James insisted on holding my GoPro for me so that my arm didn't get tired. The chivalry was touching. I'll admit I was underwhelmed by the lack of extravagance of "one of the world's most spectacular light shows," but didn't mind a bit because it had introduced me to a friendly local with whom I maintained contact long after. Before we parted ways that evening, James gave me a giant hug and some recommendations of a few more places to see before my time in Hong Kong came to an end. I was beginning to feel like traveling alone wasn't such a bad idea after all.

The next day my heart was set on several of Hong Kong's prime destinations. First was Ngong Ping, a paradise highland

and religious sanctuary on the island of Lantau. There were multiple ways to reach the peak, one of which involved a three-and-a-half mile hike up a seemingly endless set of stairs that would take about four hours and leave you wishing you had done more cardio at the gym. I didn't have the time nor the stamina to do such a thing. So instead, I decided to make the trip by cable car. I was grouped with several other travelers, each of whom let out a gasp as we were suddenly lifted into the air and could feel the car swinging with the breeze. The open waters plunged into the surface below and the trees parted to reveal the narrow hiking path. I watched as miniaturized humans navigated the winding stairs and earthy slopes. To think they actually planned to hike all the way to the top of that thing was complete blasphemy. I watched as the mountainside grew smaller and eventually shrank into a size more feasibly captured by a camera. At the top, I made my way through the tourist shops and across the property to climb the steps to Tian Tan Buddha.

I looked up at the white marble steps lined with handrails. It was hot, the stairs seemed to reach all the way into space, and I felt my stomach begin to complain of hunger. But I was determined to make it to the top. Despite being fairly in shape, the climb required several stops to catch my breath. But boy, oh boy, was that climb worth it. At the top I looked out over the Hong Kong waters and into the vast forest that spread along the horizon. It was quiet and I was oddly at peace. I meandered around the statue a few times, my feet padding along the marble infrastructure, observing as locals and visitors walked its perimeter and bowed their heads in prayer. I considered my own journey of mindfulness and practice of self-love. I thought about Buddhism and its prominent teachings about suffering and impermanence. I considered the challenges I had been through, the heartbreak that still occasionally bore deep into my chest, and the frustrations of which I've managed to let go. I thought of the places I've been, the hardships I've overcome, and the dreams I was actively pursuing. As I began to descend back down the stairs of Tian Tan Buddha, I turned around to take one last look.

It was then, staring up at the 112-foot tall Buddha, that I unexpectedly found myself beginning to cry. And this time it wasn't because I had climbed 268 steps in 100-degree heat. It seemed to hit me all at once: my childhood dream of traveling the world was a reality; those years of thinking I might never know joy were far in the past; the fears of vulnerability I never thought would crumble were very slowly beginning to give way to incredible strengths. It suddenly felt as though I was observing myself and my life as a good friend instead of through my own lens, which is usually tarnished by self-criticism. I became so instantaneously astonished at everything I had accomplished and the challenges I had overcome that it felt as though I was admiring an entirely different person. For a brief moment, I felt the weight of each and every time someone looked at me and said, "I'm so proud of you." I was fully embraced by every "I love you," and every "I believe in you."

If it's possible to experience pride and humility at the same time, that's exactly what washed over me. It was the most amount of self-love I have ever felt for even a brief moment in time. Before I could realize what my body was doing, my hands were at heart center, my head bowed, and my mouth was whispering, "Thank you, thank you, thank you." Still to this day I don't know who I was addressing. At times it was the universe for allowing me the space to grow, learn, and explore. At times it was the adversities I'd faced that taught me how to perceive challenges as learning opportunities. But perhaps first and foremost, it was myself; for persevering when I felt I couldn't, for seeking opportunities, and for making my dreams a reality.

To me, spirituality is not about one God nor one religious structure; it's about being authentic in your choices, seeking personal development, and having faith that whatever happens has a purpose. Regardless of your reasons or your 'whys,' I believe that living a virtuous life means being able to exhibit empathy and love for others despite communication barriers, cultural differences, or variable backgrounds. Whereas some may find hope and faith in a God, or even several Gods, I try first and foremost to establish hope and faith within myself. For when all is said and done, I am responsible for my choices and my opportunities. Everything happens for a reason, but I also believe we have the agency to impact change and alter our life's direction. Therefore, belief in my ability to persist has proved more valuable and motivational within my own life. Faith is about listening to your heart and following confidently with your head. Up until the moment I found myself looking up at Tian Tan Buddha, overwhelmed with love, I had been determined to let my head guide the way; to let logical reasoning overpower any emotional intuition.

Mindfulness is something I believe we should all practice on a regular basis; it helps us to know ourselves, to know others, and to create positive change in the space around us. It can be something as small as recognizing and accepting a moment of negativity, or something as profound as daily meditation. It is humbling to identify our weaknesses, and uplifting when those weaknesses become strengths. And it was on that mountain, standing in the 100-degree breezeless sun, with tears on my face, that I realized just how far I'd come. It was then that I could see my hard work paying off in leading my life down a more optimistic and open-minded path. It was then that I began to listen to my heart.

That afternoon, after paying far too much for a taxi because I got lost trying to see the Tsing Ma and Ting Kau Bridge, I ventured into a shopping mall where I located a small organization named Dialogue in the Dark. It was here that I was able to put my newfound faith into action. Dialogue in the Dark is a social enterprise that exists in 21 countries worldwide to provide visitors with an experiential introduction to a world without sight. Its website tells guests: "With the help of a white cane and guide you get a chance to explore the unseen, and learn to see in darkness." Their tour guides are locals with visual impairments who lead visitors through the exhibit and introduce them to the city through sound, taste, smell, and touch alone. The tour, which lasts 75 minutes, is done completely in the dark. No flashlights, no dimly-lit doorways, no exit signs, and no night vision goggles (although that would've been pretty sweet).

I was nervous; I was the only one in the tour group and although I'm coordinated enough to shower in the dark, I had no idea how well I would do in navigating an entire (albeit fake) city. At the beginning of the tour I was led to a dimly lit area where I was handed a cane and told that my guide's name would be Henry. I was instructed not to forget this name so that if I became stuck or afraid I could call out to him. A door was opened and I hesitantly walked through, slowly dragging the cane back and forth in front of my feet. I was plunged into darkness. My eyes strained to make out even the faintest of shapes, but the effort was dreadfully unsuccessful. Then Henry's melodic voice came floating through the silence. He introduced himself while he coaxed me forward through the dark. He spoke to me in song, his sentences hitting my ears as though musically orchestrated. I smiled to myself as he sang my name, "So HOW do you LIKE Hong KONG, A-ron?" My anxious heartbeat began to calm.

We walked through the dark until Henry instructed me to stop and investigate my surroundings. "Can you SEE where we ARE, A-ron?" I heard birds chirping and smelled fresh water, and a damp cool breeze hit my skin. Beneath my feet the ground had changed from concrete to a spongy grass. He encouraged me to explore the park, reaching out for the leaves on the trees and pressing my hand against the stone wall where a waterfall was flowing down its surface.

He then asked, "WHAT do the BIRDS look like? What COLOR are the BIRDS?" I was ashamed that my first instinct was to inform him that I did not know because I could not see. *I mean, what a silly question!* But I realized he didn't want the correct answer; he wanted to know what story my other senses had created. I came to the conclusion that my fear of being wrong was simply unnecessary in a world where the visual truth could not be known. Unless I was an expert in bird calls and could identify the types of birds by their voices, my imagination WAS the truth and I could see whatever color or kind of bird I wanted to envision. By the time these thoughts raced through my brain I think I said something like, "They're all different colors." To which Henry praised my incredibly lame answer, "Ohhh YES, A-ron. YES they are ALL different colors."

Together we rode Star Ferry where I felt the wind and water sprinkle against my face; we visited a market where I identified fruits by their smells and shapes; we listened to a musical performance in the theater; and we rang the door to an apartment building where someone spoke to me through an intercom but I left confused because I still didn't speak Chinese.

Slowly but surely this world became very real to me. Amongst my curiosities to know what the rooms looked like with the light on existed vivid images of Hong Kong and the places I'd already visited on the islands. My eyes were open, but the sites I saw were illustrated in my mind. I began to complete my new world with visualizations of the crowded street corners and tall buildings. When we crossed a street together, I imagined us in the crosswalk near my hotel. Together we listened for the steady chirping of the walk signal, and after I'd made it onto the sidewalk Henry asked me to identify the object to my left. I reached out into the dark expecting to touch the metal rails that line most street corners and separate the crowds from oncoming traffic. But instead, I winced in terror, as I identified the front of a car just inches from my hip. I was sure that I'd made it safely off the street and, despite knowing the car wasn't real, fear struck me with surprising force.

This darkened world was challenging at times, especially when I couldn't understand Henry's broken English or the sounds were much too loud to tell from which direction his voice was coming. But I kept asking for extra guidance, hitting everything with my cane (including Henry), and exploring with a hesitant curiosity. I took note of the moments in which I was frustrated that something turned out to be different than what I'd constructed in my mind. Towards the end of the tour, Henry and I sat together in a cafe where I foolishly ordered a bottled water instead of chocolate cake. I was far too worried that I wouldn't be able to find my plate in the dark and would accidentally stab Henry with the fork instead.

We sat together in darkness while he shared with me what it's like to be visually impaired in such a bustling city. He made Hong Kong sound like a quiet suburb the way he calmly eluded to his learning curves and referenced the countless occasions that people have helped to guide him. He told me about his social life and shared his experiences in communicating with friends with hearing impairments by phone. And then Henry told me something I never would have anticipated.

He loves photography.

I felt incredibly ignorant as I sat there and wondered why a man who is completely blind would enjoy taking pictures. You have to admit, it was not at all what one might expect. But my small mind slowly expanded as he began to tell me how happy his photos make his friends and family, and how much joy he feels when someone describes his pictures back to him. What I so passionately enjoy about my own work was the same thing Henry experiences when he shares his. My surprise at his hobby had been misguided and misunderstood. When Henry takes a photo, he creates a work of art that can not only be enjoyed by others, but can also be repainted every time it's described to him. And that, is a truly profound piece.

As I finished my bottled water and began to wonder if there was still time for cake, Henry said, "I'm NOW going to GIVE you a GIFT, A-ron." *A gift?* My brain immediately began to piece together what Henry must look like in the light. I was finally going to be able to see his face, and complete the story I had been illustrating in my head. Up until that moment Henry was a figment of my imagination; a character unknown beyond the melody of his voice. *That must be the gift he intends to give me.* But then, as we navigated to the exit and a slice of light shined through the bottom of a blackened curtain, Henry pulled aside the last barrier to the outside world and said calmly, "My GIFT to YOU is the LIGHT." I was immediately ashamed that I had been more excited to piece together the remaining details of my experience than to practice gratitude for the profound gift I had been given: sight.

Dialogue in the Dark forced me out of my comfort zone and into an environment where I had to trust my instincts and rely on the senses that often go ignored (or are purposefully avoided when walking near Chinese sewers). It was a unique and enlightening experience to not only enter a foreign city, but to enter it without one of many abilities I frequently take for granted. I was grateful for Henry's willingness to guide me through the dark and humbled by the stories he shared. He allowed me to discover a trust in strangers and a trust in myself as I navigated yet another world I couldn't initially understand.

I left Dialogue in the Dark with a renewed sense of spontaneity and trust. That morning I had been preoccupied by what I would do after my tour with Henry. But now, I was no longer worried about where to go next or how to get back to the hotel. So I hopped on the nearest bus outside the mall and decided to get off whenever the time felt right. I avoided pulling out my map, and instead just sat quietly as the bus whipped around tight corners and along narrow backroads. I waited patiently while people hopped on and off the bus, constantly wondering where my small dot might be on Hong Kong's virtual map. Wherever it was, I knew I could find my way home.

About an hour and 45 minutes later I climbed off the bus at Shek-O Beach. Despite being dressed in black leggings and Converse, the beach seemed like a perfect way to end my day. Although I was incredibly unprepared without much more than a tattered map to sit on, it was one of the most exhilarating moments in my travels thus far. I sat on my makeshift towel considering just how out of place I was. And yet, I wasn't the slightest bit uncomfortable. I wasn't worried about who might be judging me, or who might be snapping a photo of the strange traveler who was sitting alone, on a paper map, surrounded by a crowded beach. I closed my eyes, leaned back into the breeze, and listened to the water hit the shore. And when I later climbed barefoot up the boulders that framed the coastline, I discovered a new appreciation for living in the moment. The world was wide-open, every moment a new possibility of learning, connecting, and living with purpose. I didn't care where I ended up or how I got there; I was happy, and that was all I needed.

A few days later after R and I had finished interviewing several business and non-profit owners from around the world, I sat in the Hong Kong airport awaiting my flight back to Shanghai. I was overwhelmed by a sense of joy I couldn't describe. I no longer felt weighed down with R's unpredictable moods, commanding management style, and unforgiving personality. Hong Kong had given me the breath of fresh air I needed. The stress of work, the anxiety that simmered constantly beneath my skin, and the worries of not being enough were slowly melting away. For the first time since I graduated from Butler, I felt as though I'd accomplished something great, as though I had taken back control of my life. Navigating in the dark can be a lonely and terrifying experience. At first it may feel isolating, but as you keep exploring you find people and places that are right there with you. You discover that if you trust your instincts and listen to your heart, you might just find yourself immersed in spectacular places with phenomenal people. You might just find joy and begin to appreciate the everyday moments that make life worth living.

Hard Truths to Swallow

*The problem, simply put, is that we cannot choose everything si-
multaneously. So we live in danger of becoming paralyzed by indecision, terrified that every choice might be the wrong choice.*
~ Elizabeth Gilbert ~

Shanghai, China | August 2017

My roommate Jenny truly came into my life with spectacular
timing: when I needed a companion, craved a meaningful
friendship, and coincidentally found myself in one of the most
challenging adversities I'd yet to face in my adult life. I attempted to grin and bear it while working for R, but he continued to
drive my reputation into the ground in front of the successful
international business owners with whom I was so excited to
network. I was frequently the butt of his jokes during presenta-
tions, and if I made one small mistake I never heard the end of
it. I took every soul-crushing blow as he reprimanded me for
being "such a damn millennial," despite having done nothing
out of line. Everything I produced was below his expectations,
and as someone who needs occasional positive reinforcement,
that only made my job harder. My work was continuously and
involuntarily edited and posted online without having any re-
semblance to my authentic skill set. I constantly had to fight for
my paycheck, which came sporadically and was often lower
than agreed upon. When I would inquire about my missing pay,
I simply received a snarky, "Oh, so it's all about the money to

you, isn't it?" And to top it all off, I was reminded on multiple occasions that if I didn't like working for him, I didn't have to; I could easily be replaced by two Chinese women for the same price. The same price of seven dollars an hour. Every day felt like a battle; to get out of bed, to commute to the office, and to sit there for eight hours pretending to be grateful for everything the universe had shoved into my life.

The post-graduate opportunity of a lifetime - for which I'd spent so much time preparing and excitedly anticipating - was a complete sham. And I felt it was entirely my fault for trusting him, for taking the leap, and for not noticing it sooner. Work was becoming less and less tolerable as time went on. I was constantly walking on eggshells, wary of R's unpredictable moods and snark. He made me feel ashamed to be a Millennial and I was discouraged that there was anything I could do to change his mind. But nothing boiled my blood faster than knowing that the extensive paid travel I had been promised was nowhere in sight. And to make matters worse, R was about to embark on a lengthy business trip to India. A trip on which I had not been invited.

A few days before he left China, I mustered up the courage and messaged R on WeChat.

August 14:

E: "Can you guarantee that I will be traveling to at least the remaining locations in your proposal in the next four months?"

R: "Managing a sick kid right now. Ok to talk about this tmrw?"

E: "Sure."

Two weeks later I still hadn't received an answer, so I logged onto Skype.

August 28:

"Hi R,

Hope India is going well. I wanted to touch base and see if you still intend to have me travel to the remaining locations from your proposal. Like I said, I'd be happy to continue editing when I return to the States, but I would also love to have the opportunity to film the series while I'm still in Asia. Particularly because the opportunity to travel was taken into consideration for a lower salary. I know it's difficult to schedule since you need cooperation from interviewees, but if you could provide an approximate timeline that would be helpful. With my boyfriend visiting in October it would be great to know what's coming up.

Thanks,

Erin"

Radio silence.

So I contacted him on WeChat.

August 29:

E: "Messaged you on Skype."

And then, despite telling me several times that Skype is the primary platform on which he communicates and that I need to be better about checking it more frequently because he doesn't ever use WeChat, he responded with, "I'm not on Skype today."

So I copied and pasted my thoughtfully written message into WeChat.

He responded. "Planning Bangkok for last week in September. Still working out actual dates. October… not sure yet. Taiwan is most likely. Maybe Singapore."

He was dancing around the answers again. I embraced my inner Jenny and decided to be more straightforward, to leave no doubt about what it was that I wanted.

E: "Can you guarantee that I will be traveling to at least the remaining locations in your proposal (Singapore, Taiwan, Thailand, and Indonesia) in the next three months?"

I closed my eyes and pressed send, entirely unsure if I wanted to know the answer. If he said yes, I would have to take a leap of faith and rely on someone who had already worn my trust incredibly thin. If he said no, my heart would shatter into a million pieces and I wouldn't know how to proceed. I sat there fidgeting, staring at my phone. A few minutes later, a WeChat notification came through.

R: "No. I can't guarantee."

Time stopped. My worst fears had come right to the surface and were now punching me directly in the throat. I felt like throwing up and sobbing simultaneously. I sent a screenshot of his message to Jenny and then (and I'm only telling you this because I want you to know the unapologetic truth) started tossing back wine. My mind was reeling…. *How can someone be so apathetic? How can someone break all the promises they made to someone who so enthusiastically wants to support their business goals? Does he not understand that he was the reason I gave up six months of stability, of being able to pay my student loans, of being* *near my college friends and family, of beginning a career with a promising future, of fully investing in a brand new relationship, for him?! Does he not have sympathy for having misled me so carefully that I was willing to continue working for $7 an hour in hopes that he'll one day miraculously follow through?* Well. Apparently not. He didn't realize, and he certainly didn't seem to care.

I was defeated. I closed the door to my room, curled up into bed and threw the covers over my head where I proceeded to form a tiny pond of tears in the mattress. *Oh what my friends and family back home would think of me now.*

Several hours later a thin sliver of remaining daylight seeped through the room-darkening curtains of my bedroom window, and a collection of wadded tissues had begun to creep their way towards my pillow. Jenny knocked on my bedroom door.

"Can I come in?"

I didn't answer, but Jenny came in anyway. Because Jenny does what Jenny wants and Jenny knew that's what I needed.

"Aww honey, I'm sorry it was such a bad day. Do you want to talk about it?"

I sat up slowly as she crossed the room. She plopped down in my yellow desk chair and propped her feet on the side of my bed, a bowl of homemade stir fry in her lap.

"I just don't know what to do, Jenny. I feel like such a failure." I fiddled with a used tissue. "Nothing is going how I thought it would and I feel so lost. I feel stupid for thinking this was going to be something real."

I embraced the ugly crier in me and let it all out. By this point, shame was no longer in my vocabulary; I was hopeless and not afraid to admit it. Jenny sat back chewing her stir fry and listened as I dumped out my woes.

"Everyone believed in me. They were so excited for this trip, some I think even more excited than I was. This was supposed to be the job that started my entire career and now I'm miserable, I hate myself, and I don't think I can keep going. But I can't give up because I need the money so I don't go home completely broke. I don't want this all to have been a complete waste. I just can't believe I'm working for someone so willing to take advantage people. He has no idea how much this has hurt me."

Her calm silence inspired my own, and I sat there inspecting the word vomit I'd just spewed all over the room.

She swallowed. "I want you to consider a few things. And don't think too hard, just tell me your first thoughts." As a chronic over-thinker, that assignment terrified me. She continued, "This job. Is it benefitting your long-term career goals?"

I stumbled over my thoughts as they all simultaneously tried to squeeze through the doorframe of my mouth. "Not really. I'm not even proud of the work I'm producing; I wouldn't show this to anyone let alone a potential future employer. I don't have a thing to put on my demo reel."

She let my answer hang in the air for a moment. "What about your finances? Is the paycheck worth it?"

This was a hard one for me because any paycheck at this point seemed better than none. But I also recognized that the largest chunk of my paycheck was supposed to be coming from paid travel, of which I was receiving minimal, and it was now clear there was little hope for future trips. By that point we had only made it to Hong Kong and I was convinced the only reason was because if he didn't take me somewhere, my visa would expire and he'd have to answer to the government. Regardless, I wasn't getting nearly my share of the deal.

I begrudgingly admitted the truth. "The paycheck isn't really worth it. My last payment wasn't in full and he blamed me for not understanding how electronic transfers work. I don't like having to question whether I'll be paid, let alone paid what I'm even owed. Plus, I'm not sure we'll travel anywhere else while I'm here. I don't trust him. And apparently neither does anyone else on his team. From day one they all warned me to be careful."

She looked at me with apprehension. "How about your personal well-being? Do you feel good about your job? About yourself?" My eyes fell on the pile of wet tissues crumpled by my computer, and the lump of my exhausted body beneath the striped duvet.

Without speaking a word, she knew my answer. And then she said exactly what I needed to hear: "If you can't find even one reason to stay, then don't. Stop letting him win. You're not helping yourself by letting this drag on. You have a choice in this. You always have a choice."

This very conversation, my friends, is why I will always love and be grateful for Jenny. I knew what she said was true; I knew that ultimately the decision was mine. But I didn't want to be responsible for the negative outcomes that could result in my decision: going home broke and unable to pay my student loans; being deemed a failure for an unsuccessful first job out of college; feeling as though perhaps I had been wrong the entire time and all of this frustration and blame-placing was just a coping mechanism to deal with self-inflicted misery. I suggested to Jenny that perhaps this mess was my own fault.

"No." She stopped me mid-sentence. "This is not your fault. You didn't make him treat you this way. It's not your fault he's a terrible person. It's not your fault you trusted someone who promised to take care of you. The only thing you're responsible for is your decisions moving forward." She threw another scoop of stir fry in her mouth, and looked at me expectantly.

In that very moment, as Jenny stared back at me with an eyebrow raised, I decided that something needed to change. Despite not wanting to give up, and despite my hard-headedness in wanting to fix the world, I realized that some things just aren't worth fighting over. Especially not when it meant that my well-being was at the bottom of my own priority list.

The next day I texted our office manager and told him I was sick. I spent the day in my apartment ordering takeout and watching pixelated Netflix films. The day after that I was "still sick," and "working from home." R hadn't given me any assignments, and the office was the last place I wanted to be. I sat there trying to convince myself that this setback did not imply defeat, but was rather a blessing disguised as heartbreak.

A few nights later I laid awake trying to plan my next move, what I would say to R, and what in the world I would do if he didn't respond well. My plane ticket home was already paid but wouldn't be coming for another few months. So if I ended up unemployed, I would have to figure something out. Around 1:30 in the morning I grew restless and wandered out of my bedroom to discover a white IKEA dining chair in the middle of our living room. I padded out onto the hardwood floor of our silent apartment and circled the obscurely placed furniture. Perched on the stained plastic chair was a handwritten letter, a bag of cookies, roll of crackers, and a Belgian chocolate bar. Unfortunately, the note did not say,

"To my dearest roommate Erin,

I leave for you this midnight snack for whenever you get hungry whilst attempting to combat insomnia."

Instead, it was addressed to Lisa. Lisa was the mysterious stranger I had heard about for weeks; a friend of Jenny's who was moving to Shanghai to study at the university. As thrilled as I was to make another friend, I was hesitant about her late night arrival and intimidated by Jenny's evidently close friendship with her. Although Lisa was only staying for a few nights after her arrival from Belgium, I feared she would replace me in Jenny's life and I would have to start going to the gym alone. When you've only just recently befriended an ally in the jungle, you don't go wandering off by yourself. Although I wouldn't say I distrusted Lisa as a person, I was certainly envious that Jenny thought to put out treats for her and not me.

I picked up the note and carried it over to the coffee table that was scattered with billing statements and junk mail. Finding an empty corner, I put the paper down and wrote a small contribution to Jenny's hospitality,

"Dear Lisa, welcome to our apartment! I can't wait to meet you! - Erin".

There. Maybe now at least she'll share those cookies….

Just as I placed the note back on its perch I heard the high-pitched beeps of our apartment door keypad. My heart thumped through the walls of my chest. *Lisa.* I dodged back to my bedroom as though I'd just peed my pants in the middle of a supermarket but didn't want to draw any attention. Which, by the way, was ironic, because in that terrifying moment I wasn't wearing any pants at all. As I hurled myself behind my bedroom door it dawned on me that if she had walked in even five seconds earlier she would have been welcomed by none other than a half-dressed weirdo drooling over her snacks in the dark. I'm not one to worry about first impressions, but that would've left quite a mark. Once my breathing had slowed and I heard Lisa close the door to the adjacent bedroom, I crawled back into bed and fell fast asleep.

I woke up to the smell of feminine shampoos and strong perfume. For the first time in a long time my shared bathroom actually smelled... good. I slid on some shorts and slowly opened my bedroom door. Pretending it was a morning like any other, I padded into the bathroom where I brushed my teeth, washed my face, and ran my fingers through my hair to make it look a little more, "I woke up like this. My hair is just naturally tamed and drop-dead gorgeous." As I walked back down the hallway I paused at Jenny's room to find Lisa occupying the extra space in her bed. I awkwardly said hi and wondered if jumping into their cuddle puddle would be more or less weird than being caught in my apartment at two a.m. without pants on.

That afternoon the three of us explored Shanghai together and I began to warm up to the idea of incorporating Lisa into my daily life. A few nights after her arrival we ventured out to Found 158, a maze of subterranean bars and restaurants that catered to the international population living in Shanghai. We descended the winding staircase to find ourselves immersed in cultures from all over the world: we walked by a European pub, an Italian cafe, a Vietnamese eatery, a Mexican cantina, and a Turkish restaurant. It was like an upscale, adult-only Epcot submerged beneath the Earth. If I had walked casually by this spot on the street, or biked alongside it on the road, I never would have noticed it existed without curiously peering over the street-level railing. It was seriously the fanciest concrete hole I've ever visited.

In the short amount of time Lisa and I spent getting to know each other I concluded that making friends abroad is far easier than at home. Here's why:

- True travelers are a certain breed, so when you meet one it's like running into a long lost friend at the grocery store - you ask where they've been, where they're going, and what their stories are. None of that, "What's your major?" or "Which rung of the corporate ladder are you?" bullcrap. It's mutually understood that none of those details are important. Those details don't change the person underneath.

- People come and go without warning, so there's very little pressure to find a "forever friend." Most of the people you'll meet are in-the-moment companions who may or may not even be in the same country tomorrow. They are "circumstantial," if you will. And without pressure, there's more room to be authentically yourself. Because of that, you learn pretty quickly whether or not you're compatible.

- Once you've grown accustomed to being alone and vulnerable in a foreign country, being vulnerable with people doesn't seem so hard. It's easy to tell your story and be authentically yourself because, number one, if they don't like you, who cares? There are plenty of other fish in the sea. And number two, you have a world to see; if you find a travel partner, great! But if not, the journey will go on without them.

My connections with Lisa and Jenny were fairly instantaneous considering most of my friendships back home took several months or even years to reach the level of, "Please bring over pints of ice cream and watch Rom Coms with me. I will not be wearing pants. Kthnxbai." In fact, Jenny and I reached that level so quickly I was almost astonished when she came flitting into my room the week after she moved in and announced, "I just had the best poop! Let's go to the gym!" So on September 4th, less than a week after Lisa and I had met, it hardly felt unnatural to ask if she was interested in joining me on an adventure. I messaged her on WeChat while riding the metro home from work.

E: "Hey! Thinking about taking a trip to Nanjing this weekend - want to join?"

L: "Sure! What day?"

I'd never traveled with Lisa, much less spent time with her sans Jenny. To book a trip with someone I knew little to nothing about was truly an act of spontaneity and vulnerability. But Jenny had been tied up with work, wanderlust was chewing at my feet, and the journey was sure to be a lot more fun with a friend. I had nothing to lose. So Lisa and I packed our day packs, and boarded a high speed train to the south.

Nanjing was an adventure in and of itself, let alone the experience of navigating a new city with someone I'd barely just met without so much as a vague idea of where either of us wanted to go or sought to accomplish. I had booked the train tickets only knowing that I needed to get out of Shanghai; I knew the rest would unfold with time. As we sat on the train watching the Chinese landscapes soar past our window, I showed her photos of my family, my childhood home, my friends from college, and my boyfriend, Josh. Without intending to, we scrolled through the entirety of my cell phone camera roll. And when we had finished mine, we began scrolling through hers. It was a fun pastime and an incredibly interesting way of getting to know someone. Without meaning to we learned about each other's perceptions of the world and most valuable moments in life. We quite literally witnessed each other's recent history through the lens of their own eyes.

When we arrived in Nanjing, Lisa and I faced one road bump after another. At first, we struggled to exit the train station, unsure of which direction we needed or where we even wanted to end up. When we finally found ourselves outdoors, we somehow also found ourselves in the middle of an AED (Automated External Defibrillators) convention. There were tents, giveaways, demonstrations, and even a dance team who created a unique visual reference for anyone learning how to perform CPR. Lisa and I watched the dancers in amusement until, much to our surprise, they invited us to join them. Lisa and I took one look at each other, and jumped into the group. Our first accomplishment in Nanjing was learning an AED dance. It was, to say the least, a memorable experience and a good reminder that dance requires no common language.

Lisa and I found ourselves walking along the streets of Nanjing beneath the shadows of the trees. Unlike Shanghai, this city was draped with greenery and its streets were mellow and lightly trafficked. It was a breath of fresh air from the big city smog and concrete landscapes. As we continued exploring, Lisa's demeanor only further contributed to what was becoming a truly tranquil and carefree adventure. Lisa exuded a type of composure that eased my stresses and made decisions far easier.

Traveling with others can be overwhelming, particularly when interests differ and opinions clash. But Lisa and I hardly butted heads; in fact, we were far closer to a couple of overzealous puppies walking each other on a leash shouting, "Where do you wanna go?"

"I don't care, where do you wanna go?!"

"I don't know! I'll just go wherever!"

"So will I!"

And that is precisely how we got around. We ended up eating lunch at a chicken joint named Big Face, wandering through Zhanyuan Garden, visiting the presidential palace, climbing the stairs to the top of the city wall, and leisurely biking through the city on rented Mobikes. In the afternoon, as we walked along the sidewalk, an elderly local insisted on reading Lisa's palm while another passerby rolled up next to us on his scooter and declared that he would come visit me in the United States and that I should be prepared for his arrival. I never said the things we did or came across were all normal... In fact, if you travel with me, I can almost guarantee you at least one experience that is completely out of the ordinary. I couldn't make these things up if I tried, but if I could, I'd have twelve more books out by now.

Every time we faced a new challenge - struggling to unlock our Mobikes, getting lost in an attempt to locate the entrance to the city walls, and almost missing our train home because we couldn't find our platform - Lisa provided a poised and dignified energy that seemed to lighten the very air that we breathed (which was great because breathing in China is like sucking play dough into your lungs). By the end of the day Lisa and I were satisfied with merely spending the time we had together wandering a new city and going where the roads took us. Before we headed back to the train station we decided to hunt down an afternoon snack and check out some local shopping. So we ended up in a cafe inside a department store where we indulged in yogurt parfaits.

Had it been anywhere in the United States, or even in Europe, it would have been odd that our primary source of entertainment from the table was a cafe manager chasing flies around the restaurant with a bug zapper. We watched in amusement as he crept up on the unsuspecting intruders and quickly brought them to justice. Every time we heard the familiar ZAP, of the swatter, we shouted "AAYYY" from our seats and applauded as though our home team had scored. It was one of many experiences best explained with, "Only in Asia...". We headed back to Shanghai that night running on all that was left of our adrenaline. As the train pulled out of Nanjing South Station, I realized just how fortunate I was to have embarked on an adventure with Lisa. I had fulfilled my need for exploration, learned what it was like to travel with no real plan or intention, and established a brand new friendship along the way.

All it took was one (very long) day trip outside of the city and suddenly my world became an open map. A welcomed anxiety came hurtling towards me as I realized I could go anywhere, do anything, and spend however long I wanted wandering aimlessly through a part of the world I'd never seen. I was finally able to embrace just how grandiose and exciting my next adventure could be. As Jenny so boldly reminded me, I am in control of my life and the decisions that guide it.

A few weeks later R surprisingly came through on one of his promises. He booked interviews for Bangkok and Hong Kong; the plan being to send me to Thailand a few days early, conduct several interviews, and then stop in Hong Kong on the way back to China. It was one last paid trip I could take before gracefully exiting with some remnants of dignity. So I agreed to take one final trip with R, if for nothing other than to reset my visa and try one last time to make something more of my crumbling post-graduate career. If all else failed, I knew there was another route I could take. And just as the buildings in Shanghai would continue to reconstruct themselves, so, too, would my future. As I began to prepare for Thailand, I sensed the beginning of many new adventures to come.

Tuk Tuks & Selfie Queens

Perhaps travel cannot prevent bigotry, but, by demonstrating that
all peoples cry, laugh, eat, worry, and die, it can introduce the idea that
if we try and understand each other, we may even become friends.
~ Maya Angelou ~

Bangkok, Thailand | September 21 - 27, 2017

I spent my first day in Bangkok trekking in the hottest of Thailand suns from the airport, to the metro station, to my hostel, back to the metro station, to a tuk tuk (a three-wheeled taxi) that tried to quadruple charge me for a ride to Wat Pho where I continued to walk for over an hour until I'd toured the entire Grand Palace and then some. I had immediately exhausted myself. But Thailand was unlike any Asian city I'd visited thus far, and I wasn't about to sit still. The city was bustling with heavy traffic and constant noise from street vendors, passersby shouting into their cell phones, the metro as it sped along the rails above the street, and the horns of impatient cars. The first serenity I found was within the Grand Palace, where visitors were few and the architectural wonder was adorned with intricate designs and embracing colors. I wandered through temples and along the outskirts of the palace walls, my spirits high but my feet beginning to complain.

As soon as I'd begrudgingly decided to make the 20 minute walk to Khao San Road, a friendly local waved me over to his tuk tuk. He was tall, young, and starry-eyed.

"Did you like the palace? It's very beautiful, no? Like you maybe."

I decided to take the compliment instead of question the 'maybe' tacked onto the end of his incredibly inauthentic pick-up line.

"Yes, it was incredible. So many colors and designs. I could spend hours here!"

"Where you go now, beautiful?" He leaned back casually against the frame of his tuk tuk.

My parents would have told me to be cautious of the incessant flattery, but I knew by now that 'beautiful' was just another word for 'clearly lost and vulnerable foreigner who is uninformed of fair tuk tuk pricing.'

"I'm going to Khao San Road."

He grinned at me. "Oh Khao San Road, yes, good place, very good place. Tell me, have you seen the 32 meter Buddha?"

Considering there were thousands of Buddha statues in this city and I'd likely already encountered 472 of them, I had no idea which statue he was referencing. So he offered to take me, 'for fair price,' and then said we would finish the trip at Khao San Road. He was friendly enough, but his asking price was still at least triple what my currency converter deemed as "fair." After some seriously hard bargaining and my final threat to walk, he made his final offer.

"I give you better rate, very cheap, but you help me, too."

I looked at him suspiciously. "What do you mean?"

"I give you low low price but we visit my friend's shop. You go in, look around, don't have to buy, but pretend. For a little time. Just a little. Pretend, and then come back outside." *Oh boy.*

I thought about how persuasive salesmen could be, and how little money was in my wallet, but figured the experience might be interesting. "I don't have to buy anything?"

"No. Don't buy. But I get ticket for gas. You shop, I get ticket."

I understood that 'ticket' meant voucher, of which he would be able to redeem for free or discounted gas. I had heard of this tourist trap before, a method of getting shopaholic tourists in front of pushy salesmen who then make your tuk tuk trip far more expensive than originally intended. The drivers got gas and the shops got business; it was a win-win. The rate my driver offered me now was far cheaper than what I'd ever hoped for. So I climbed in, shrugging away the 20 minutes I figured I'd spend inside the shop, and he pulled his tuk tuk into the streets of Bangkok.

Fast forward to entering an upscale fabric shop wearing black capri leggings, bright blue mesh Nike tennis shoes, a Butler Bulldog tank top, and a whole lot of sweat. I was out of place, confused, and not as prepared for the onslaught of persuasion as I had thought. If you've survived this experience, you are truly a hero. When I walked through the door I was immediately bombarded by a suave man in a freshly pressed suit. He asked what brought me into his store today.

What I wanted to say was, "Oh let's not play games, you know your commissioned tuk tuk driver brought me here. Now give him his freakin' coupon and spare me the sale."

What I said instead was, "I'm thinking about buying a dress."

Now, if you know me and dresses, and you know how big of a pushover I can be, you are aware that this was suddenly a very dangerous situation to be in. He piled books on the table in front of me and asked what kind of style I'd prefer. I flipped through them patiently, wishing I actually had the spare cash to make this happen. There were ballgowns, cocktail dresses, and, my greatest weakness, dresses with pockets. I pointed to a few "potentials" and then he led me upstairs to look at the fabrics. I ran my hand along the different makes of silk, dreaming of slipping a dress of that material over my head. But when I asked how much, the price tag dragged my jaw to the ground. Even though I wasn't intending to make a purchase, the very idea that someone would pay so much for clothing was beyond my comprehension.

"Ohhhh no, no, no, sir. I'm sorry I don't have that kind of money." I looked down at my sweaty torso in an attempt to emphasize just how out of place I was. But he didn't care a bit, so he tried a new tactic.

"Miss, look. Okay. Good quality, I give you for 25% discount. Best I can do. Beautiful dress, really, you should take home. We work fast." He held out a purple fabric from the shelf; my favorite color.

"I'm sorry, I just don't have that kind of money…"

He sighed. "Okay, okay, you win. I give you 35%. But no more."

"I would need a much bigger discount and a lot more cash."

For some reason, this got him excited. "Okay maybe we make dress for you and you come back to pay tomorrow. You come back tomorrow, yeah? You can bring more money."

He must have been convinced I was traveling with a secret safe conveniently stashed with hundreds of dollars in it.

I reassured him, "That's okay… the dresses are beautiful, really. I just didn't know the cost. I'm not really able to afford it…"

He seemed frustrated and suggested that I should check my wallet. So I smirked in amusement as I pulled out my wallet and opened it to show him the few bills I had tucked in my backpack before leaving my hostel. It was barely enough for dinner. There are many reasons I don't carry much cash and, if I do, keep a minimal number of bills in my wallet with the rest in a hidden pouch, and this just happened to be one of them. In any bartering situation, it's one thing to tell them you don't have the cash, but it's another to physically pull open your wallet and prove your lack of funds. Sure enough, my suave salesman looked incredibly discontent.

"Okay." He had me cornered. "Maybe you like to take a tie for your boyfriend. You have boyfriend?"

"How much?"

He led me over to several stands along the front wall that were draped with every fabric and color of tie. He informed me that one would only set me back $25. I pretended to think very seriously about it, all the while wondering what I might need to say in order to get out of there without spending a single penny. My brain was in overdrive, trying to get myself out of the mess for which I'd volunteered. I pointed to a stand close to the door that was lined with pairs of harem pants. I oo'd and awe'd over the intricate designs before using my strategic placement to get closer and closer to the exit.

And finally, after one last persuasive attempt to ask, "How much you can pay?" I muttered a quick, "Thank you for your time," and darted out the door.

Forty-five minutes of my life was gone and I thanked HIM for his time.

I climbed back into the tuk tuk while my driver made it clear he was quite pleased with my willingness to help. As he drove me through the streets of Bangkok the sun sank lower and lower until night overtook the sky. He dropped me off at Wat Intharawihan as promised and told me he would be waiting in the parking lot. I walked along a fence that led into the 32-meter Buddha and then followed the sounds of captivating rhythmic chanting through a darkened alley to find myself in front of a prayer hall. Now, I don't frequently follow the sounds of chanting through ominous darkened alleyways. BUT WHEN I DO, I discover an entire Ubosot (the holiest of prayer rooms) of practicing buddhists reciting prayer in such unity that it caused goosebumps to run up my spine, where they remained for the next 17 minutes. At first, I stood before the temple admiring its marble structure and letting the waves of prayer wash over me. I was intrigued, but intimidated. *Is it okay to go closer? Is it rude to listen in on a prayer? Am I dressed appropriately?* I had so many questions and not enough answers to make a reasonable decision, so I waited.

A few moments later a middle-aged man, seemingly foreign, confidently removed his shoes and walked into the hall. So I threw a t-shirt over my tank top (so as not to offend anyone with my shoulders) and then allowed my legs to carry me up the steps where I, too, removed my shoes, and approached the entrance. I stood observing from just outside the door until I noticed another woman sitting across the room. *It must be okay to go in.* I stepped over the threshold and kneeled in the back. *So far so good.* I was blending in.

What I had failed to realize before reserving my space in the hall was that the only other foreigners in the temple were mouthing the chanted prayer in a silent unison. I was the only one in the room who had little to no clue what was going on or what anyone was saying. Anxiety began to stab at my chest with the same rhythmic beats of their chanting. *I don't belong here. I should leave. They know I'm a fraud. What if I offend them?* I tried sending out positive energy so that they might understand I came with good intentions, but I wasn't confident they got the message. *Curse my natural curiosity and incessant desire to be a part of something bigger. Why couldn't I have just shied away and gone instead to Khao San Road with the rest of the tourists where I belong?!*

Yet, despite my hyperactive inner-monologue, something held me there. Perhaps it was the fear of everyone realizing what a fraud I was if I left a mere few minutes after my arrival, or perhaps it was because the chanting that once felt intimidating had begun to embrace my ears in a comforting rhythmic melody. I allowed my breath to slow and the panicked thoughts drift from mind. I let out the air I'd been stashing in my lungs. *Okay, I can do this. I'll just meditate. That's acceptable, right? I don't need to know what's being said to at least pretend to fit in.* I closed my eyes, bowed my head, and tried to clear my thoughts. The vocals washed over me like an embracing waterfall, the tones falling in and around the contours of my body. My thoughts kept barricading the back of my brain, wishing to feel something different, something magical. I wanted to be transported to another world in which these notes hitting my ears meant something more than just syllables. I wanted to come to some epic conclusion about my purpose in life and what Thailand would mean to my adventures. I wanted to spontaneously find out that I can levitate. Oh, and also that I had achieved nirvana. That would've been great. But ten minutes later I was retying my shoes, stuffing my t-shirt back into my bag, and walking back to the tuk tuk. Spirituality, my friends, just doesn't come that easy.

A life of gratitude and faith requires much more than observing one prayer. Rome wasn't built in a day, and neither should anything worth working towards in your life. If I sat down to write a book on the first try, we wouldn't be here, primarily because I wouldn't have much to say. It would read a little something like, *Try something and you shall succeed and become famous and everyone will love you. Congrats. The end. You win.* But instead, this book is full of the challenges and adversities faced throughout an adventure. It is a testament to the journey that I was on, and am still on. Ask me how many times I've legitimately tried to meditate. I'll let you in on the truth now and tell you maybe three. I knew walking into that Ubosot that I would not connect with the space as deeply as others, and I wasn't about to lie to myself trying. But if there's anything I learned from Tian Tan Buddha in Hong Kong, it was that those moments of true understanding and tranquility are never too far from reach.

By the time I made it to Khao San Road I was starving and willing to drool over the first street food cart that came my way. I handed over some bills in exchange for a takeaway box filled to the brim with carbs, and promptly sat down on the sidewalk where I shoveled veggie fried rice and mini egg rolls down my throat as fast as they would slide. Chewing, at this point, was a thing of the past. The shops and restaurants on Khao San Road were vibrating with energy. I watched from my perch on the sidewalk as groups of people gathered at nearby bars, gawked at the giant insects on display (only $3 for a photo), and purchased cheesy t-shirts that read, 'Same Same, But Different.'

Despite my assumptions that being surrounded by other travelers would be a welcomed relief, I felt strangely out of place, with zero to no interest in looking at the same pairs of pants or cell phone cases at every stall on the street. And I certainly wasn't about to pay $7 to drink a beer by myself. I observed as backpackers from all over the world shook hands with strangers and sat down to enjoy live music together as the night went on. My skin crawled with the sudden reminder that I was alone, that I had no one to share in my spontaneous experiences and adventures. Could I have gone over and shaken some hands? Sure. But I was so tired and grungy that even a handshake seemed like a daunting task, let alone elaborating on the backstory I knew they'd ask for. I realized that it was both a blessing and a curse to travel alone; if I didn't have the energy to talk, I didn't have to, nor did I have to debate plans with anyone or feel rushed to accomplish everything a group wanted to do. But sometimes, in all honesty, I just wanted someone to gawk at giant insects with me. I began to feel self-conscious; I became acutely aware that I was the only loner eating dinner on the sidewalk. Like any outsider at a middle school dance, I shoved one more spoonful of food into my mouth before picking myself up off the ground and looking for the first ride out of the area. I was exhausted and slightly embarrassed that I'd tried to blend in on a street where loners were far from few.

"Taxi, you need taxi? I have taxi for you!" A middle-aged local shouted at me from the road.

"I need the metro." It was a bit of a walk to the station and I knew my feet could no longer carry me that far.

"Yes, yes I can do for you!" After some standard bargaining I was following the driver to his car. He slid an orange vest over his shoulders and handed me a helmet. *Um. What?* I stood in awe as he threw his leg over a motorcycle parked on the side of the road and steadied it so that I could climb on.

"Whoops, sorry!" I panicked and began to ramble, "I meant a taxi-taxi, my parents would murder me if I got on this thing. It's not at all safe and I would never do anything they wouldn't approve of. Thanks though!" I turned and walked away as quickly as I could.

Just kidding! I snapped on my helmet, climbed on without a second thought, and rode off into the night. Sorry, not sorry, mom and dad.

We sped through the darkened streets so fast tears started to trickle from my eyes. The wind braced steadily against my face while my thighs gripped the seat so hard my legs started to tremble. It was exhilarating; I felt so alive! I felt completely out of control and yet knew I was entirely responsible for making the very decision that got me here in the first place. It was the perfect balance of living life on the edge without putting myself in harm's way. When we finally parked next to the National Stadium metro station I shoved my payment of 200 baht into my driver's hand and ran towards the ticket booth, adrenaline still pulsing through my veins. So much adrenaline, in fact, that when I got off the metro to find a monsoon suddenly blowing through the city, I simply pulled a thin poncho from my backpack, tossed it over my head, and decided to make a run for it. No amount of rain could compete with my renewed spirit. *My tired feet can't hold me back now!* Well, maybe not in that very moment, but I did have some serious regrets as my only pair of tennis shoes were now soaked and, as I would shortly come to find, unwearable for the next three days.

The following morning I begrudgingly heard my mother's stern disapproval as I headed out for the day wearing the only other pair of shoes I had available: flip flops. You probably already know this, but unless you intend to ride only in a tuk tuk or taxi and be in no way self-sufficient, flip flops are a horrible, horrible, horrible plan. But I had places to go, sights to see, and nothing was going to stand in my way.

Weeks prior, during a particularly dull few hours in the Shanghai office, I had posted in a Facebook group of female travelers requesting recommendations for things to do in Bangkok. One of the many comments in particular had caught my attention.

You should take a day trip to cycle around the Ancient City in Samutprakarn. Called Muangboran. It is a huge park in the shape of the country and they have rebuilt all the famous temples so you can 'see all of Thailand in one day.' Very few western tourists know about this place. I live close by and take all my friends and family; they all say it's been their favorite day out by far.

If you tell me tourists don't know about a place, you'll definitely find me there! Not because I'm trying to be a trendsetter and do all the things no one else has discovered yet, but because I seriously enjoy the lack of selfie sticks and fanny-pack-wearing loud mouths who can't seem to grasp the concept of common cultural courtesies. *No, this historical site does not offer free WiFi, get over yourself.* Rant over. I happily grabbed my daypack from the hostel room and headed to the very end of the Sukhumvit Metro Line where I then hailed a cab. After I hopped inside, the driver began to pull around the block while I enthusiastically recited, "Muangboran" in the best Thai accent that I could. He looked at me like I was from Mars. I tried writing it phonetically, repeating it with other types of accents, charismatically pretending I was a giant temple or palace; nothing was working. The driver looked like a saddened deer in headlights. The poor guy was clueless, and all because I was incredibly unprepared.

What surprised me the most was that instead of kicking me out, like most taxi drivers in Southeast Asia would do, he simply kept driving around the block and looking at me like I would eventually start speaking his language. So I finally had to give up for him and signaled to pull over where he regrettably left me standing there on a street I didn't recognize. Knowing I had no other options, I hesitantly approached a few locals taking a break outside of an antique shop and once again attempted my poor pronunciation of Muangboran. When they didn't initially understand, I threw in a little charades, performing the 'A' of YMCA over my head and snapping some photos on my imaginary camera. Ten minutes later a kind woman I'd somehow befriended in the process held my hand and walked me back to the street corner. She flagged down another cab, spoke quickly to the driver in Thai while pointing down the road, and then opened the back door for me. The driver nodded, she closed the door behind me, and he pulled away from the curb. I watched as she disappeared behind me. She and the driver were both confident, but I was completely oblivious of what had just happened. It dawned on me that this woman could have misunderstood my charades and was sending me halfway across the city only to find myself paying an absurdly high taxi bill and never reaching Muangboran. But the general direction we were headed felt right, so I decided that the only thing I could do was enjoy the ride. Since communication was obviously not an option, I once again threw myself into the trusting hands of the incredibly friendly locals and sat silently in the backseat as my driver navigated through traffic. About a half hour later I was graciously delivered right where I had wanted to go.

Muangboran was a paradise of agricultural and historical wonders. At the entrance I rented a bike that I rode through the Thailand-shaped park for over four hours, blissfully unaware of the world outside its borders. My hair whipped around my sweaty neck as I sailed past miniature ancient palaces, tributes to the great Buddha, intricately designed monasteries, and gardens of yogis. I hiked up the infinite steps of the reconstruction of Prasat Phra Wihan and gazed in wonder at the Mondop of Bodhisattva Avalokiteshvara. I ate a delicious home-cooked meal of fried rice and egg under a small snack hut along one of the side roads, ducked under intricately designed archways, and meandered through crumbling hallways that were part of the magnificent architecture of Thailand's rich history. And all of this without running into any crowds or, really, anyone else for that matter. The silence was nearly deafening. And it. Was. Incredible.

I headed back towards the exit where I spotted one last temple and decided to park my bike out front to explore. I smiled and nodded to the nearby security guard at which point his expression changed from boredom to one of concern as he mumbled something in Thai and pointed to my bike. One of my tires was going flat. I knew the ride had gotten a bit bumpier, but hadn't thought anything of it because my adventure would soon be over and I could let them know at the front office that the bike could use a little air. I wasn't quite riding on the rim so I wasn't worried about doing any damage to the frame.

So I laughed and waved my hand dismissively, reassuring him, "It's okay, it's okay," and then disappeared into what is most closely translated to "Wachiratham Cathedral, The Buddha of Anat Universe," (or พุทธาวาสแห่งอนัตตจักรวาล if you know how to read Thai). As I walked into the courtyard I looked up to see the most magnificent structure I'd ever seen, covered from roof to foundation in a gold finish that glistened in the sunlight. A statue of Buddha stood towering over me as I paced the perimeter of the grounds. I was overcome by the sensation that I was not worthy of being here, that I was not noble nor spiritual enough to be in the presence of something so spectacular.

By the time I left, my bike had vanished and the security guard was proudly standing next to its replacement, both tires full of air. Without knowing my story, without being able to communicate, without so much as a notion of what kind of person I was, he had demonstrated a sincere care for my well-being and overall experience in the park. He went out of his way to help a stranger regardless of whether or not it directly affected him. I grinned with appreciation, placed my hands at heart center, bowed my head and said, "Khob khun ka, khob khun ka." *"Thank you, thank you."*

Khob khun ka was a phrase I frequently found myself repeating in Thailand. Although Bangkok was an overwhelming and crowded city, I learned to take refuge in the momentary connections I formed with locals. The security guard at Muangboran was not the first nor the last to show me unconditional kindness. First was a staff member at my hostel, Weeping Willow, who walked me all the way to the store herself to make sure I found the best mango sticky rice there was to offer. Every time I walked into a 7/11 (which was frequently because they are quite literally on every corner), I received a friendly bow and a genuinely welcoming, "Sawahdeeka." There was the waitress at a restaurant who watched as I dumped the entirety of my wallet onto the counter to pay for my takeout, but, when I still fell 300 baht short, waived her hands and said, "On me, I pay. No worry." And there was the bartender who, when I declined the drink menu because I only had enough cash for food, brought over the traditional welcome drink - on the house - and told me to have a good night. No matter where I went or what I did, I was sincerely cared for. The energy was contagious and the overwhelming generosity was truly touching.

So when I walked into Malai Massage and Beauty to see if I could tend to my tired and abused feet, it was only fitting that I was soon befriended by two enthusiastic and chatty nail technicians. I was eager to pamper myself and give my feet the love they deserved after having put them through so much adventure. And I'll be completely honest, the only reason I chose this location over every other nail salon in Bangkok (which may be in close competition to the number of 7/11s) was because all of the technicians wore purple button-down shirts. Yes, I chose my nail salon simply because they all wore my favorite color. Sometimes, decisions need to be made with a little less logic. Following Thai customs, I took my shoes off at the door, and one of the girls led me to the back of the salon to a puffy recliner where she placed a pillow behind my back and handed me a cup of warm tea.

She placed a few polish choices on my lap and I immediately pulled out a shade of radiant purple. She smiled widely and pointed to her shirt, "Same same."

I nodded and thoughtfully enunciated, "My favorite color."

She pointed to herself. "Me same. Nice color miss." Thus began the kindling of our odd friendship.

I introduced myself, "My name is Erin. What is yours?"

She took a brief pause from stripping some unbelievable calluses from the bottom of my feet. "I'm Yok. Happy to meet you."

It was so strange to communicate with another adult using such simple words and sentence structures. I kept wondering what kind of conversation would have been possible had we shared a common language. Yok continued grooming my poor and abused feet while I opened my backpack to inspect the souvenirs I had purchased from Chatuchak Market earlier that day.

I'd been struggling to locate a set of gifts I could bring home that were both meaningful and personal. The touristy keychains and t-shirts were cute, but not at all unique to the places I had been and the experiences I'd so enjoyed. I didn't want to bring home something that would sit on someone's shelf and eventually be tossed in a donate pile or, even worse, the garbage. While I was hunting for souvenirs that morning I became hopelessly lost in Chatuchak Market. The 27 acres of land swallowed me whole and the 15,000 and some odd booths began to pull me in every direction. One of them happened to be a leather shop manned by three exceptionally charismatic local men. They danced to music while they collected order forms and by the inflections in their voices and the laughter of other customers I could tell they were quite the comedy routine. They had a collection of various items including luggage tags, passport covers, purses, wallets, laptop covers, and wristlets. Each item came with a customizable name plate and a charm from one of the many bins displayed in front of their booth. I stood admiring the colorful passport covers and the ideas started flowing. I picked out a different color cover for each of my fellow travel junkie friends and family members back home and selected several charms that reflected their personalities. Then I adorned each of them with a token of my own: a small compass that rested on the inside corner of each cover. It was a representation of my own passion for travel and a wish for each of them to continue their own adventures. The booth owners were thrilled every time I thought of someone else to spoil and happily got to work crafting each of the passport covers I'd designed. By the time I walked away I had a grin on my face, from the entertainment of the booth owners and for finally finding a gift worth giving.

Yok looked up from her diligent application of purple polish to my now pampered feet. Without missing a beat she pointed to the compass emblem on the inside of one of the passports.

"Same same. You see?" She then pointed to my shirt. I suddenly realized I had been wearing my Modo Yoga tank top which featured a giant compass on the front, almost identical to the ones I'd picked out for the inside covers. I face-palmed a little too hard and nearly took out my eye. Those guys at the leather shop must have thought I was a narcissistic weirdo for decorating what were clearly gifts for people back home with an image I was already so confidently wearing. Yok and I had a friendly laugh at the ridiculousness of the entire situation.

As she continued painting my toes another technician came by and began enthusiastically chattering to Yok.

Yok turned to address me and said, "She say pretty eyes."

"Khob Khun ka," I grinned and bowed in gratitude. It was the only way I knew how to thank her.

"My name Fay." She tipped back on her heels and wrung her hands tightly in front of her. It reminded me of a young girl finally telling her crush that she liked him. We added each other on WeChat (it wasn't unusual to find users outside of China) and began swapping photos of our families. Both of them melted over the images of me and my mom, and I shared with them pictures of my boyfriend and my best friends from college.

To each they said, "So beautiful, so beautiful."

By the time Yok had finished painting my toes, I had several invitations to visit their homes and received a handful of adorable GIFs from them on WeChat. Before I left we took a photo together out front of the salon, and as I headed back into the bustling streets I shouted, "Khob khun ka, khob khun ka!"

A few days later I returned to the salon after an unfortunate fall in the shower in which I chipped an entire chunk of that beautiful radiant purple from my big toenail. I wasn't even upset with the fact that my hip was horrifically bruised and all five toes on my right foot were now throbbing. No, I was crushed that Yok's hard work had gone to waste because I was such a klutz. So when I approached her that evening to show her my damaged toe, reenacting in comical format the sheer clumsiness with which I tumbled onto the shower floor, I reassured her that I would be happy to pay for the fix. I kid you not, three minutes later I was sitting on a bench outside the salon surrounded by a group of giggling Thai women as Yok repainted my toenail and Fay applied tiger balm (arguably the world's most effective itch relief) to the countless mosquito bites covering my legs. I sat there for an hour while these women lovingly played with my hair and mindlessly massaged my tired legs as they conversed with a local who was walking the street selling clothes from her arms. I watched at they took turns disappearing into the shop to try on different outfits, and then arriving at the doorway like a runway model. Each new outfit brought a rush of new laughter. Despite having no comprehension of what was being said, I felt like I was one of the girls. They knew I couldn't communicate, yet included me in their laughter, and it made all the difference in the world.

That following morning, as I pulled my suitcase down the uneven street, I passed by Malai one last time to say goodbye. But unlike the night before, when the light from the salon cast spotlights on the vibrant energy of the women sitting outside, the shop was quiet. A metal garage door hid the giant glass windows in front. I stood there for a moment smiling, in appreciation not only of the hospitality of Yok and Fay, but also of the thoughtfulness of the security guard, the kindness of the antique shop owner, the generosity of the waitress and the bartender, and the selflessness of the hostel worker. As my metro car left the station and headed towards the airport, I considered just how unique these international connections had become. I found myself united with people from around the world with whom I could not possibly communicate without a translator. We were brought together by mere coincidence and in it discovered an authenticity born of our shared experiences and basic human needs. They took care of me not because I paid them, or had any authority over them, but because - whether I intended to or not - I asked for help. I practiced vulnerability; they recognized someone in need, and they helped the best they could. No matter how introverted or extroverted we might be, there is a place in all of us that craves the intimacy of human vulnerability and connection. Bangkok, Thailand was just that; an overwhelmingly busy city, yes, but a city filled with people who love unconditionally and embrace opportunities to build meaningful relationships, even with short-term visitors.

Every month, sometimes more frequently, Fay sends photos upon photos of her and her many friends and family members in Thailand. I've received videos of her home during rainy season, pictures of her trying on clothes at the mall, selfies with her friends at work, and even photos of her parents taking naps on the floor during a particularly hot afternoon. I have been given digital tours of her farmhouse and been invited to stay with her family on multiple occasions. I would send her back photos of my apartment and selfies in my work attire. She would tell me, in very broken English, about the men that broke her heart and how it made her sad. I would reassure her broken heart with GIFs of hugs and cute animals, and she would later comfort my sad emojis with hearts and confetti. We found ways to portray the emotions we felt with imagery and, even without words, our love and support were understood. I embrace the days that Fay sends me 26 WeChat messages all at once, because they represent an authentic connection that crosses over oceans, cultures, and even languages. They represent a sincere compassion and empathy from someone who doesn't even know my last name.

Chocolate Cake
& Serendipity

What is that feeling when you're driving away from people and they recede on the plain till you see their specks dispersing? - it's the too-huge world vaulting us, and it's goodbye. But we lean forward to the next crazy venture beneath the skies.

~ Jack Kerouac ~

Shanghai, China | September 28 - October 10

By the time I left Thailand, I had affirmation that it was time to distance myself from R. Despite several enlightening interviews and a few brief moments of laughter with him, I could no longer maintain my cool in the face of R's blatant hypocrisy. Enter the story of the infamous chocolate cake… It all began with a casual conversation in the cafe that sold the delectable dessert R had been talking about for weeks. I had skipped breakfast as per R's recommendation and, although the hunger pains were stirring in my belly, I knew it would be worthwhile in the end. We passed the pastry case on the way to our table and I can't tell you how tempting it was to sneak around the counter and start stuffing my face. It would have been a new rendition of the chocolate cake scene from "Matilda".

We sat in a corner of the cafe chatting with a woman who began a travel program for kids that provides opportunities for cultural immersion to those who otherwise wouldn't be able to afford it. I was fascinated; she spoke of her motivation behind the organization and how she managed to build such a successful program. I asked her about the development of her curriculum and as she answered my question I looked over to find R scrolling through his phone. I watched from the corner of my eye as he ignored her completely and instead answered emails, responded to messages, and searched for directions to the next location. This was, unfortunately, not unusual behavior from him; too often he had an attitude that proclaimed, "I'm only interested in what you have to say if it's interesting or helpful to me," and I frequently found myself compensating accordingly. I tried my best to give her my full attention so as to distract her from his apparent disinterest in the conversation.

When he finally set his phone down and checked back in, he began inquiring about the sustainability of her business plan. It was then that my own mind wandered off. I began to wonder if I had discovered my next job opportunity. Her energy was captivating, the work aligned precisely with my passion for helping others, and it would be a career that involved fulfilling travel and connection. *This is the one....* I pulled out my phone to find her on LinkedIn while she continued to answer R's questions. As soon as I hit 'connect' on her profile, I put my phone back in my backpack.

After we shook hands and parted ways my mouth began to water in anticipation of chocolate cake. Just as I was envisioning taking my first fork-full, R decided that he no longer wanted to eat there. He suggested we go somewhere else and headed straight for the door. I suppose I could have spoken up, I could have stood my ground and told him I needed breakfast, I could have told him I'd been waiting for this for weeks and it wasn't fair for him to change his mind now. I could have even thrown the toddler tantrum I felt boiling beneath my skin. But I let it go. I didn't have the energy nor the motivation to fight him. I was done.

When we left the cafe, he confronted me. "You really need to put your phone away during interviews. It's incredibly rude and disrespectful. She kept looking over at you and it was really embarrassing for me."

My face became flushed with anger. It took every ounce of me not to turn around and walk in the opposite direction; to curse his name, flip him the bird, and head back to Shanghai without him (and probably stop back at the cafe on my way). Not only was he criticizing me for something he failed to see in himself, but I was becoming incredibly hungry and frustrated. *How dare he nitpick a momentary flaw in the face of so many of his own heartbreaking failures.*

I followed him to the metro several paces behind, and it suddenly dawned on me why the chocolate cake had made me so upset. It was yet another representation of every broken promise he'd ever made. I listed them in my head: new computer, networking opportunities, fulfilling work, paid travel to up to five different countries, a steady paycheck, and meaningful adventure. I realized that while some of those promises were more difficult to uphold than others, that business and scheduling can occasionally get in the way, chocolate cake was the one thing on which he easily could have followed through. We were already there, already hungry, and it would have been effortless to flag down a waiter. But he couldn't do even that. He couldn't fulfill a promise so simple as a piece of chocolate cake.

We stood silently swaying back and forth on the metro. I decided in that moment that it was time to initiate a change. R had made the worst management mistake any leader could. By not following through on even the simplest of promises, he lost my trust entirely. So I strategized my next moves, and casually asked R if he wouldn't mind sending my paycheck a little earlier since my usual payday would fall over the upcoming weeklong national holiday.

"I want you to enjoy your holiday and not have to worry about processing a payment for me." I tried to make my own needs about him instead. "Plus, the extra cash would be helpful during vacation."

In all reality, I just wanted to be paid before Josh arrived in Shanghai. By the time I picked him up at the airport I wanted to be free of preoccupied thoughts and stress. I wanted a fresh start and I wanted to share it with him.

Before I left the United States I had used a good portion of my savings to pay for Josh's very first passport and international plane ticket. If that wasn't a bold move within the first two months of a relationship, I honestly don't know what would have been. But he had been so supportive of my adventures and demonstrated a sincerity that I had yet to find in another man; I wanted to share this part of my life with him. It was his first international trip, let alone solo voyage overseas, and I could not have been more excited to share with him my new home in Shanghai. The last thing I wanted when his plane landed, was for my mind to be far off in a place that was still worried about work.

R scrolled thoughtlessly through his phone but replied, "Sure, I can pay you when you get back. Just send me the invoice."

I was surprised at his cooperation, but incredibly grateful for a small win. Feeling good about our compromise, and reassured that I would receive my final paycheck a little early, I graciously joined R as we flew into Hong Kong where we conducted several more interviews. R then remained in Hong Kong while I flew back to Shanghai alone.

Shanghai, China | September 29 - October 7

I sent R my invoice as soon as I got back to my apartment in Shanghai. It was long after midnight, but I wanted to be sure my part was done. The next morning, I messaged R on WeChat. I felt confident that he would follow through but wanted to provide a gentle reminder.

E: "Emailed you my invoice - thanks for paying today!"

R: "Ok. Will pay on 5th as always. Have a good holiday."

And then a few minutes later,

R: "Also. Please drop equipment off at office today or tomorrow. I'll need it over holiday. Thanks."

I rolled my eyes and messaged back.

E: "I thought you said the other day you'd pay today so we didn't have to worry about it over the holiday." I waited impatiently.

R: "Erin. I didn't say that." My stomach rose into my throat.

I messaged with determination.

E: "Yes you did. On the metro. I said I'll send you the invoice the day I get back so you can pay it sooner and you said, 'yeah that's fine.' Otherwise I wouldn't have sent you the invoice yet."

And then, after 15 minutes of waiting, I messaged in jest.

E: "Perhaps I should start recording our conversations? *insert winking emoji here*"

Fifteen minutes later I had biked to the office and dropped off the equipment. As I did, I grabbed my personal belongings from my desk and stuffed them in my backpack. My initial plan was to resume my freelancing status with R so that I could be more flexible and avoid his unpredictable moods, but if that didn't work for him then I'd find something else. Either way, I wouldn't be coming back to the office and I was beyond ready for a week of uninterrupted bliss as I introduced Josh to my life in China. In just a few hours I would be headed to the airport to pick him up, and there wasn't a single thing R could do to ruin that for me.

I messaged him.

E: "Equipment is at the office. I would greatly appreciate the follow-through on paying today as you said. Let me know."

Fifteen minutes later when I arrived home, I followed up.

E: "I would not have stayed up until 4 a.m. putting together the invoice if you had said you wouldn't pay today."

Several hours later on my way to the airport, I sent one final attempt.

E: "You said you would pay today since it is a working day. Please let me know if you will do so."

And then I put my phone down and watched the Shanghai skyline fly by my window, my heartbeat thumping out of my chest in anticipation of finally seeing Josh in person for the first time in over three months. It was crazy to think that in the five-and-a-half months we'd been dating, only two of those were spent in the same city, let alone the same country. And yet, somehow, our relationship only grew stronger. He encouraged me when I felt uncertain, loved me when I was lonely, and applauded every bit of my success. He knew all the right words to say and just how to say them. And as he walked around the corner of the arrivals gate, I felt as though my world had finally become whole again.

Josh and I spent an unforgettable week exploring Shanghai. Although the October national holiday made for an interesting first visit to China, Josh took in every new experience with enthusiasm and curiosity. I felt like a proud parent watching their child walk alone for the first time. What had become routine and mundane for me, was so new and invigorating for him. I got to vicariously relive my first experiences in China.

The benefit to it being a national holiday was that the city streets and local businesses in Shanghai were fairly quiet. We could wander the local markets without bumping shoulders, and bike on the main streets without much anxiety over traffic and hordes of pedestrians. The downside was that any and every tourist attraction was host to what felt like the entire population of China. Yuyuan Garden turned into standing (and slightly wiggling) room only, and nearly every road and metro station downtown were inaccessible. There were areas where bikes were banned due to the high foot traffic, and you couldn't go within a mile of a main attraction by car without sitting on the road for an hour. If you haven't been in Shanghai (or any primary Asian destination) during October holiday, I certainly wouldn't recommend putting it on your bucket list. After Josh and I finally made it to the Bund long enough for a photo with the Shanghai skyline, we made a beeline back to my apartment for some much needed peace and quiet.

Two days after Josh arrived, R finally messaged me back.

R: "Will pay tonight/tmrw morning."

Josh and I spent the rest of the week detoxing and resetting my mentality. No, not detoxing in the way of juicing and sweat lodges, but rather epic Netflix binges (albeit quite pixelated), Papa John's pizza, and more than our fair share of Magnum ice cream bars. At first we tried to blame Josh's sesame allergy for our inability to eat local cuisine, but in all reality I just wanted an excuse to gorge myself on some home-inspired 'za. We spent endless hours curled up in bed together. For the first time in a while it felt as though I could breathe deeply. The stress and anxiety I had built up inside melted away within just a few days of being with Josh. And it wasn't so much the fact that it was my boyfriend (although, honey, I'm very grateful it was), but rather simply being near someone who knew me outside my life in China. Someone who could remind me of the person I was before my dream job was shattered and my trust jaded. Someone who could replenish my heart with unconditional love and revitalize my spirit with just one hug. As we lay next to each other on my IKEA mattress, I held onto him tightly. For, if I let go, I was afraid he might disappear.

R and I never rekindled our working relationship; After a long conversation with Josh and some advising from my parents, I asked R if he would allow me to resume my remote editing position. The goal was to continue making money while on the road and not completely sever an opportunity to remain connected to Asia. It was a professional, courteous, and well-thought out plan. I anticipated R would still need the help, and hoped he would allow me to temporarily keep the external hard drive so that my laptop could handle the work load. I would return it before I went home to the States, of course, but it would make editing on the road much easier. It was supposed to be a win-win; R would get the edits he needed with someone who already knew the workflow, and I would be able to travel while still making an income. When I originally proposed the idea, he was surprisingly open to it. But when he asked for me to return the external hard drive, and I tried to explain that without it I couldn't edit his content, things went south.

R: "Sorry, Erin. You are going to have to work that out on your own. The drive is property of (the company), and you chose to end the arrangement."

Despite trying endlessly to explain that I would still be working for him and his company remotely, and that I would return the drive before I left in December, he refused.

R: "You chose to accept this assignment, and you are choosing to end it. The drive, and the work, is the property of (the company)."

E: "I'm not ending anything, I am continuing to work for you. I may not have internet access on the road so having the files locally would be more convenient."

He wasn't happy with my response.

R: "I'm not going to continue this conversation. The drive is to be returned before you leave. Including all working files for all work, introductions, events, interviews, etc."

I had a hard time understanding how he expected me to edit without the hard drive that kept my computer running, let alone without any of the content. It no longer felt as though he wanted me to edit for him at all.

By the time Josh and I sat huddled together on the metro as it sped towards Pudong airport, I was no longer receiving answers from R on WeChat. I concluded that because of his blatant disinterest in making it possible for me to edit his projects on the road, our contract had ended. He clearly had no intention of cooperating or discussing further solutions to help meet his needs, so I considered our working relationship over. I didn't even have the chance to resign, because his cold shoulder told me I had already been let go.

Saying goodbye to my position with R's company was hard only because it left me stranded and unsure about my future. The empty space that had once been occupied by projects and assignments - no matter how mundane - now felt threatening. But saying goodbye to Josh was a new level of difficulty. Watching him disappear behind security check-in was like watching a piece of me leave. When people we love physically distance themselves, it can feel like losing a part of your identity. This doesn't mean you aren't secure with yourself, or don't know who you are without others, but more so that the person you are when you're with them temporarily fades. When I first started getting to know Josh, I remember how worried my friends were that I appeared to be falling for him so quickly. But as we sat there one night, talking about Josh and my past relationships, I suddenly realized why Josh felt so right. Everything I did, and everything I said, was authentically me. Unlike my past relationships in which I would sacrifice pieces of myself to appeal to my partner (even something as small as switching up my favorite flavor of ice cream), I realized that, with Josh, I hadn't changed a single thing. Perhaps it was because, right before I met him, I had decided to focus on myself and my future. Or perhaps it was knowing that Asia was around the corner and I didn't have much hope he'd stick around. Whatever the reason, I didn't hold back and I didn't adapt who I was. And Josh still wanted to be with me all the same.

When people in our lives leave, we lose a piece of ourselves, because the person we are when we're with them is unique to that relationship. No two people are the same, so different relationships bring out different parts of ourselves. This applies to both positive and negative relationships. When things ended with R, I lost the part of me that was angry and hurt. I felt the weight of instability and confusion lift from my chest. But I also walked away stronger, having learned a valuable lesson in self-empowerment and respect. Watching Josh leave, I felt the part of me fade that was confident that no matter what I said or did, I would be unconditionally accepted. I lost the security blanket of having someone nearby who understood who I really was behind the language barriers, and unfamiliar customs. I recognized the absence of someone who, despite all the adversities I faced, knew which direction my heart wanted to go. It wasn't quite loneliness, but rather a sudden realization that I was, once again, alone. The silence was unbearable and my unplanned future was looming.

I watched the Shanghai airport fade off into the distance as the metro car methodically sped its way back into the city, and I soon began to cry. I was overwhelmed with joy and devastation all at once; my heart didn't know whether to feel broken or whole. There were so many endings met with so many beginnings that my emotional stability was wavering. I sat sniffling while a young Chinese mother watched unapologetically from across the aisle. She dug through her purse and pulled out a pack of tissues. I watched from beneath my heavy lashes as she opened the package and began to take one out. And then, she reconsidered and handed me the whole pack.

With kind eyes and a well-intentioned smile she said in broken English, "Cry not on the outside, only on the inside."

Somewhere beneath my tears a quiet laughter bubbled up from my chest. It is still, to this day, the strangest comfort I've ever been offered. *Do my tears make me appear weak? Does she pity me? Should I be suppressing these overbearing emotions?*

I learned a very significant cultural difference between Americans and Chinese in that moment, but I also came to realize that her words could be impactful nonetheless. I could cry all day but that would not change reality. If I wanted to create something new, begin a new chapter, or make strides towards a new frame of mind, I had to stop crying and start processing. I can't cry on the outside if my inside isn't working to change anything. The person who existed when Josh was nearby was someone I could rediscover and establish on my own. Josh recognized me as my true self, and I knew with the right experiences and conversations I, too, could recognize and be-come that person. No amount of adversity, discomfort, or fear would change who I was. And no amount of crying was going to change that, either. I had to start altering my perceptions and seeking joy in the life I had already created.

As Josh's plane took off I had no idea that my upcoming ad-ventures through Southeast Asia would not only teach me how to find that confidence in myself, but also would build me up to face the world with a renewed perception of trust, vulnerability, and love. The first morning I woke up in which R did not await my arrival at the office, was the day I came to embrace a pro-found gratitude for impermanence. It was the day I recognized that just as joy can be stripped away so, too, can the pain and frustration. It was the day I began to appreciate the adversities and challenges that the universe had tossed my way. It was the day I understood that with all pain comes resolution, but the choice in creating that is up to us. It was the day that I truly be-gan to live.

A Traveler in
Western China

It's On My List

You can't make decisions based on fear and the possibility
of what might happen.
~ Michelle Obama ~

Shanghai, China | October 10

In the weeks leading up to my so-called "resignation," I had been thinking about my next adventure. In the early days, I considered going home. I was devastated at the end of what was supposed to have been my dream job and, frankly, embarrassed to remain in Shanghai alone and unemployed. The thought of having been so successful throughout my years of academia only to end up stranded in a foreign country with zero income a mere five months after graduating, was appalling. Although I recognized the triumph of having moved to Asia alone in the first place, I still felt the weight of being deemed a failure in the eyes of America's white-picket-fence society. I was supposed to be climbing the ladder of success, not flopping around aimlessly halfway around the globe. My alma mater would be so disappointed.

When R first booked my flight to Shanghai he had included a return ticket for December. It was cheaper for him to purchase both at one time and since we had agreed upon no longer than six months we thought it appropriate to have an end date. But even though I had a free ticket home I considered paying to change the date. I figured it would be better to mourn my loss in the comfort of my own home than to be a sad, unemployed young adult living in Shanghai. If I went home, I could take the next three months to recover and get a head start on my new career move in the States. And, to aid my healing, I could watch a lot of un-pixelated Netflix and eat pints of ice cream to my heart's content. *Sounds like okay therapy to me!* But after some thorough research I realized that changing my departure date would cost a lot more than simply remaining in Shanghai. And then, in a moment of clarity, an epiphany that would have lasting repercussions, I realized that instead of purchasing a new ticket home, I could purchase a ticket to somewhere new and exciting. Rather than going home or staying in Shanghai, I could do something far more daring and adventurous. *I could travel the world.*

After taking the journey to Nanjing with Lisa, and seeing how easy it was to navigate alone in Hong Kong and Bangkok, I wondered what the rest of Southeast Asia might be like on my own. R may have failed in following through on his promise of flying me to Taiwan, Singapore, and Indonesia, but each of those countries were just a flight or two away. And, after a few quick searches, I realized those particular flights weren't nearly as expensive as I'd thought. As I sat on my bed with my computer resting on my thighs, I scrolled through page after page of travel destinations and blog sites. I felt from deep within me an impulse, a sudden lack of control, beginning to itch beneath my skin. I glanced up from my laptop, looking out at the cityscape of Shanghai apartments and office buildings that clustered just beyond my bedroom window, and realized exactly what I needed to do. I made a vow to myself: I wasn't going to board a plane home without having experienced the countries I came for. R may have taken my paycheck and equipment, but I still had my GoPro and a passion for adventure. He may have destroyed my chances at a secure job, but nothing could destroy my determination to make the most of what I had in that very moment. I was going to make the sweetest lemonade out of the sourest of lemons.

I had $3,000 left in my savings, money I had hoped to save for my transition back to the United States to establish my life as a "real" adult and begin paying off my student loan debt. But it was money that could also take me to a few of the countries R had left out, and then some. I knew Singapore, Taiwan, and Indonesia were on the list, but the more I searched the longer my list became, growing to include Malaysia, Cambodia, Laos, and Vietnam. I also wanted to see more of China. After all, the Terra cotta warriors had been a curiosity since 8th grade social studies and there was no amount of cuteness that could beat the giant Chengdu pandas. I spent hours at a time reading backpacker insights and researching the top destinations all over Southeast Asia. As I continued planning, my mind drifted to visions of touching the sands of the Gobi Desert, reclining on a beach in Indonesia, and stuffing myself with food from a busy hawker center in Singapore. By the time I finished making my list I had seven countries and twelve different cities to visit. Using Trip.-com, Google reviews, and Hostelworld, I found cost-effective accommodations and convenient inner-city transportation. I took screenshots of the sights I wanted to see, and made note of any travel tips I found online. I felt like a madwoman plotting my next scheme as handwritten notes overtook the thin lines of my paperback notebook.

Had I come to Asia prepared for backpacking, I may have dived in head first and booked a one-way ticket to my first destination of choice. But because I was less than prepared, I decided to separate the adventures into three different journeys to allow myself time to repack according to the climate and restock on supplies. I could feel the anticipation of adventure bubbling beneath the nervousness of a solo endeavor. And the more excited I became, the less worried I was about taking a path less traveled. I no longer cared about what was "normal" for adults my age; I wasn't anxious about remaining on the bottom rung of a corporate ladder or not being able to afford the apartment I wanted when I got home. I didn't care if the first six months of my post-graduate life wouldn't count towards a resume or LinkedIn profile. Whatever happened after Asia would happen as it was meant to be but, in the meantime, I had a world to explore.

First up was Western China. I decided to stay within the country for multiple reasons:

> 1. I was already comfortable navigating Chinese trains and public transportation.
>
> 2. I would have reliable cell phone service which meant my translation apps were guaranteed to work.
>
> 3. I already felt confident in my knowledge of the culture, food, and social standards.

It was a small first step towards a much more grand adventure, but a step that would still challenge me within the safety of a country with which I was familiar.

My itinerary was based on the minimum number of days I would need in each city based on recommendations I found online. I booked as many trains as possible to keep the costs low and to see more of the country as I made the trek. I reserved several hostels, a handful of flights, and packed a 60-liter hiking pack with CLIF bars, mini travel toiletries, four changes of clothes, a light jacket, and my GoPro. I had no idea what I was doing or how well my plans would work, but it was an adventure that was mine and that made all the difference. I felt overwhelmed with wanderlust and a giddy anxiety as my departure from Shanghai grew closer. The day after Josh headed back to the United States, I set out for Western China to see the Terra cotta Warriors, the beloved Chengdu pandas, and to touch the sands of the Gobi Desert.

The Yellow Scarf

Let us always meet each other with a smile, for the smile is the beginning of love.
~ Mother Teresa ~

Xi'An & Lanzhou, China | October 11 - 13

Whenever I say goodbye to my grandpa Chuck, he always reminds me of two very important things: do well in school, and never stop smiling. While the former may no longer apply (phew!), the latter continues to be an important practice in my life. We often forget about the incredible power of something so simple as a smile. It's a demonstration of vulnerability and openness; an action of unconditional kindness and the quickest way to start a conversation. A smile goes right along with a, "How are you?" and, from there, the directions are limitless. And if you somehow find yourself smiling at someone with whom you share no common language yet they still want to feed you dinner, show you pictures of their children, make sure you get on the right bus, and take a silly photo with you, then you are all the more fortunate. Sometimes, especially when traveling alone, a smile is the only one-line opener you can think of. And - let me tell you - it works wonders.

Adrenaline pulsed through my veins as I hoisted my hiking pack onto the luggage rack of a high-speed train headed towards Xi'an, China. It was the first leg of my two-and-a-half-week journey to the Gobi desert and back. I folded my ticket into my passport, tucked both into the pocket of my thin black jacket, and settled into my seat clutching one of the gifts Josh had sent with me: a Rubik's cube. I figured I could make use of the seven-hour journey and finally teach myself how to solve one of those pesky blocks of plastic he was so passionate about. Josh had been so excited to give it to me before I left the States and after several months of staring at it on my desk I had yet to figure out how it actually worked. So I plugged in my headphones, turned on my favorite travel music playlist, and got to work. Unfortunately, I'd seriously overestimated the amount of time it might require and, within an hour, I had solved it multiple times, memorized the algorithm, and was beginning to grow bored. Yes, you read it here first: this was the historical train ride in which yours truly solved her very first Rubik's cube. Twenty-two years old and making serious waves in the land of nerds.

By the time hour four rolled around, I was desperate for amusement. So while I sat there impatiently wondering what to do with myself, my eyes began to drift over to my seat mate's phone as she scrolled through one of her social media platforms. We had hardly acknowledged each other before the train departed from the station, but she seemed kind and had a very gentle presence. It was interesting to see what kinds of photos and videos not only showed up on her feed, but also which ones she spent time on. I couldn't read any of the Chinese symbols, of course, but I didn't really need words to comprehend the hilarity of one of the albums she soon began flicking through on her screen. I watched in amusement as she closely inspected an image of what appeared to be a thin man wearing a fanny pack designed to look like a stomach sticking out beneath the bottom of his shirt. If you haven't yet discovered the "Dad Bod Fanny Pack", please Google it now. I'll wait.

My seat mate chuckled at the picture and then leaned back into her seat, at which point she noticed my obvious intrusion of privacy. We awkwardly made eye contact before I pointed down at her phone, giggled, and acted as though she'd invited me to join in on her scrolling-binge hours ago and had only just forgotten. Surprisingly, this worked. Now, I wouldn't recommend this tactic with just anyone, especially not in the United States where people are so hyper-protective of their screens that they dim the backlight so low they forget they even have battery life. But instead of being completely freaked out that this blonde girl was stalking her news feed, the starry-eyed Asian woman turned to face me, gave me a huge smile, and opened the first translation app she could locate on her phone.

Thus commenced a lengthy conversation between two strangers on a train (brought to you by Google Translate and whatever the Chinese equivalent was). Over the next few hours I got to know 牛红权. I wish I could tell you how to pronounce this, but evidently my limited months of learning Mandarin has failed me. The closest thing I have to a pronounceable name was her nickname on WeChat, Niu (which, may be Pinyin for her actual name, but seeing as I cannot read Chinese characters I may need some assistance in confirming this). Niu went on to tell me about her middle school teaching career and how she was traveling to Xi'an for an annual history conference. She showed me her hometown on a map and invited me to visit so that she could take me to Mount Huangshan. It was the same mountain that had, at one point, been on my list of things to see in China, but was ultimately passed up when money became an issue. She eyed the Rubik's cube I was still fidgeting with and launched into a text frenzy about how her son loves to solve cubes, is incredibly handsome, happens to be my age and, oh bytheway, would think I'm very pretty. When she began showing me pictures of him I thought for sure I was about to receive a marriage proposal from a 43-year-old Chinese woman. Fortunately, if she had asked, it was all but lost in translation.

After watching three of Niu's choir concert videos, I decided to find the dining car for a snack. My stomach had starting to complain with hunger but I was already actively avoiding my backpack full of Clif bars. Besides, it was just the beginning of my journey and I wanted to fully immerse myself in the experience of traveling across China. Unfortunately, however, the dining car's primary options were vacuum-sealed chicken feet and Lays potato chips in the flavor of "Hot & Sour Fish Soup". *No, thank you.* I reluctantly stared at the food cart for several minutes, trying to work myself up to try something new, but ended up - for lack of a better phrase - chickening out. *Perhaps those vacuum sealed feet would be fitting after all....* But when I returned to my seat with just a bottle of green tea, Niu went full-blown mama bear. She spent the next ten minutes begging to let her buy me food; whatever and however much I wanted. She tried to hand me money, coerce me back to the dining car with her, and even offered me a bite of the burrito she was consuming. Then, in one final attempt to feed my poor starving soul, she handed me a tiny yellow package from her purse. And, I suppose I could chalk it up to immersing myself in the local culture, but after being offered a generous gift multiple times I finally accepted it.

Niu sat eagerly waiting for me to eat whatever was in the lumpy vacuum-packed treat. The yellow wrapping warped itself tightly around the chunk of food inside. On the front, a stick figure hung happily beneath a parachute of what appeared to be layers of bacon. *Well, if this guy likes it so much, then it must not be so bad.* As I opened the package it smelled as though a bottle filled with the aromas of a meat shop had fallen onto the ground and smashed into a million pieces, leaving me with the odd scent of braised something-or-other. I squeezed gently from the bottom and up slid a dark blob covered in a slippery gel-like coating.

Now let me be clear:

1. This is not a food I would have dared tried had my own mother handed it to me.

2. I don't usually take food from strangers but when I do they are the nice motherly type. And,

3. I didn't want to be rude since she was obviously so invested in my well-being.

I pretended to be thrilled about the dark slimy blob she had handed me. She motioned for me to be careful, so I approached it cautiously and attempted a nibble. She watched eagerly from her seat. The substance was tough to pull at. I tried to take a larger chunk between my teeth. The seasoning burned the corners of my mouth. I still had no idea what I was eating and still to this day I can't be sure. I'm fairly confident it was braised duck neck jerky, but after my hefty online research, trying to locate the company and the product, I did not find anything conclusive. It could have been a myriad of other vacuum-sealed meats. The world may never know....

Of course, despite neither my love nor hatred of this gift, when Niu gave me a thumbs up and gestured curiously with a nod of her head, I grinned back, jerky in my teeth and all, nodding happily over her thoughtful gift. So, naturally, she took this as a go-ahead, and proceeded to pull out a larger, unopened bag of individually wrapped snacks from her giant mom purse and stuck it in the pouch of the seat in front of me. I was now burdened with an entire Costco-size bag of the individually wrapped mystery meat. Having fed the lonesome traveler and provided nourishment for the rest of my journey, Niu went back to her phone, incredibly pleased with herself.

I sat there staring at the yellow packaging as it poked out from the holes in the mesh pocket, wondering what I had done to deserve such selflessness. Here I was, traveling alone through China on what was only just the beginning of my journey, and I had already been taken under a local's wing. Niu seemed to deeply care about me, and did all she could to ensure I was happy and healthy. Despite not being able to communicate verbally, she felt it her duty to watch over me. I thought about how we often rely so heavily on language that we forget how easily we can become united simply through meaningful intent and a friendly smile. Although technology certainly assisted Niu and me in forming what became an odd friendship, our common language appeared to be only that of vulnerability and open-heartedness; one in which we had nothing to lose but everything to gain. It was an unprecedented friendship that began my journey with authentic compassion and joy.

The train finally came to a crawl and passengers began to hurriedly collect their luggage and occupy a space in the aisle. I watched in confusion as everyone pulled out winter coats and wrapped heavy scarves around their necks. I was well aware that Chinese natives were stereotypically always cold, and that they were used to such hot temperatures that 65 degrees is practically winter, *but seriously?* I wondered how soon it would be until someone pulled out earmuffs. I stood up to collect my backpack and Niu shot me a concerned look from the aisle. She pointed to my light jacket and then tugged on the fabric at my elbow. She pulled up on the neckline of her fuzzy pink sweater, brought her fists to her chin, and shuddered in an imaginary arctic tundra. I understood that she was worried I would be cold, but I waved my hands and said reassuringly, "It's okay, it's okay," with a giant smile slapped across my face. 65 degrees was perfect weather for me; I was hardly concerned about my choice in attire. Niu looked at me as though I had told her I was going to do naked snow angels on an iceberg. But when the herd of passengers began to move, we were forced to follow suit and the topic was dismissed.

I stepped out onto the platform where I was faced with a harsh reality. I wasn't quite sure how we'd crossed over into an entire new climate so quickly, but the air outside those protective train walls was beyond frigid. The weather was dreary and the air smelled like cold relentless rain. It certainly wasn't 65 degrees; in fact, I would have been lucky if it were anywhere above fifty. But of course, to protect my pride, I pretended as though I hardly noticed. Niu and I hugged goodbye on the platform and I bowed my head in an untranslatable gratitude. But just as I thought we might begin to walk separate journeys, she tugged at my arm and unzipped the outside of her suitcase. From within a small pocket she pulled out a beautiful sheer scarf. It was lightweight, with various hues of yellow flowing within the folds in its thin fabric. Faint bursts of orange spattered themselves along the middle. Yellow was not my color, and I had a feeling that fabric wouldn't offer much protection from the cold, but neither one of those thoughts went through my head in that moment. All I saw was a generous gift, one that was intended to demonstrate love and nurture toward a complete stranger. It was an unexpected gesture that left me with a full heart and a giant goofy smile on my face. Niu stood on her tip-toes and carefully wrapped the scarf around my neck as she returned my smile with one that said, "You know I was right. Now don't get sick." I gently clutched the fabric and watched as she proudly marched herself toward the exit.

I stood in the middle of a train station immersed in chaos and buzzing with travelers, suddenly feeling very alone. After being fed and quite literally clothed, I was not ready to let go of the comfort Niu had provided. It dawned on me that I was now by myself in a city I'd never been to, surrounded by symbols and sounds I couldn't understand. I tried to focus on the task at hand but was swept up in the anxiety of everyone else seeming to know exactly where they needed to go. There was nothing worse than feeling like everyone else had a purpose, but yours was yet to be determined.

When I had been researching transportation and planning out my itinerary according to how long it would take to accomplish everything on my list, I had read that the Terra cotta warriors were just a bus ride away from the main train station in Xi'an. My plan was to head directly to the warriors and then eventually find my way to the hostel I had booked. But amidst the chaos of my arrival I had no idea where to locate the bus I needed. So I did the only logical thing I could think of and got in line for the nearest ticket booth. It was a large and intimidating box that sat square in the middle of the station, manned by several locals who sat shouting at customers through small holes in the glass barriers. I stood patiently behind a man exchanging tickets with a woman speaking rapidly in Mandarin. When he had finished his transaction he turned without care and hurriedly brushed past me on his way to the metro.

I nervously stepped up to the window, shifting the weight of my backpack on my hips, and asked, "How do I get to the Terra cotta warriors?"

She looked at me as though I had a raw fish stapled to my forehead.

I repeated the important part of my question, careful to enunciate each syllable. "Terra cotta warriors?"

She looked longingly to the attendant on her left who was assisting another traveler, as if hoping he had overheard my question and was willing to jump in and take over. I quickly pulled up a webpage I had been perusing on my phone earlier and pointed to a photo of a stone warrior shooting an arrow into the sky. She dismissed me, waving her hands in front of her face frantically as if I'd offered her some of the fresh fish from my forehead.

"Go there."

She pointed apathetically to a tourist booth across the station. How I hadn't noticed the 'I'm not from here and need directions' booth beforehand, I have no idea.

The two women sitting at the table seemed like a train station was the last place they wanted to be.

I smiled politely and spoke with patience. "I'm trying to get to the Terra cotta warriors, can you help me?"

One of them answered without even looking in my direction. "Today, no."

"I'm sorry?" I thought for sure I misunderstood because my careful research had clearly stated I could get to the Terra cotta warriors from the station.

"Today, no. No bus."

Oh. Well, that's not what the Internet said....

I stood, dumbfounded, not sure what move to make next as this was my only plan for the day. *Are they wrong? Am I wrong?* Either way, it didn't seem like I was going anywhere anytime soon. I thanked them and turned my back, defeatedly meandering deeper into the station.

I felt an uncomfortable sadness wash over me. My plans were already ruined and it wasn't even 24 hours into my trip. I had intended to see the warriors the day I arrived so that I could hike the Huashan Mountain Death Trail the following day. Although my parents were not exactly pleased with the second part of that plan I was convinced it would be an adventure I needed to make my journey all the more epic. The Huashan Death Trail would have involved scaling the side of a mountain via a series of narrow planks less than a foot wide. In addition to the thrill-seeking element of scaling death-defying heights protected by only a harness and carabiner, this trail is known for its magnificent views from the summit in which you can see the four other peaks of the mountain and the Yellow River below. Daring travelers from all over the world risk their lives for this unforgettable experience. It was terrifying, but surely stunning. And nothing said, "I'm having a pre-quarter-life-crisis" than climbing that mountain.

I had a decision to make; since I couldn't take the bus directly to the Terra cotta warriors, I no longer had time to both see them and hike the Death Trail while I was in Xi'an. The two were located just far enough apart that the timing would be a disaster. So I had to prioritize. Of course, it went without saying that I knew which one my parents would be thrilled to hear I skipped.

And, after all, if I was unprepared for the cold weather in a train station I certainly wasn't prepared for wind chill on top of a mountain. Since I wasn't heading to the Terra cotta warriors anytime soon, and I certainly wasn't setting out to climb a mountain, I decided to find my hostel and lighten some of the load from my shoulders. I wandered over to a transportation map displayed on a large tiled wall and located the Xi'an Bell Tower, the only metro stop close to the accommodation I had booked. I defeatedly bought a metro ticket and sulked my way to the trains.

By the time I made it to the hostel I was frozen and soaked to the bone. Niu had accurately predicted my misery and, despite her generous gift, I was feeling the full wrath of Xi'an's dreary weather. Because, what's worse than a cold day in China? A cold, rainy day in China, that's what. My travel size umbrella protected me from the rain, but couldn't protect me from the bitter chill and continuously deepening puddles. I carelessly navigated to an alleyway where my hostel - according to the Hostelworld.com description - was somewhere behind "dark wooden doors and two dragon statues." Considering I was in the heart of China, where just about every business featured dark wooden doors and dragon decor, it was not a very helpful clue. After attempting to check into the wrong hostel, I was finally redirected to the correct building a few doors down.

I stumbled into the Han Tang House where I dropped my umbrella into a pile of wet rain gear at the door and set my backpack down at the check-in counter. The lobby was eerily embracing; dimmed hallways were lined with panels of dark wood and red bursts of Chinese decor dispersed splashes of subdued color. People from all over the world were chatting loudly at a large central tabletop as they learned how to play mahjong from several locals. The check-in desk was littered with pictures of local attractions, glowing Trip Advisor reviews, detailed tour information, and doodles from the travelers who'd passed through. I noticed one of their featured tours was an all-inclusive trip to see the Terra cotta warriors. Although I wasn't usually one for tours, I momentarily considered the benefits of not having to make another attempt at navigating the city on my own. After handing over my payment of $7 a night, I found the six-bed female dorm on the second floor where I stripped off my wet clothes, hung my socks and leggings from the spare hooks along the wall, and collapsed at a wooden chair and table to reevaluate my plan.

I quietly admitted that I hadn't exactly packed for the weather and was beginning to question my spontaneity on account of being completely and utterly unprepared. I had packed my Rubik's cube and a reasonable stash of Clif Bars, but apparently that wasn't all one needed for a successful trip out West. *Who knew? Well... Niu did....* I was unable to shake not only the cold from my bones, but also the uncomfortable truth that I had no idea what I was doing. What should have been the easiest part of my journey was already proving to be far more difficult than anticipated. But as I sat there reconsidering the decisions that led me to sitting alone in a Chinese hostel, I realized that there was nothing I could do but carry on. The adventure was mine; I didn't have to worry about anyone else being miserable or cold. I didn't have to become preoccupied by changes in plans because the only person it would affect was me. *Who cares if I don't get to check something off the list? Who cares if nothing works as I thought it would? Heck, who cares if I even leave the hostel at all?* I had complete and total control and, as I sat alone in that quiet hostel dorm, I was hit by an overwhelming sensation of joyful liberation.

With a renewed sense of adventure I was determined to make the most of what could have ended up a regrettably subdued evening. I could have stayed indoors and watched a movie, or gone to bed early, but as it continued to drizzle I instead hiked to the Xi'an Bell Tower, through the Muslim Quarter, and back to the hostel through narrow alleyways. I ate a variety of food on sticks (couldn't tell you what they were), sampled pretzels from a kind old man who gave me a place to sit and rest for a bit (while his employees took photos of me sopping wet), and paid a small fee to have fish eat the dead skin off my feet (it felt as weird as it sounds). I don't quite know what compelled me to step into the fish spa that day, but my feet were soaked with rain anyway, so I figured a pedicure would do me some good.

Despite the rain, and the fact that I could no longer feel my feet, by the time I got back to the hostel I was quite proud of myself. I hadn't spent the evening curled up in bed as I'd envisioned myself doing back at the train station. A day that began so beautifully, with Niu and her incredible kindness, hardly deserved such a mundane ending. It made me think of all those nights I stowed away in my college dorm or in my bedroom back home watching Netflix, eating Ben & Jerry's ice cream, and listening to the rain on my window. How frequently that weather kept me indoors and yet, had I done that in Asia, I would have been guilt-ridden at the waste of an opportunity.

Rather than complain about what hadn't worked out, I tried to practice gratitude for what did. It was a lesson I could certainly take home with me; if I didn't make excuses halfway around the world there were no excuses to be made at home. That night, after taking a hot shower and crawling up into my top bunk, I felt a sort of accomplishment not usually experienced at the end of a long and very wet day.

The bed shifted below as my bunkmate flopped down next to her pillow. There were six bunk beds in the female dorm, so I knew it was only a matter of time before I had to share my own. I rolled over to identify the newcomers: two English blondes and a French brunette. They chatted quietly as they shuffled through their belongings in the dark, so as not to disturb the young Chinese girl sleeping on one of the beds in the corner. I whispered down an introduction and asked what brought them to Xi'an. I learned that Eleanor, Alice, and Marion had been in the city for several days already and seemed to know their way around. They had already seen the Terra cotta warriors, traipsed through the Muslim Quarter, and visited several of the local markets. They spoke of bargain hunting, street food vendors, and bartering with locals. They recommended foods to try and temples to visit.

One of the many benefits of meeting travelers and asking about their journey is the gift of learning from their mistakes and gaining insight into how to make your own adventure a success.

I leaned over the railing of my bunk bed as I whispered down, "Should I go see the Terra cotta warriors on my own, or book a tour?"

Eleanor suddenly appeared from her bunk beneath mine and replied, "Book a tour. That's what we did. It's a bit more expensive than going on your own, but it's a private bus and you have a tour guide. It might be more difficult to understand the context of the site if you go alone. Plus, our guide was incredibly friendly and made it a lot of fun."

Alice and Marion nodded in agreement as Eleanor disappeared again beneath my top bunk. The thought of following around a guide was less than thrilling, but I was still at the beginning of my adventure and had already become frustrated that my research wasn't paying off. So I heeded their advice, grabbed my wallet, and headed down to the front desk where I booked a group tour to the Terra cotta warriors.

The next morning the skies had cleared and a gentle sun warmed the damp sidewalks. I departed the hostel on a bus with several other travelers and our spunky guide, Jia Jia (whose English name was apparently, 'Lady Jia Jia'). She imparted not only her contagious and energetic hilarities but also her knowledge of Emperor Qin and the historical significance of his tomb. We followed Lady Jia Jia through the dig sites like ducklings, listening intently as she rattled off tidbits about how each of the statues were unique and often reflected the artisan who had sculpted it by hand. I walked along the outskirt of the pits, peering down at rows upon rows of stoic warriors, some still protruding through the earth as they awaited their excavation. It was a sight I had been enthused to see for years, and as I finally stood before it I could hardly believe my eyes. I took photo after photo, trying to convince myself that I was really there, standing before such a significant piece of China's rich history.

I'm a strong believer that everything happens for a reason. And to this day I'm glad I didn't miss out on seeing the Terra cotta Warriors. As much as I wish I had been prepared for a death-defying hike, having two feet safely on the ground next to an extraordinary historical phenomenon was a reasonably fair trade. When our tour came to a close, Lady Jia Jia offered to drop off anyone who wanted to walk the Xi'an city walls before the van headed back to the hostel. Not ready to turn in for the day, and wanting to take advantage of the nice weather, I hopped out with several others and approached the entrance with anticipation. The sun hovered low in the sky as I meandered the expansive brick walkways that stood forty feet above the surrounding city. I looked out through the gaping slats in the brick as everyday life continued to hum below us.

I arrived back at the hostel to find the girls from my dorm seated around the common room table eating homemade dumplings. They had opted to stay in the hostel that night to participate in a cooking class and play games with other travelers. Despite having done absolutely none of the work myself, they invited me to join them at the table and gorge myself on homemade food. *Don't have to ask me twice!* We sat sharing stories from our day until late into the night when I finally retreated to the dorm for a good night's sleep before my departure to Lanzhou the next morning. I was sad to be leaving so soon, but eager to continue my journey out west. It was then that Eleanor announced her next destination: Chengdu. After a brief discussion we realized that we would soon be in the same city again later that week, so we connected over WeChat, and I promised to message her when I arrived. I fell asleep that night comforted by the notion that someone familiar would be awaiting my arrival in Chengdu.

At promptly six o'clock the next morning I was the lonesome backpacker sitting on the ground outside a gated metro station entrance, waiting for it to open. In similar fashion to the rest of my transportation snafus thus far, I had made an incorrect assumption that I could at least make it downstairs to the ticket booths even if the trains weren't yet running. Much to my chagrin, however, I didn't make it much farther than the metro sign. The gates were closed and locked. I rarely found myself in positions of standstill but, when I did, I knew I had no choice but to wait it out. So I waited alone on the dark, cold, empty streets of downtown Xi'an. And as I sat there shivering I considered the extensive travel ahead of me. Once I took the metro to Xi'an North Station, I would board a three-hour train to Lanzhou West Station. Once I arrived in Lanzhou, I'd have seven hours to make my way to the main Lanzhou Railway Station before a fourteen-hour overnight train to Dunhuang. It was going to be a long 24 hours and - if it was anything like my first leg of the trip - it was bound to be unpredictably interesting.

Upon arriving in Lanzhou I was immediately lost; I couldn't find the bus I had intended to take into the city and had no idea where I was headed on foot. But I had seven hours to kill and no particular path in mind, so I picked a direction and started walking. I spent the rest of my day meandering through a city devoid of other foreigners and dripping with Chinese characters. I understood even fewer signs than in Xi'an and yet somehow wasn't bothered in the slightest. I boarded buses just to see where they ended up, followed paths into gated parks hoping to find an exit at the other side, and wandered into an old mill without a clue of its history or purpose. And, despite the significant language barrier, I quickly found that smiling was all I needed to communicate with the locals. It was in Lanzhou that I met a crowd of merchants who insisted on taking photos with me and doting over my blonde hair. I met a couple taking a stroll near the river who requested through charades that I take a photo for them. I wandered into a fruit shop to purchase a snack, but when I approached the counter to pay, the two employees immediately insisted I take the banana for free. Over and over again I was met with smiles and sincerity, despite a lack of verbal communication.

It was also in Lanzhou that I hopped on a Mobike and peddled it through the busy streets while weighted down by an overstuffed hiking backpack on my back and a regularly stuffed backpack strapped across my chest. My desire for faster transportation simply could not be stopped by the amount of stuff I carried. Now, if that wasn't an amusing sight I'm not sure what else would be. And if I could figure out how to bike around a city with such a burden, I could also figure out how to use a squatty potty while holding all my gear. Now THAT was a leg day I hadn't signed up for, but I was unusually proud nonetheless for conquering such a task.

As I walked through the streets of Lanzhou it dawned on me how joyful I felt. Despite having no true direction, constantly having to turn around and reroute myself, and not being able to communicate verbally with people around me, I was completely at peace. People were friendly and welcoming regardless of whether or not I could introduce myself. Although, when I did attempt my poor pronunciation of, "Wǒ jiào Hǎi lì" (a friendly introduction using my Chinese name), they immediately assumed I knew Mandarin and began chattering away with excitement. It wasn't until I looked at them with fear in my eyes when they realized I had only memorized that singular phrase. I learned very quickly that perhaps it was best I stick to English.

I wasn't stressed about getting to my next destination, nor did I care how I got there. Lanzhou made me realize that my love of travel ran much deeper than exploration and adventure. Travel means that you are inevitably going to get lost, have to double-back, and even rebook some tickets. You're going to make mistakes but you will also learn crucial lessons about yourself and the world around you. As I stood looking out at the Yellow River that afternoon, I understood that was my 'why' behind traveling in the first place. Was I disappointed that I couldn't climb Mount Huashan? Absolutely. Was I perplexed by Lanzhou's city layout? Yup. Was I worried about finding my way despite language barriers? Yeah, of course. But at the end of the day I sincerely enjoyed having to adapt and reroute. I found it exhilarating to communicate across languages. It was invigorating to see just how far I could push my limits before feeling even an ounce of frustration. I recognized that, because I was on my own and without a particular plan, needing to redirect or start over was not a negative experience; it was a learning opportunity.

Even at the very beginning of a much longer journey, I realized that the only strength I need to travel was the determination to keep going. Despite my rapid itinerary (just a day or two in most cities), I began to gain confidence that I would still find the adventures fulfilling. I was going to miss out on opportunities - that much was a given - but I knew that it would be what I did with that challenge that truly counted. Perhaps getting things wrong would be far more exciting than getting everything right. After all, we wouldn't learn a thing if we were never forced to adapt.

Sand Dunes & Google Translate

Not all those who wander are lost.
~ J.R.R. Tolkien ~

Dunhuang, China | October 14 - 16

Out of all the planes, trains, and taxis I took through Asia, the only trip that truly made me anxious was the overnight sleeper train I booked from Lanzhou to Dunhuang. By the time I reached the train station across the city it was beginning to set in that I had booked myself an inescapable fourteen-hour journey during which I would be shut in a small cabin with up to three other strangers. Although I had purchased the tickets with excited anticipation, thrilled to experience something new, I suddenly dreaded not knowing what lie ahead. As I sat in Lanzhou

Station a half-hour before we departed, I realized that I had not done nearly enough research. *Do the train cars have electrical outlets? Hot water dispensers? Do I need my own toilet paper? Should I have purchased more food? I don't even know the social standards for this kind of journey. Should I keep my shoes on? Who decides when to turn off the cabin lights? What am I supposed to do for fourteen hours if I can't sleep?* It was the first time I was truly afraid of being miserable should things not work out.

Fortunately, I had done enough research to know that booking a soft sleeper instead of a hard sleeper meant I would be far more comfortable both physically and mentally. A soft sleeper meant sharing a larger room with in-cabin luggage storage, a locking door, and two sets of bunk beds. It also meant access to a western style toilet which, although I didn't mind embracing the squatty potty, I certainly didn't mind the prospect of not having to cling onto the walls while the train rocked back and forth. Hard sleeper cabins, on the other hand, are smaller rooms with open luggage storage and zero privacy. It also meant two, three-bed-high bunk beds which appeared impossible to conquer as a five-foot-four individual. Ladder or not, that top bunk was much too high from the ground, and the surface was far too narrow for restful sleep. Nothing like the fear of falling off a bed to keep someone from getting any rest. As someone who struggles to sleep on transportation as it is, I knew the hard sleeper would be a bad idea. Without reassurance that someone wouldn't sneak into my luggage overnight, or that I wouldn't be forced into the highest bunk, I would have been guaranteed a journey heavily weighted by insomnia.

I boarded the train, squeezing me and my backpack through narrow doorways as I navigated to my cabin. I was the first passenger in our group to arrive, so I took advantage of the extra time to get comfortable. I stepped into the cabin, suddenly feeling quite claustrophobic as the edges of the bunk beds were within just a few inches of me on either side. My backpack hugged my body tightly as I turned around in a circle, inspecting the slight curve of the stark white walls and deep blue coloring of the bunk beds. A small table draped with a thin lace tablecloth was tucked tightly beneath the window. An electric water kettle was plugged in to a single outlet below, and a vase of flowers added a touch of class to the decor. Several fluffy pillows were stacked at the top of each bed, and one of the white down comforters was calling to my tired body. I listened as other passengers found their way to their cabins, their voices growing louder only to once again fade as they passed by my door. I hoisted my backpack up onto the luggage rack above the door, and climbed up onto an upper bunk. I figured, without knowing who would be joining me, that I would leave the bottom bunks to them. Plus, being on the top bunk would make it far more difficult for anyone to reach me while I was sleeping. I placed the little tin box I packed with earplugs, medicine, and a sleeping mask in the woven bedside pouch near my head. Then I took off my shoes, folded up my legs beneath me, and waited.

Within a few minutes I was joined by a middle-aged Chinese couple who noticed me in the top bunk as they entered. The man, a well-dressed and seemingly kind individual, nodded a polite but silent greeting, while his wife bashfully looked away. I understood right away that we would not be communicating much; their assumption that I did not know Mandarin would prove to be correct, and my assumption that they spoke very little English was also likely accurate. The only time we came close to speaking was during an awkward encounter as I attempted to lean over the edge of my bed railing to plug in my computer charger to the outlet below the table. The man quickly stood up from his bottom bunk, smiled at me, held out his hand to collect my charger, and leaned over the table to plug it in. I thanked him in English to reinforce that whatever assumption he had made about my ability to speak Mandarin, was correct. The cabin remained quiet; he simply nodded and smiled. For the next several hours as my cabin mates laid down to sleep, I worked on my computer, editing videos and preparing posts for social media until my eyes grew tired. Once I could no longer stand the thought of staring at a screen, I plugged in my phone, put in my earplugs, curled up underneath the soft down comforter, and fell asleep.

Ask my parents, boyfriend, or even my cat, and they will all tell you with certainty that I am not a heavy sleeper. I am such a light sleeper, in fact, that a bug could fart and it would probably wake me up. And to make things more difficult, I have a very hard time falling asleep in unfamiliar territories. So much so, that when I was taken to the emergency room several years ago in need of a migraine concoction, no amount of heavy intravenous medications could knock me out. I was loopy, but determinately awake. So to have fallen asleep on a moving train in China was an honest to goodness miracle. But a crew member having to literally shake me from a deep sleep in the morning to check my train ticket, was just plain unbelievable. I had been sleeping so hard I hadn't even noticed the overhead light being turned on in our cabin. She must have been poking and prodding my leg for several minutes before giving up and instead simulating an earthquake by shaking my entire lower body until it awoke. It was perhaps one of the best night's sleep I'd had yet.

I pulled back the window curtain to reveal an unsettling yet serene sight. Our train was just outside of Dunhuang and there was nothing but sand for as far as I could see. I could feel the chilled air against the glass as the desert landscape was brushed by the subtle pink of a sunrise. The noisy chaos of Chinese cities had been replaced with wide-open spaces and silence. The world had gone quiet and all that was left was the serenity of endless sands and the soft clicking of the train wheels against the tracks.

As the train crawled to a stop, my tranquility was interrupted by a phone call. I answered with a cautious, "Hello?", only to be bombarded by a man speaking rapidly in Mandarin. *Just what I was afraid of.* The only people who ever called my Chinese phone number were people I couldn't understand.

I must have looked frightened because as I tried to explain to the man babbling on the other end that, "I speak English. Do you speak English? English. No Chinese," the kind man from my cabin stood up from his lower bunk and motioned for me to give him my phone. I leaned over the railing and handed it down.

He spoke with patience to the man on the other end, hung up, and then gave me back my phone. "Your driver. I help you."

I understood from those five words that it had been the courtesy shuttle to my hotel attempting to locate me at the railway station. Without any other options and an odd sense of trust, I nodded and thanked him for his help.

The man's wife followed along as my generous translator not only directed me through the train station, but also insisted on carrying my bags. He answered my phone when the shuttle driver inevitably called again and graciously led me right to the van waiting outside. I shook my benefactor's hand, handed my bags to the driver, and climbed in. Still to this day I am 100% confident I would not have located my ride had it not been for the unconditional generosity of a complete stranger from my cabin. My driver navigated through the empty streets of Dunhuang, the open sand giving way to pop-up shops and small-town buildings. The smooth paved road seemed to disappear into the horizon in front of us, and I watched as trees began to dot themselves along the side of the road. The world was tranquil, free of chaos, and consumed by a calming bliss. By the time we pulled up in front of my hotel, I had a permanent smile on my face.

Dunhuang was the first place I booked an actual hotel, and I couldn't have been more excited for a private room with a private bathroom and a quiet place to rest. My reservation at The Aegean Sea Zhen Pin Hotel cost a whopping $20 per night. It was a three-star accommodation but, compared to the hostels I had been staying in up until that point, it felt like a five-star. This part of my journey was going to be the most rejuvenating of all.

This particular Chinese city might have been popular with tourists, but it wasn't highly trafficked by Western tourists in particular. In fact, I was not only the sole Caucasian female for miles, but also none of the locals appeared to understand English. Unlike Shanghai and Xi'an, I had only my translator on which to rely. I had been so spoiled by the frequency of encountering English speakers (or at least, great charades players), that when the locals in Dunhuang just stared back at me blankly as I tried to repeat myself in the simplest English known to man, I knew this destination would be a bit more challenging. But, to their credit, these same locals also demonstrated the most patience when it came to communication barriers. Checking into my hotel was the first of many trials. The front desk staff sat with me for almost an hour as I used Google Translate to ask them countless questions about how to get tickets for the Mogao Caves, where to catch the bus to Crescent Lake, and recommendations on places to eat. Unlike the big cities, where I would have been shoo'd away due to being a complete and utter inconvenience, these locals made every effort to communicate. And when they didn't know the answer, or couldn't think of a proper translation, they just smiled silently and waited for me to rework my question. They were the global award-winners of customer service.

Finally, with several sets of directions from the friendly hotel staff, I meandered outside to get something to eat before heading towards the Gobi desert where Mingsha Mountain and Crescent Lake awaited my arrival. As soon as I stepped outside into the cool sunlight, I heard a woman shouting in Mandarin. I looked over to see an exuberantly excited local flagging me down as though I were a rescue boat drifting by her desolate island. She grinned as I hesitantly wandered closer, came over to grab me by the arm, and hurriedly escorted me into a small cafe where I came face-to-face with several other locals. The restaurant went silent while everyone paused in place to assess the new arrival. My host positioned me in front of her counter and rushed around the other side to point at a list on the wall behind her of what I could only assume were different foods. She enthusiastically fiddled with the cash register, awaiting my selection. I smiled, but was unsure how to respond.

There's a reason I normally avoid restaurants that don't have pictures of food on the menu. This was a perfect example of why. Although having photos available usually means the establishment is more touristy, at least I would know what I was ordering. I pointed at the menu and shrugged my shoulders, making it clear that I couldn't understand the characters. But she just stared back at me, waiting. I pulled out my phone and attempted to use Google Translate to at least identify anything that said, "Beef" or "Noodles." Usually, the live translation feature was helpful in providing what was at least near-comprehensible English. But this time, the density of small Chinese lettering was confusing the program. I tried angling my camera every which way but there were too many characters for it to pull out specific words.

My enthusiastic host watched with curiosity before finally dismissing my effort with several waves of her hands and rounded the counter only to grab my arm and pull me into the seating area. She began to lead me around the restaurant, approaching table after table, pointing at the foods her customers were eating. I tagged along uncomfortably while the locals stared with apathy. Every time we reached a new table the petite Chinese woman would look up at me and grin, nodding in question about my thoughts and opinions. After several awkward moments I found the first food that looked vaguely familiar and pointed to it as quickly as I could; anything to end the 'tour-de-tables.' She clapped happily, showed me to a table, and rushed off to the kitchen. I nervously played with my phone until she appeared moments later with a bowl of noodles and several dumplings. With my stomach rumbling, I began to eat, and the entire restaurant crew took turns poking their heads out into the dining area to observe. My host watched in joyful anticipation as I gave a big thumbs up and smiled with a mouth full of noodles. She practically danced back to her counter.

Since I wasn't yet familiar with the city, I decided to hail a cab to the bus station. I knew I needed bus number three, but had little to no idea which direction I was supposed to be heading. So when a taxi promptly stopped for me, I climbed into the back and pulled out my phone where I had already translated, 'Bus Station.' I then said in articulate English, "Bus station, please." The driver looked at me funny, but nodded his head and pulled away from the curb. A few moments later, as we drove into town past small shops and markets, I heard him muttering beneath his breath, "Bus. Busssss. Buuuhhhsss."

Oh boy, I thought. *He has no idea where I want to go. He's just driving aimlessly until he figures out what bus means.* I sat pressed against the backseat and closed my eyes, hoping I wouldn't end up all the way across town. As he circled a roundabout downtown he repeated, "Bussss. Bus. Bus." And then, suddenly, within a mere three minutes of getting in the car, he pulled over. Right in front of a bus stop. *I guess it was closer than I thought....* I opened my wallet to pay my fare, at which point my driver proudly pointed out the window and grinned back at me, "Bus!" His eyes were lit with anticipation of my response. I found myself grinning. He hadn't been confused in the slightest; just exuberantly excited to have learned a new English word.

I boarded a bus that transported me to the edge of the Gobi desert. I watched from my seat as the long empty highway disappeared into the sand dunes that became visible in the distance. We came to a stop outside a series of open-air shopping booths, but souvenirs were hardly on my mind. No, I was on the hunt for some sand. After purchasing a ticket and slathering sunscreen on my frighteningly pale ligaments, I approached the entrance to the sand dunes with tears in my eyes. I can't explain why it was such an emotional experience, but as I looked up at the towering dunes and imagined the expansive sandy abyss that continued behind them, I was overwhelmed with a resounding sense of wonder. I was standing on the edge of the Gobi desert, a place I'd only ever seen in textbooks and *National Geographic* documentaries. It was for the same reason the Tian Tan Buddha had been such a moving experience; to realize I was standing in a place so phenomenal, and to have made the journey entirely on my own, was an accomplishment that filled me with pride. I could hardly believe I was touching the sands of the Gobi desert, a geographical location so far removed from my every day world; a place I had only dreamed of one day seeing.

I spent the entire afternoon trudging through the dunes as sand enveloped my every step. My bare feet hit the sun-warmed surface and then quickly sank beyond the surface to touch the cooled layers below. I climbed the side of Mingsha Mountain, bracing my feet against the rungs of a wooden ladder as the sands grew steeper. I made it halfway up the incline before my heart began to pound against the walls of my chest. Had it not been for the cool breeze, the sun combined with my labored breathing would have made for quite a miserable hike. It took a bit longer than I would like to admit, but I kept my eyes on the peak and didn't stop. And by the time I reached the top I was out of breath for more than one reason. I stood tall and watched the city of Dunhuang spread itself out along the horizon. When the heavy breathing finally subsided my ears were met with the muted sounds of distant voices as they traveled along the sands and amongst the bases of the dunes.

From the top I could see Crescent Lake, a paradoxical desert oasis that has survived thousands of years and numerous sand storms. The water wrapped itself around a temple that was comfortably settled at the base of Mingsha Mountain. Greenery embellished the temple yard and gently framed the still waters of the lake. It was truly an oasis; a refreshing glimpse of color in an otherwise beige landscape. A cool breeze dried the beads of sweat from my forehead as I began to walk across the peak. Dunhuang's tranquility had reached a new level.

Now, I'm no yoga professional, but I've dabbled enough to appreciate how grounding and physically beautiful it can be. So when my eyes caught the elegant lines of the cascading sand dunes, I decided it would be the perfect place to practice.

I balanced my GoPro in the sand and started working through some poses. And from that point forward, my GoPro was the only thing that remained balanced. Sand yoga, particularly on the soft sand of Mingsha Mountain, was hardly a walk in the park. The slightest wobble left me tumbling, and the sand constantly shifted beneath my wavering stance. I kept trying, but it was hardly the successful session I had imagined. Just as I was about to laugh it off as a comedic attempt at an artistic endeavor, a young Chinese mother came wandering over to me. She had been observing from across the dune while her son played with a water bottle full of sand.

I smiled at her and she smiled back. She pointed at herself and then at me, and said, "You and me? Together?" I understood she wanted to do yoga together, but had little to no idea what that might look like. So I said, "Sure!" and nodded with enthusiasm. I let her take my hand to lead me further up the peak. She held onto my arm as she pulled her foot behind her into a pose commonly referred to as Lord of the Dance. It involves an exceptional amount of balance on stable ground let alone shifting sands. She pointed and nodded at me; it was my turn. We both struggled to find stability as we simultaneously pulled our legs into the air behind us and grasped at each other's free hand. It was a sight to see, I'm sure. For several moments we were one; our torsos bent in towards each other and our hands clasped with interlocking fingers. I thought about how, as soon as one of us stumbled, the other would no doubt follow. She looked up at me and smiled. Yoga needed no translation and, despite our language barrier and wobbly knees, I felt more grounded from sharing that experience than from any practice I've ever done alone.

I began to stumble back down the side of Mingsha Mountain at which point I caught sight of a child sledding down the bottom half of the slope in a wooden toboggan. Now I don't know about you, but any opportunity to embrace my inner child is an opportunity I wouldn't miss. So I wandered over to the guy handing out sleds and he helped me climb on before sending me sliding down the side of the mountain. Just as it was difficult to find stability in the shifting sands so, too, was it tricky to maintain a straight course. My sled twisted and turned beneath me, sending sand flying into my shoes and down my pants. When I reached the bottom I stood up and watched the grains seep from my clothes like a broken hourglass. Despite the gritty taste of the sand that had snuck past my lips, I looked up at the sun and smiled.

The weather would have been a perfect spring day back home. The warm sun beat gently against my skin while the breeze offered enough to prevent me from sweating. So instead of taking the bus back to the station, I started to walk. I became the epitome of what everyone thinks when they hear the word "backpacker." I walked along the side of the highway, dodging beneath the shade of the trees, while my solar-powered battery pack soaked up the sun's rays from its strategic place on the outside of my backpack. It was perhaps one of the greatest gifts I was given for my travels (that, and purse-sized toilet paper rolls); as long as I had sunlight, my phone charger never needed an outlet.

Down the road I came across what appeared to be a small town. Curious, I ventured off the road and made my way into what turned out to be a haven of unique shops, restaurants, and art galleries. But unlike most of the artisan towns I'd stumbled upon, this one was entirely devoid of crowds. It was so barren that some of the shop owners were nowhere to be found. I wandered in and out of quiet stores, decorated with colorful pieces of culture and history. It was eerily desolate, yet somehow comforting. I was so used to being followed through markets or supervised by distrustful shop owners that to navigate a town without a single eye upon me was refreshing. I spent some time examining hand-made works and artisan gifts, and listening to rhythmic beats pour through a speaker on an empty café patio. I passed by lanterns that hung from the light posts and kiosks with scarves that fluttered in the breeze. No one shouted prices at me, or pulled me into their store. I was the sole occupant of an artistic oasis.

It was late afternoon when I started back towards the main road. And as I walked, I thought about my two best friends and study abroad companions from college. They had been there when, in each new city we ventured to in Western Europe, I made it my mission to locate a perfect spot to watch the sunset. We watched it from a park bench in Edinburgh, the top of the Eiffel Tower in Paris, from a rooftop overlooking St. Peter's Basilica in Rome, and from the crowded streets of Dublin, Ireland as a street musician played Ed Sheeran on his guitar. With every new destination there was a new sunset, and the tradition never grew old. It was such a tradition that, a few nights before we graduated from college my best friends came over to my house, blindfolded me, and led me to a car that drove all over campus before ending up at the top of an empty parking garage. I took off the blindfold to reveal a picnic of homemade cookies, glasses of champagne, and one of the prettiest sunsets I'd ever seen on campus. One of my best friends looked at me and said, "Erin, whenever I see a beautiful sunset, I think of you." It is one of the greatest compliments I've ever been given.

Before heading back to my hotel in Dunhuang I did a quick search on my phone for a place to watch the sunset over the desert horizon. Supposedly, the best place was on top of Mingsha Mountain, but I had accidentally passed up that opportunity when I ventured outside its gates. My only other option was a hotel not far from where I was on the main road. I scanned through an article that mentioned I would need to navigate through the hotel and locate a staircase to the rooftop café. While it made me nervous to sneak into a four-star hotel where I didn't speak the native language nor knew the policy regarding non-guest visitors, I figured the worst that could happen would be someone asking me to leave. I opened the heavy front doors and embraced my inner Jenny as I confidently marched past the check-in desk and through the lobby. I beelined past the hotel restaurant where I saw a sign pointing to a set of stairs and decided to take the chance. Sure enough, at the top of the stairs was a door that opened out onto a rooftop terrace that faced the sand dunes in the distance. It was breathtaking, and just like the town I'd stumbled upon on the way here, the patio was empty and quiet. I sat down at a table near the ledge of the terrace and watched the sun as it set behind Mingsha Mountain, casting pink and orange hues across the tranquil sky.

The next day I woke up and headed to the café next door for a quick breakfast before departing for Mogao Caves. I'm not sure who was more excited to see me when I walked through the door, the woman who had so joyously guided me into her restaurant the day before, or the restaurant staff who had taken a sudden and strangely bold interest in my blonde hair. I was led to a table where I sat obediently until, without prompting, I was brought a bowl of grits, four steamed buns, several deep-fried dough sticks, and a bowl of soybean milk. I learned later that these were items considered to be a traditional Chinese breakfast. It wasn't exactly bacon and eggs, but it was filling nonetheless, and I was honored by their efforts in sharing a local custom with a stranger. While I ate, the restaurant staff took turns approaching with giddy smiles as they handed me their phones with poorly translated greetings and questions like, "Where your home from?" and, "How long in China you?" Fortunately, my experience with translators was extensive enough I was able to answer with, "I am from America," and, "I live in China for six months." Each time I handed back the phone they would huddle in a group and giggle over my replies.

When I pulled out my Google Translate app they went bonkers over my ability to point the camera at Chinese characters and see it translated directly on the screen. They brought me labels and papers with characters to see them transformed into English lettering. One of the women grabbed my phone from me and typed hurriedly into Google's Chinese keyboard. She handed it back to me, beaming. It read, "The I wish the beauty to play happy welcome beauty come to Dunhuang." No matter how poor the translation, their intentions were clear; the positivity and kindness with which they welcomed me into their world was unprecedented. The lack of verbal communication skills was no match for their enthusiastic spirits.

At Mogao Caves I was one of four other English speakers on a tour of the UNESCO world heritage site that features over one thousand representations of Buddha within a system of 735 caves. We stood in the confined space of darkened grottos as our guide shared with us the significance of the Silk Road and its influence on religion and culture throughout Asia. She elaborated on the history of Mogao Caves, a prominent cultural emblem that features artwork ranging from the fifth to the thirteenth centuries. Elements of Indian, Western, and Chinese styles of art can still be found on the fading murals and statues. In addition to the intricate designs of the caves, several tens of thousands of manuscripts were found hidden within the walls of the temples. I was walking through a time capsule of religious, cultural, and artistic traditions throughout Asia. While we waited our turn to enter one of the caves, a middle-aged woman in our group tapped my arm and offered me a grape from her bag of snacks; an odd, but not unusual gesture from another traveler. Robyn, I later learned, was an American who had been living and teaching in China for four years. She was on one final adventure before heading back to the States later that month. We chatted as we continued the tour, and when it came to an end, Robyn and I sat down in the welcome center's cafe for lunch. We discussed social behaviors, cultural norms, and experiences we'd had since moving to Asia. After we finished eating we ventured back into the city of Dunhuang to explore the night markets and meander through narrow side streets lined with food stalls.

And with the sun beginning to make its final descent behind the buildings, Robyn thanked me for my company and headed back to her hotel.

What surprised me the most about Dunhuang was the incredible patience and generosity of its people. Despite my confusion checking into the hotel, and my indecision with ordering food due a lack of images on the menu, everyone I met took the time to sit down and help me work through the barriers with translators and maps. Maybe it was the off-season, or maybe I happened to catch them on a particularly pleasant day, but every individual I met in Dunhuang exhibited sincere kindness and an eagerness to help. The few Westerners I found were pleasant and kind; they were on a journey of their own and spoke of their travels and adventures with a passion familiar to my own. As I sat in my hotel room, preparing for my flight to Chengdu the next day, I embraced the remaining hours of solitude as a gift; a refreshing change of scenery from the usual overwhelming crowds of Chinese cities. When I boarded my plane to Chengdu the next day, in a small desolate airport, I looked out at the vast sands of the Gobi Desert, longing to stay just a few more days. The quiet streets, the tranquil desert, and the cool embrace of Dunhuang's small town charm would surely be missed.

Mahjong, Tea, & An Abacus

A good traveler has no fixed plans and is not intent on arriving.
~ Lao Tzu ~

Chengdu & Leshan, China | October 16 - 19

If I came back from Asia believing in anything, it was that I never, ever, ever, ever want to be called a tourist. Tourists are the ones filing complaints about the lack of public WiFi, moaning that the shops are inconveniently closed during siesta, that the curry is much too spicy for their taste, and that using a squatty potty was not the kind of leg day they signed up for. The bottom line is that tourists are just that, tourists; they breeze through, snap their photos, ooh and awe, then go home and move on with their lives. Perhaps most notoriously known for hosting these types of visitors, are guided tours. It is for this precise reason that I'm not usually one to follow a guide anywhere. Even though all tour goers may not be tourists, first impressions matter and I don't want that to be mine. So when Eleanor and I met up in Chengdu on my journey back from the Gobi Desert, and she suggested we book a tour of Leshan together, my first thought was, "Oh hell no." But I am not one to deny myself a potentially enlightening experience, so after much thought and discussion, I agreed to give it a try.

The next morning, I joined Eleanor in the backseat of a cab that tore through the streets of the Sichuan province. I watched as the city of Chengdu disappeared and the bustling streets turned into hilltop tea gardens. We arrived in Leshan several hours later where we were met by our guide, Patrick Yang. And, unfortunately, things didn't exactly start off on the right foot. We began our tour by boat where we drifted toward Leshan's Giant Buddha just across the river. Eleanor and I looked down at our bright orange life vests and started to wonder where on the tourist scale we might be. We were surrounded by other Westerners, gabbing on and on about their lunch plans and their "treacherous" flights to Asia (they thought having no leg room was bad? Try a death threat…). A local woman stood behind us screaming about how we'd better take a $25 professional photo right now or, so help her, we won't have a single memorable moment on this trip. We turned our backs to her and craned our necks as we silently looked up at the 71-meter, *ahem*, 233-foot-tall, intricately carved figure protruding from the Redrock. It was an astounding sight. I mean, the pinkie toe was the size of a Love Sac (although arguably far less cozy). The entirety of it was so massive I probably could have crawled inside Buddha's ear and taken a reasonably comfortable nap.

But as Eleanor and I looked at the crowd surrounding us on the top deck of the boat, we read each others' minds. We wanted to interact with the local people, experience the traditions, and become a part of the Leshan community. Despite our tour guide's extensive knowledge, Eleanor and I felt a lack of deeper connection with the space around us. The screaming photographer and complaining tourists didn't do much to close the gap between us and Leshan. It seemed our bright orange life vests symbolized two different kinds of safety: the kind that prevented us from drowning, and the kind that kept us at arm's length from meaningful connection.

Our guide, Patrick, was quite the memorable individual, and he did his best to bring us into everyday life in Leshan. As he drove us from the riverside and into a nearby village, he shared his own story about growing up in a quaint home and pursuing a life of purpose and joy. He narrated his time spent training at a monastery, and admitted that although he enjoyed his practices and deeply desired a simpler, more charitable life, he was kicked out of the monastery for drinking and smoking too much. Oh, and apparently women. Patrick obviously hadn't gotten the memo about the essence of monkhood.... He told us about his family and his childhood dream of becoming an engineer. But, he explained, when a neighbor recommended he study conversational English and tourism, he decided to pursue a more viable option in a rapidly diversifying world. And as we drove past it, he pointed out the school he had attended twenty-three years ago. We were finally getting a glimpse into the life of a local.

And then, out of nowhere, Patrick excitedly shouted from the driver's seat, "Oh! Dog died!" He pointed out the window frantically, satisfied with the abrupt change in subject. "My god. Died. Died. It died." He rolled down the window, slowed the van to a stop, and leaned his head out, "Can you see?" He craned his neck as he spun to face us while Eleanor and I stared wide-eyed at each other, unsure of how to respond. Last I checked, roadkill was not a worthwhile spectacle, let alone something you got excited about. But Patrick was all riled up. And then, in usual tour guide fashion, he went on to inform us about the vast number of people who believe it is good for your body to consume baked snakes, cats, and dogs. He explained that each of them have unique tastes and offer variable health benefits like physical strength and sexual drive. And just when we thought we'd heard it all, he began to educate us about the proper wine pairings. Like the Westerners we are, Ellie and I sat in the backseat with our jaws resting comfortably on the ground.

Patrick pulled off of the main road and into a small village nestled by the river. We walked together through streets that were humming with locals cooking food, gambling over decks of cards, drinking tea, and playing mahjong. But this scene was much unlike the usual streets we wandered. No one approached us or shouted for us to come inside their shop, nor did anyone take photos of us as we walked; they simply observed with apathy. This, my friends, is exactly how you know a place is untouched by tourism. Eleanor and I started our afternoon with lunch at a family owned restaurant where they served us water buffalo, eggs and tomato, bok choy, grits, and rice. To say I could've eaten four more meals right then and there would nearly be an understatement. It was unforgettably delicious. And after we'd consumed all that we possibly could in one sitting we followed Patrick through the winding concrete streets while he relayed the history of 'Old Town'.

Just as Patrick began to dive into stories of the Red Guards, we stumbled upon an elderly woman hunched over a worn bamboo chair, weighing a package of noodles between her feet. She wore a pair of black slacks and a thick navy blue coat, her short whitened hair pulled back with two barrettes. I noticed that there were soft wrinkles where the smile in her eyes had once been. And layered on top of her already bulky ensemble was a sweater vest scattered with bursts of colorful flowers and circles. From beneath her slacks appeared a pair of bright baby blue socks.

Patrick explained that locals frequently weigh their purchases from market to ensure the shop owner had been honorable in their sale. We watched as she meticulously moved a metal weight back and forth along the rod in her hand. Below, the packaged noodles sat nestled in a rounded silver tray that hung from one end. Every so often she would look up from her work to study our presence from behind her thin framed glasses. But when Patrick began to translate the Chinese symbols that decorated her front door, she came to life, waving her arms from left to right and pointing to her home. She continued to speak passionately over Patrick's voice as he translated the story of her once beautifully painted door that was taken from her home during the cultural revolution in 1968. The old woman watched as Patrick described the door that had been painted with colorful birds and elegant calligraphy. She eventually went back to sitting with her package of noodles, but continued to watch Eleanor and me with reservation. While Patrick recalled stories of the cultural revolution, I could see a certain sadness in her eyes that I hadn't noticed when we'd first arrived. After several moments of absentminded observation, the old woman stood up, made her exit through her now barren wooden door, and disappeared in the darkened corridor of her home.

Eleanor and I continued through the village, passing by a middle-aged man shaving a customer's beard. The owner of the barber shop had transformed an exterior wall of his home into a salon; a large mirror hung precariously by a nail, a hairdryer dangled from an external electrical outlet, and a small sink braced itself against the grey cement wall. Service prices were written in chalk on the upper lefthand corner of the wall. Patrick explained that this shop was a family business; the wooden chair on the sidewalk had belonged to the barber's great-grandfather and has since been handed down for generations. He introduced us to the barber's wife who took several photos with us and admired our matching blonde hair. Apparently, the owner had asked if we wanted our hair cut, but Patrick preemptively (and thankfully) declined.

We later wandered into a small shop where we met a 97-year-old man who was far too happy to be selling funerary supplies for a living. Eleanor and I admired the simplistic storefront as Patrick began to introduce us to the old man and his son, who stood observing from the other side of the room. It was helpful to have Patrick there to provide a foundation for each of the stories we were encountering; he shared with us their ages, details about their family, their occupations, and the stories he knew from earlier times.

The old man welcomed us into his shop with an enormous smile and open arms as he shuffled over to the entrance in his blue track jacket and pageboy hat. Patrick leaned over to us and whispered, "This man, he love foreigners. He get so happy when foreigners come to his shop."

I had heard about Chinese funerary traditions before, but hadn't yet been inside a supply shop; I tend to avoid death-related concepts since my own immortality isn't exactly a fun idea to entertain. Although, the Chinese belief in reincarnation is certainly a more ideal and less morbid way of thinking. When a loved one dies in China it is believed that their souls are reincarnated into another life, and their gravestones serve to mark their earthly residence, or passageway to the afterlife. On Ghost Day, which occurs during the seventh month of the Chinese calendar, it is believed that ghosts of the deceased come back to visit Earth. Throughout the month families of the deceased offer things one might need in their second life by placing food on their grave and burning necessary supplies like paper money, clothes, and cardboard house replicas. Although, in my opinion, things have gotten a bit flashy lately as our friendly store owner proudly showed us his collection of cardboard iPhones, laptops, mansions, and even luxury cars. Perhaps the dead really do have better lives than the living....

While we stood investigating the items that lined his shelves, Eleanor noticed an abacus resting on top of a glass display case. Patrick explained that many people in China, particularly in smaller villages, still prefer the ancient tool to modern technology. Taking notice of our curiosity, the old man sprung to life, excitedly clutching the abacus and racing around the counter for a demonstration. Patrick asked us to provide a multiplication problem on which the old man happily got to work, his unsteady fingers sliding each bead purposefully across the frame of the abacus. We watched as he mumbled over the ancient calculator and when we showed him that his result matched the number on Eleanor's iPhone calculator, he grinned as though he'd won the lottery. He was youthful and child-like in his sincere enthusiasm to make new friends and teach us about his life, and we were beyond thrilled to have shared in that experience. Before we left, the old man told Patrick how much we reminded him of his great-granddaughter, and he gave us each a small sesame biscuit as a token of gratitude.

We continued wandering down a narrow alleyway where we came upon a 98-year-old woman selling spices. She had set up shop in a small wooden booth at the end of the road. The wooden shutters opened wide to display racks of homemade spices, all neatly categorized in glass jars. She waved us over to sample her concoctions, one of which was definitely pepper and left Eleanor and me both wheezing for air. The old woman chuckled under her breath and offered us a different jar to try. Patrick had known this woman for a long time, and shared with us that she only continues to work in her old age because she is afraid that, if she stops, she might die.

Farther down the road we watched a younger woman mix spice blends on a tarp inside her garage. Eleanor bent over the pile and confidently identified pieces of cinnamon, nutmeg, clove, and anise. We then meandered into a small warehouse where we watched a pair of sisters handcraft a full-size duvet by layering string through the pegs of several giant wooden frames. Patrick claimed they could finish an entire duvet in under an hour. I began to wonder if behind the warehouse walls there were hidden machines keeping up with the workload. We stood patiently observing as they strategically laid each strand back and forth across the frame using long, thin sticks of bamboo.

Across the street we entered the home of an 89-year-old man who had invited us to join him for tea. We stepped over the raised stone threshold, a traditional feature of Chinese homes, and were instantly plunged into a dimmed entryway where a group of locals sat around a card table playing mahjong. The darkness lifted as we continued into the open-air courtyard where a tree sprouted from its cement pot and several oversized tea kettles were nestled within a stone hearth. An assortment of large metal pots and pans had been stacked on top of a knee-high stone wall. The space resembled an abandoned venue; extra chairs scattered around the rooms and leaned against the walls, worn curtains masked doorways and storage spaces, and single lightbulbs hung suspended from the high ceilings. On the other side of the packed dirt courtyard, Patrick waited for us at one of the tables.

We sat sipping hot green tea, watching our host become distractedly preoccupied by his long tobacco pipe. He stood tall and thin, with his neck slightly bent as he puffed on the pipe's mouth piece. A chunky gold ring hugged his middle finger, and his long yellow fingernails had begun to curl. His ears poked out from beneath a black fur cap worn tightly around his head, and his leather jacket clashed tragically against his grey woolen trousers. The old man shuffled as he paced, seemingly unaware that we were waiting for him. He meandered aimlessly through the courtyard making one attempt after the other to light his pipe successfully.

Patrick waved a hand over his steaming cup of tea and shared that the house we were sitting in had been part of the family for hundreds of years. It was the same home that had been built by the old man's great-grandfather, and was the very home in which he was born.

Patrick then leaned over and let us in on the neighborhood joke. "People ask him how tall you are, and he says, *(I've converted these numbers from the metric system for you)*, 'five-foot-six.' But his friends, joking to him say, you are only four-foot. A boy, he's a boy."

I watched as the old man's eyes wandered the room in curiosity and thoughtfulness, like the eyes of an absentminded child. He went over to look at the tea kettles, inspected the structure of an adjacent wall, and after some more time spent lighting his pipe, finally took a seat at our table. His body was present, but his mind was far away.

Patrick elaborated on the expansive courtyards of the old man's home. He shared that during the cultural revolution it was forbidden for families to have several courtyards, but this home always had two. Right before the guards arrived in their city, however, the father had been gambling and lost one of the courtyards to another family. So when the guards arrived, they arrived to a single courtyard home. Little did he know he had accidentally saved his house by gambling away a portion of his property.

"His brother," Patrick started on another story, "his house taken by Red Army. He joined wrong party."

Eleanor and I listened with intent.

"It's funny," Patrick continued, pointing to our absentminded host. "He told me, every day on Ghost Day, his mother burning the paper money, paper clothes, paper car, took his older brother these things."

I understood that his mother had been mourning the loss of her son by burning offerings for his afterlife. For thirty-four years she did this in remembrance of her child. But then one day she received a letter that said he was alive and living well in Taiwan.

"And his mother cry," Patrick wiped imaginary tears from his cheeks. "Too happy, until she cry. Because thirty-four years his family think he died. Right before she die, she knows son is alive."

Patrick turned and pointed to an area in the back of the house, guarded by a light blue sheet draped from the ceiling.

"She there now. She has space back there, with son's picture. They are together."

Eleanor and I looked at the old man as he focused on his pipe and let out a sigh. He didn't understand English, but he didn't have to in that moment. This house was his place of birth and his mother's final resting place. It was a home in which he survived the cultural revolution. And now, it was a space shared by friends and passersby as his family's history was carried on by the art of storytelling. The old man's mind was far away, but his heart was still very much alive in the stories shared amongst visitors. By the time we thanked him for the tea and crossed over the threshold and back into the street, it was about an hour later, and the sisters had successfully finished their duvet.

Patrick hailed a bright orange tuk tuk that drove us back to the van where we piled in and began to drive towards the tea farms. Eleanor and I sat quietly in the back, reflecting on the stories we had collected. I considered the people we had met and the lives they've lived; a woman whose spice shop was her only lifeline, a man whose funerary supplies did not sour his joyful persona, and a brother whose home is his living memoir.

Everyone we met had a story to share, and graciously welcomed us into their lives. It was an experience that most guided tours couldn't orchestrate if they tried; an experience that was authentic and honest; one that felt like coming home to old friends. All of this was in thanks to Patrick, whose personal relationships and long-term friendships had allowed us the space to truly immerse ourselves in local life. And just as we began to wonder what generosity could possibly be coming next, Patrick decided to stop for oranges and, despite declining his offer multiple times, gifted each of us with a handful of fruit anyway. It was a day of unconditional giving.

By the time we reached the tea gardens I desperately needed to pee. So Patrick arranged for us to use the restroom before we hiked up to the plantations. He pulled into the driveway of a small cement farmhouse and directed Eleanor and me around a corner, towards the end of a dark hallway. A quick search for the light switch revealed a severe lack of electricity. We hesitantly rounded a corner to find ourselves standing before what I assumed Patrick had considered to be a restroom. The closet-sized room was illuminated only by narrow gaps where the top of the walls met the roof. A small hose was protruding from the wall where the sink would have been, and in place of a toilet was a triangular gap in the cement floor.

Eleanor and I let out a synchronized, "Oh no...". But by then, the urge to pee was far more upsetting than the hole in the ground. So I closed the door behind me and as I crouched over the endless pit of darkness I did my best to ignore the gut-wrenching scent and the maggots that swarmed at my feet. And, just as I thought things couldn't get any worse, I heard the distinct snorts of a very large animal. *Is that a...?* I heard Eleanor shriek from the other side of the wall. And then, as if we came to the same conclusion in that very moment, we burst out laughing until our sides began to ache. While our friendly neighbor the pig continued to snort. There was now truly nothing in Asia I hadn't yet experienced, and I would never, **ever** complain about a Port-a-John again.

Up at the tea plantation we met a couple who had been married for over sixty years. They lived in a modest home on the edge of the fields where they made their livelihood growing tea. Eleanor and I were each given a traditional bamboo hat and basket before we set off to gather tea leaves with the couple's daughter. We slid through the mud as we competed to see who could fill their basket the fastest. Spoiler alert, Eleanor and I both lost by a landslide. #Amateurs. Back at the house the couple demonstrated how to steam the leaves over a fire and then roll them over a woven bamboo mat. We watched in amusement as the old man, whose stature was permanently bent in a 90-degree angle, shuffled around the courtyard with haste and then dropped down into a low Asian squat as though it were the most natural ability to have at 89 years of age. If any of my grandparents tried to squat like that they surely would have displaced a hip. We crouched down beside the elderly couple as she meticulously rolled and he pulled out stray leaves to show us. Eleanor idled over the leaves and took them gently into her hands. When the leaves we had prepared were sent off to the oven to finish drying, we sampled a few of the teas ready for market. And as dusk turned into a crisp evening, we purchased a few bags of tea, bowed in gratitude for their hospitality, and headed back down the hill.

Eleanor and I sat silently in the backseat while Patrick drove the van into the city. We watched as fireworks lit up the darkened sky far off in the distance.

"A wedding," Patrick said calmly. "Big fireworks for weddings."

I watched the colorful reflections on the blackened waters below as we passed over a narrow bridge, and replayed the day's events in my head. I pulled out my phone and began listing the moments I wanted to preserve; the stories I couldn't afford to forget. The people we'd befriended and the generosity with which we'd been met was beyond any expectations of "just another guided tour." Patrick had immersed us in local life by introducing us to the storytellers of Leshan, China, and there was simply no proper way to thank him for the impact of that gesture.

So often when we travel, we seek out the stories from the lives of the extraordinary: kings and their palaces, criminals and their cells, or works of architecture that wowed the world. So often we forget how phenomenal the lives of the ordinary can be. Eleanor and I stepped into the worlds of barbers, herb sellers, shop owners, tea makers, families, and neighbors. Together we heard stories that will likely never make the front cover of a newspaper or be published in a bestseller, but were impactful nonetheless. The storytellers of Leshan opened their homes to us, expected nothing in return, and shared some of even their darkest days with strangers.

As the saying goes: "You can't buy happiness, but you can buy a plane ticket, and that's pretty close."

Well, yes, but you can't buy interpersonal relationships and cultural connection. That, my friends, is where the division between tourism and travel lies. You see, tourists take their photos, buy their souvenirs, and see parts of the world others only dream of seeing. But travelers capture moments, buy a round of drinks in a local bar, and experience parts of the world others only dream of experiencing. Tourists believe that if they've paid for a trip, the destination and their tour group owes them a memorable experience. Travelers know that neither the destination nor its local people owe them anything.

Tourists perceive adversity in travel (such as flight delays and lack of translators) to be an inconvenient hassle. Travelers embrace the opportunity to learn from being lost and confused. Tourists stick to the beaten path of civilization and familiar comforts. Travelers intentionally push themselves beyond their comfort zones. Tourists treat the locals as objects of a giant museum; a means to an end for memorable photography. Travelers treat locals as an opportunity to further understand local culture and tradition; they create relationships that last longer than their trip. **Tourists take everything and leave nothing**; their local impact is minimal as a result of their surface-level experience. **Travelers take nothing and leave everything**; their local impact is meaningful and purposeful, and they understand how a location and a story can shape who you are.

Tourists act as though it's their right to be there. Travelers understand it's a privilege. But don't be fooled; you can look like one and in fact be the other. Just because you're on a tour, doesn't make you a tourist; the title is dependent on your perspective, intentions, and your level of gratitude. Everyone has a story to tell, and every story is uniquely phenomenal. It is in those ordinary moments that the most extraordinary stories can be found. And the storytellers of Leshan will never know quite how profoundly they impacted my own narrative.

An Explorer in
Malaysia, Singapore,
Indonesia & Taiwan

Yin, Yang, & Monkeys

The main thing is to be moved, to love, to hope, to tremble, to live.
~ Auguste Rodin ~

Penang, Malaysia | October 25 - 28

When I was in preschool I had a favorite stuffed doll that went everywhere with me. In fact, she got so filthy from spending too much time on the playground that I'm confident my parents finally laid her to rest somewhere far away from my immune system. I can't remember what she actually looked like beyond her dark brown hair made of yarn, pulled back into a neat braid on which I'm sure my mom had spent far too much time. But, in my mind, she was the cloth replica of Degas's "Little Dancer". She was the little dancer who had come to "life" to inspire my passion for dance and be a wonderful listener as I told her all of my four-year-old problems. A few years later some family friends, likely seeing my desperate need for a new (much cleaner) companion, gave me a storybook about the little dancer and a limited edition doll that took its rightful place front and center on my wooden bookshelf. Every time I put on my ballet shoes, despite my innate frustration with ballet being too "dull" and "slow" for my taste, I danced as I imagined the little dancer would. I grew up so in awe of her iconic story that years later when I unsuspectingly came face to bow with one of the bronze renditions at a museum in Europe, I actually started crying. So when I met a man in Asia who adored Degas's "Little

Dancer" as much as I, the world as I knew it took an unexpected pirouette.

After my adventure to Western Asia, I had decided to take my newfound independence overseas and soon found myself embarking on a journey through Malaysia, Singapore, Indonesia, and Taiwan.

It was my first day in Penang, Malaysia and I was 100% in need of a shower. I had been wandering through the Batu Ferringhi beach area for over an hour and was now aimlessly pacing the streets waiting for the night market to open. The sand from the beach settled in between my toes as my damp socks stuck to the inside of my shoes. I considered the list of attractions I'd researched prior to my arrival. I wanted to watch the sunset from the highest point on the island - a tradition I embraced in every city I visited - so naturally, Penang Hill was high on my list. There was an art gallery that boasted handmade handicrafts and world renowned paintings. The butterfly gardens were somewhere nearby, and something called Adventure Zone, that I later came to realize was simply a room of children's slides intended to amuse a much younger set of world travelers. And then there was Kek Lok Si Temple, a stunning emblem of Buddhist culture and esteemed architecture. Frustrated that my indecision left me directionless, I stopped on the sidewalk to pull out my city map. Running my fingers along the edge I scoured the page for anything of interest. And then I looked up.

A stark white building with windows that stretched from floor to ceiling presented itself inconspicuously across the street. The driveway extended beyond a chain link fence and spilled out carelessly onto the road. Inside, an unkempt yard camouflaged two parked cars. Had it not been for the branding above the second floor balcony, I may have dismissed the building for someone's home. The Yahong Art Gallery had appeared during my planning, but certainly wasn't of higher importance than Penang Hill, the temple, or the butterfly gardens. After all, my time was limited, and I was determined to hit my top three before leaving for Kuala Lumpur. But, somehow, my aimless wandering had dumped me directly in front of the place for which I thought I wouldn't have time. Somewhere in my mind I knew this gallery had appeared in front of me for a reason. Plus, the sun was getting hot and I desperately craved some shade. So I followed my intuition and stepped into the street.

As I walked through the double doors I was instantly blasted with a frigid breeze pouring from the mega-fan that oscillated in the entrance. It took everything I had not to just oscillate with it for the next hour. I nodded at the gallery curator as I passed through the entrance, and smiled at an old man sitting in a low-sitting folding chair against the wall. He was disinterested in my arrival and sat tirelessly fanning himself with a newspaper. *He must not have heard about the arctic tundra happening in the entryway.*

The dimly lit building was spacious, yet underwhelming. Large staircases lined the adjacent walls, leading to an ominous second floor closed off by heavy wooden doors. I perused the first-floor shelves that were lined with handicrafts of every variety. Sculpted wooden animals, silk scarves dyed with pulsating colors, multiple collections of intricately decorated chopsticks, miniature vases, antique bowls, and handmade greeting cards.

Each no more expensive than a mass-produced tourist souvenir, yet far more beautiful than any keychain or bumper sticker. I contemplated just how many things I could delicately stuff into my hiking pack and carry with me for the remaining three weeks of my adventure. Behind me, I could feel the eyes of the gallery owner drifting in my direction, observant although reserved in her approach. It was normal to be followed by shop owners in Asia, but knowing that didn't make me feel any less of a criminal.

I made my way to the far back room and found myself standing amongst delicately carved bones, statues that stood taller than my 5-foot-4 self, hand-painted clocks, custom-made dining tables, ceramic urns, giant wooden masks, clay figures with animal hair, and intricately cut metal works. Don't even get me started on the price tags. My wallet cried before I even had a chance to consider a purchase. I was afraid to breathe, much less walk around in sheer admiration of the talented local artists. I weaved cautiously through the back rooms, the curator silently following behind.

I wandered back to the shelves out front and picked up several wooden animals that had caught my attention. They were small, durable, and easily transportable; a traveler's dream. As I approached the counter the Malaysian shop owner kindly asked if I was interested in seeing some paintings. Although my wanderlust had no particular schedule, I didn't want to spend the entire afternoon in one shop. If this place had fallen unexpectedly before me, what other magic might be out there waiting for my arrival? But I didn't want to appear rude or dismissive, so I agreed. *What's the harm in a quick detour?* She signaled to the old man who had been relaxing in the corner. He immediately pulled himself out of the chair and bounded toward the steps with renewed energy. He wore a blue and white striped shirt, the breast pocket sagging with a collection of ballpoint pens. His white hair was slightly yellowed, with specs of dark natural coloring still peeking through at the roots. Together we climbed the steps and, after ushering me in with a wave of his arm, the old man followed me into the studio. As he reached for the light switch I suddenly found myself surrounded by canvases decorated with vibrant dyes.

The old man showed me to a bulletin board filled with newspaper clippings and began to recite his spiel. The studio, I learned, featured a collection of works by Chuah Thean Teng, a Chinese artist considered to be the father and master of batik style painting in Malaysia. He was known around the world for his innovation of style and the repurposing of a fine art technique originally used for designing garments. My gallery host pointed to pieces hanging on the wall, noting their linear attributes and detailed structures. Despite the age in his eyes, he was exuberantly youthful in his storytelling; his arms waving with the eloquence of a maestro and his voice revealing an emotional connection with the works. I appreciated the intricate stories, but had a sudden growing suspicion that I was now trapped in an art gallery with a man who could drive a hard sale. I might have had time, but I didn't have money. And if there's anything I've learned since moving to Asia, it's that I tend to crumble in the hands of a good salesman. Yes, I can, in fact, be intimidated into buying things I don't need.

Just as I considered fabricating an excuse to leave, he said something I never would have expected.

"This artist is my father." He looked at me as though it had been the most natural thing for him to reveal in that moment.

My mouth fell open and my eyes wandered around the room, suddenly aware of the gravity of this spontaneous encounter. Here I was, casually chatting with the man whose father filled this gallery and many others around the world with an impeccable collection of historically and culturally influential art.

And then, pointing to a canvas in the corner adorned with softer lines and free-flowing colors, he said, "And this is my self-portrait."

Chuah Siew Teng explained that, much to his father's dismay, he had also pursued a life creating art.

"My father say art is no good for career, doesn't make much money. But you can't deny love."

Unlike his father's classic style of batik, Chuah Siew Teng instead found inspiration from artists like Van Gogh and Degas.

"Art is not art if you copy, it's only real art if you innovate, so I make different style than my father."

I stood in front of his self-portrait: a pair of monkeys sitting on a tree branch.

Chuah Siew Teng explained that he was born the year of the monkey, and that the two animals symbolized an idealistic life.

"One time, a man told me he likes men, and I could not understand. Man is not to be with man. Man and woman make babies, man and man do not. Is not natural, you see? Man and woman, balance. But man and man, no balance." He shook his head with angst.

"So these monkeys, my monkeys, they are one man and one woman. The woman monkey whispers to the man, 'Tomorrow we will marry.' You see?"

He looked at me proudly, "Balance."

He pointed to the other elements of harmony in his work; the location of the leaves, the earthy colors, and even the strategic placement of his Chinese and English signatures.

"Life is balance, you see?" He gave me a toothy grin. "Man, woman. Light, dark. Good, bad. Happy, sad. Peace, fight. Like yin, yang. You know it?"

I nodded.

While I may not have agreed with Chuah Siew Teng's belief that heterosexuality is the definition of a balanced life, or that there is one idealistic way to achieve happiness, I did appreciate his fundamental value in finding harmony. He had managed to illustrate through visuals the unconditional support experienced when we find our partner in life; the love that is created when one discovers their true equal.

"But to find balance," he searched my eyes for understanding. "You must be balanced. Love comes to another when you love yourself."

He explained that only when each side has established a sense of balance in their own lives, can they fall in love and find success in a relationship with someone else. I thought about Josh; how eager he was to support my adventures and how confident he was in my ability to take on the world alone. I considered just how monumental our relationship could be if we continued to thrive even after living six months apart. Chuah Siew Teng felt passionately that individual balance has to be established before a stronger, more unified balance can be created for both.

"Because of this, the piece, it reminds me of the song "You Raise Me Up" (by Josh Groban). You know it?" He sang a few bars. I grinned.

As we walked through the gallery Chuah Siew Teng told me about his studies in London and his extensive international travels, which explained his proficient English. I flipped through scrapbooks full of newspaper headlines and certificates of honor for having donated works to charities all over the world. He revealed the background stories to several of his works, including a piece in which - to great shock and amusement from his professor - he unexpectedly painted his peers in the nude. We talked about Degas and our shared love of dance. He rattled off phrases in Italian, Chinese, German, English, Russian, Malay, French, and Spanish simply because he could. He talked about how important it is to find and appreciate the beauty in people's bodies; not out of lust, but rather sincere admiration for the naturally occurring artistry of human life.

"You should make love because you love, not have sex because you lust." He pulled several paintings of dancers from beneath a stack of canvases.

"Love is knowing how beautiful a body is. You have to appreciate the beauty to feel the love." He believed that too many people cannot love because they cannot see beauty.

Chuah Siew Teng believed that painting the human body was a meditation of awareness and appreciation for natural beauty. To him, painting someone was just as intimate, if not more so, than making love. He could not fathom the idea of using a body for anything other than love or art. I was infatuated; his artistic intuition shimmered through every sentence he spoke. The words themselves seemed to become a work of art. Just as though I were watching a paintbrush pull colorful paints across a canvas, I was entranced.

In the far corner of the studio I stood observing a few works in progress as he demonstrated the process for creating batik paintings; molten wax strategically placed on a canvas and each color of dye applied in separate layers. Depending on the level of detail, one piece alone could take two to three months to complete. He led me over to a table where he handed me canvas after canvas of his most recent works, each one more beautiful than the last. I set aside a few of the pieces I loved, only dreaming of hanging one on my walls at home. I shuffled through the remaining canvases, knowing full well that my wallet was hardly large enough for any of them.

"And you sell these?" I asked.

He nodded.

"How much do you usually…"

"Which one you like?" He smiled.

It was the question most conscientious travelers hate to hear. Although, it's more often heard as one attempts to flee from a particularly aggressive marketplace seller who is yelling, "I give you good price! Hey! Lady, I give you discount!"

But this time, the question seemed to hit much harder. I looked at Chuah Siew Teng and hesitantly pulled two pieces from the stack; a peaceful scene of a noodle shop in Hong Kong and another version of his monkey self-portrait adorned with purple flowers.

He chuckled and pointed to the monkeys. "This is one of my favorites. I love purple."

A man of my own heart....

He affectionately offered to give me a good price. But still I winced when I asked how much.

Pointing to the noodle shop he said, "This one I sell to someone for 10,000." Without pulling out my currency conversion app, I knew right away it was beyond my budget. And before you go reaching for a calculator, I'll tell you that at the time of writing this chapter it was equal to over $2,550.

My heart broke as he sat proudly overlooking his art. I asked how much for the monkeys; out of every piece I'd seen it was the only one with which I truly felt a deep connection. It was not only a phenomenal work of art, but also a representation of a meaningful conversation and deep friendship.

"This one, same price." He had a gleam in his eye. "But for you, maybe I give half price. You know?"

As I sat in a perplexed silence on the couch another traveler wandered into the studio. She admired the canvases and again he offered me the piece for 5,000 Ringgits. The new traveler and I caught each other's gaze, and instantly I could tell we both agreed. This kind-hearted man genuinely wished me to have a piece of his life's work, but it was at a price I simply could not afford. And to bargain further would not only be an insult to his talent but would leave me with a guilt I could never shake.

I felt a deep sadness build in my chest as I admitted, "This is worth so much more than I can give..."

He interjected, "But because of friendship, I don't care." He reiterated that sometimes he gave his paintings to museums free of charge.

I looked him in the eyes as tears swelled behind my own and said, "I could not possibly pay you so little for something so beautiful. I cannot pay you what this is worth."

Unlike the pushy marketplace sellers, he didn't push back. He too, recognized the value in his work and, despite his disappointment, understood why I could not accept his bargain.

We took a photo together before I left. I hardly even cared that I was covered in sweat, wearing eighteen hours worth of travel and beach sand on my clothes. It is still one of my favorite pictures from those six months of adventures. I promised that when the day came that I had the money to repay him for his time, stories, and talent, that I would return to buy one of his self-portraits. *In the meantime,* I thought, *until I win the lottery and magically pay off the student debt quickly accruing in my absence, I'll just stock up on notecards and savor the videos I've captured.* In the end, a price tag means nothing if the story behind it doesn't move you.

Chuah Siew Teng reestablished a relationship to art that had been developing over the past twenty-two years of my life. From the influence of my grandmother, great aunt, and my mother, to my time spent wandering the museums in Paris, Amsterdam, and Italy, from the moment I cried upon seeing the "Little Dancer" in person, to my love of Van Gogh since I was a kid, nothing could have prepared me for the deep connection I felt looking at those monkeys or imagining myself reflected in the silky lines of his female figures. He truly sees life through an artist's eyes, and to catch even a glimpse of that world was a sincere honor and a truly humbling experience.

As I left the gallery, I glanced down at the MyIntent bracelet I wore on my wrist, stamped with the word, "Synchronicity," and smiled. *Everything happens for a reason.* And for whatever reason it was that I wandered into this gallery and met Chuah Siew Teng, and learned from him the art of life's balance and true love, I am so deeply grateful. The ten-pack of post cards I picked from the shelves will hardly fill the space of an original piece, but they will forever carry the representation of a conversation and experience that left the artist within me feeling that much more inspired.

Stranger Danger & Parasails

He who does not trust enough will not be trusted.

~ Lao Tzu ~

Penang, Malaysia | October 25 - 28

Fear is not a motivator. If that were the case, I wouldn't have pulled off half the stunts I did in Asia, especially not alone. You see, when we are afraid of something we take precautionary measures to avoid our fear becoming a reality. I was scared when I began to realize that my post-graduate job of a lifetime was a sham. I was scared of what people back home might think, scared of what my future would become, and scared to admit that life wasn't working out the way I'd planned. For a while, this fear paralyzed me. I tried endlessly to turn the situation around and learn how to cope with my anger simply because quitting was the scariest possible outcome. This fear installed a set of blinders; I was so focused on fixing things so as not to lose my job that I couldn't see the beautiful open world in front of me. It took a few months too long for me to realize that my greatest joys would be found by overcoming my fear of failure and facing the reality that things just weren't working out as expected.

Growing up, we hear the same words of caution as we learn to navigate this crazy and unpredictable world on our own: don't talk to strangers, watch your drink, don't accept gifts of food from people you don't know, and if a stranger picks you up from school make sure they know the secret password. Oh, and don't get into any unknown vehicles. Now, don't get me wrong, there is validity in teaching your kids not to trust strangers. The world can unfortunately be a terrifying place. Which is why, when a middle-aged local Malaysian man with limited English asked me to hop on the back of his motorbike and ride into the jungle where we would then hike to a remote lighthouse together, I could hear my parents in the back of my mind screaming, "HAVE WE TAUGHT YOU NOTHING?!"

It all started after my spontaneous detour to the Yahong Art Gallery. I had wandered back to Batu Ferringhi beach in search of some dinner and, after gorging myself on chicken satay drizzled with peanut sauce, I found myself lounging on the coast. I sat there on the sand listening to the shrieks of young children playing in the brisk waters, and to the soft hum of distant jet skis as they sped along the horizon. Up in the clouds, someone was being hoisted into the air by an oversized parachute tethered to a speed boat below. I imagined what the shore must look like from up there, the sparkling blue waters contrasting the panoramic spread of thick jungle. The skeptic in me jumped straight to the conclusion that, however neat the experience might be, a tourist trap like that had to be stupidly expensive. But the adventurer in me considered how likely it would be that I'd soon again find myself hanging out on a beach in Southeast Asia with a water sports company in arm's reach. *What is it the kids say these days? YOLO?*

I gathered my belongings and traipsed over to a stand where several local men were chatting in the shade. After negotiating a price that was about half of the outrageous number listed on their sandwich board, I grabbed my GoPro, hoisted up my pant legs, and awkwardly stepped into a harness. Strapped to me in my parasail was a guy named The Man. Or... Zee Man. Maybe Zemahn. There might have been a bit of a language barrier.

I clutched my GoPro against my chest as we were yanked up into the breeze. I watched the horizon expand before me, the depth of the thick jungle growing rapidly as we gained altitude. The crisp fresh air hit my face and I felt what was becoming an overbearing exhaustion begin to drip away entirely. The sun began to sink behind the trees as the sky dimmed peacefully behind me. It was such a serene space that I'd nearly forgotten I was attached to another human. Although he wasn't the most talkative, I managed to find out that between working for the water sports company during the day and the beachside bar at night, my parasailing guide was living a pretty good life in Malaysia.

After an awkward landing in the sand, of which I unfortunately have video evidence, I joined my parasailing guide in the shade for a drink at the beachside bar named Riverstone Bistro. We were served by his friend and coworker, who proudly announced that our drinks were, "on the house." But just as awkward as our landing had been, so too was the conversation. I attempted to make small talk with my friendly guide, despite his introverted and bashful personality. He shared with me, in simple English, his passion for cooking and being outdoors. He mentioned that he used to hike through the nearby national park quite frequently, but hasn't been in a while due to a lack of interest from his friends. And that's when he told me about Monkey Beach.

"You hike there," he said, turning and pointing to the trees that lined the distant shore. "There you find Monkey Beach. It's a nice beach, very nice. Quiet." He looked at me. "You are going?"

I confessed, "I don't know. I don't really have a plan. I just got here today." I thought of the long list of sights and activities I still wanted to cross off. Street art, night markets, art museums, butterfly gardens and, of course, the notoriously delicious hawker centers.

He looked at me curiously, "We can go if you want. I can take you to the park. We can hike together."

I could hear every adult from my childhood screaming, "NOT HIKING INTO REMOTE JUNGLES WITH STRANGERS IS A RULE YOU SHOULD NOT DISOBEY."

So I decided to administer a quick test.

I looked at him and said as confidently as I could, "I have a friend back at the hostel, can they come too?" I wondered if he could see through my blatant lie.

He waved his hand in a casual and friendly dismissal, "Of course, no problem! They come too."

Well… in this theoretical scenario he'd have to kill us both at the same time and he doesn't really seem capable nor interested in doing that. So, it must be okay. Right?

I smiled. "Sure, we'd love to."

He put his number in my phone (finally confirming that his name was Zeman) and we agreed to meet at the beach the next morning. I spent the entire rest of my evening wondering if I'd made a horrific mistake and even considered contracting a good old case of fake food poisoning to get out of it. I thought about what my parents would say, what my friends would think, and what would happen if things went wrong. Yet, despite all of my doubts, there was an instinctual pull to follow through on my promise. My intuition reassured me that I would be okay. The decision had been of my own will, one that I made with confidence, and for some reason I felt I could trust Zeman. So the next morning I booked a car and headed back to the beaches of Batu Ferringhi.

As I waited for Zeman to arrive I messaged Josh on WeChat: "I'm going hiking with the guy who works at the beachside bar I was at last night".

He responded, seemingly unconcerned: "That will be fun!"

It was just like Josh to be enthusiastic without worry. He trusted me, which was a wonderful feeling, but in that very moment I wasn't even sure that I trusted myself. So I provided him the information he might need just in case I disappeared in the jungle.

"I know this may be a tad paranoid of me but I'm playing it safe. Haha. This is the guy's phone number who I'm going with. His name is Zeman. He works for the bar and on the beach taking people on parasailing trips. I have no reason yet NOT to trust him - too many people have seen me here and know I'm going, so I'm not too worried, but it's still a stranger sooooo…"

Josh continued to show very little concern that I was heading off into a national park with a man I'd just met. He texted back: "One can never be too safe!" Thanks, Joshua.

I looked out across the water where the forest met the shoreline and anticipated a quiet and very awkward hike. But all I had to do was survive two hours of anxiety and it would all be over; I could go back to my hostel, take a nap, find some street art, and eat nasi goreng (fried rice) until my stomach exploded. I was afraid, but not afraid enough to miss out on an interesting experience. And certainly not enough to pass up the chance to see more of Malaysia. As great as eating my way through hawker centers sounded, so did an epic adventure. I was still daydreaming about food when Zeman rolled up to the beach on a motorbike. *Well, if anyone is going to kill me now, it will probably be my father.*

Zeman strolled over to hand me an extra helmet, then impatiently waved me onto his bike. *What a chivalrous guy.*

He looked around and asked, "Where is your friend?"

"Oh, she couldn't come today." I tried my best to pull off the fib, "She wasn't feeling well."

He nodded in dismissal and turned back to his bike. Zeman was certainly a man of few words. I took a few deep breaths and mentally prepared myself for an adventure I'd never forget. *It wouldn't be travel if I didn't do something that scared me, right?* And if I lived a life unable to trust anyone I certainly wouldn't be making any friends! Besides, it was a straight shot to the Penang National Park. No turns, no bridges, and not even more than four miles down the coast. Not a whole lot could go wrong!

The paved roads in Penang were smooth as glass, and I leaned my head back into the wind as it braced itself against my body. We cruised past the seafood restaurants and Hard Rock Hotel Penang, past night market stalls and art museums, and flew through several intersections devoid of traffic. I felt the sun pulse against my skin through breaks in the shade, and breathed in the crisp ocean air when we neared the coast. I imagined our path to the park as though watching Google Maps track our vehicle with a little blue dot; a straight shot and then a right. Easy peasy. I took a refreshing deep breath.

And then Zeman turned left.

No no no no no. I panicked. *There is no left on this route. He wasn't supposed to turn. There's no possible way this is a local short-cut because the only way is straight and he just turned left.* My mind went full spaz-mode. *Oh my god, he's taking me back to his place where he'll stow me away and probably murder me. Or maybe he's driving me to a buddy's house where he'll hand me off and I'll disappear forever. No, he's probably driving me into the jungle where he'll force me off the bike and I'll have to fight my way back to the main road and probably be lost for so long that it'll be dark by the time I find anyone and OhMyGodImTooYoungToDie.*

I was about to throw myself from the bike in dramatic fashion when Zeman turned to yell into the wind, "I need gas."

I could hear my heartbeat in my ears. Thoughts sped through my brain at an alarming rate.

But instead of revealing my true level of panic, I simply replied, "Okay," and held on tightly as he leaned the bike through several roundabouts. He then pulled into a gas station where he filled up his bike and promptly led me inside so he could buy me an orange juice for the ride. *Well, if I've ever met a killer, this is the nicest one by far. Courteous, AND concerned about my Vitamin C intake.*

We walked back outside to the bike where he strapped his helmet on and said nonchalantly, "We'll go to the park. But first, I want to show you Penang. Very beautiful."

Of course, me being me, I only managed to spit out an overly enthusiastic and slightly uncomfortable, "Okay!"

Despite my panic just moments earlier, I realized Zeman had yet to break my trust. I mean, he bought me OJ. And my intuition hadn't yet picked up any odd vibes beyond my confusion when we turned left. Zeman and I sped along local backroads that, quite frankly, reminded me of Ft. Lauderdale, Florida. Palm trees dotted the landscape while modest ranch-style housing spread itself out along the road. The apartment complexes and school buildings were all painted in light pastels, reminiscent of a seaside neighborhood. I watched as civilization turned into coastline, and coastline turned into winding jungle roads. The temperature dropped instantaneously and the humidity began to climb with us.

Zeman yelled back into the wind, "You like waterfalls?"

I responded with a resounding, "Yeah!"

He slowed to a stop and parked his bike on the side of the road.

Zeman strapped his helmet to the handlebars of the bike and started off into the trees. He hurried me along with a wave of his hand. We crossed halfway over a rickety bridge before ducking beneath the railing and lowering ourselves onto the rocks below. I cautiously followed Zeman as he crouched below branches and straddled moving waters to maneuver from boulder to boulder. He would leap onto a distant rock, turn around, and watch as I followed suit. Together we climbed strategically, albeit quite dangerously, up the falls. By the time we made it to the top I was convinced he might actually be a ninja; the way he jumped and always landed silently on his feet was just not normal. At the top we perched on a large boulder that overlooked a beautiful swimming hole, complete with its own set of falls. We sat for several moments in a serene silence before walking back down to the bike. But instead of climbing back down the falls, Zeman led me to a perfectly cleared, easily accessible hiking trail.

I looked at Zeman, who was grinning back at me, knowing very well the trick he'd played. "You like adventure, don't you?" I gave him a skeptical look.

He shrugged. "Makes life more interesting."

Zeman was an explorer at heart. He made me feel at ease while at the same time inspiring my own adventurer that lived inside. He drove us to a lookout where I observed the red-roofed villages below and the ocean waters that stretched themselves longingly toward the horizon. He bought durian from a local fruit stand and demonstrated how to eat it as he pried open the shell with his bare hands. I had avoided Asia's stinkiest fruit for so long, but Zeman insisted that I could not leave Penang without trying a fresh one from the durian farms. So I gave it a go and sucked the stale-mango flavored flesh from the seed. Honestly, it wasn't that bad, but it's not something I'd do again. The oddly soft, custard-like texture made me gag more than the flavor itself. And the flavor, my friends, was not great.

On our way back down the coast, Zeman slowed to a crawl and pulled his bike off onto the shoulder. I sat there confused while he hopped off and removed his helmet.

Then he turned to me and said, "Your turn."

"Um, what?"

"Your turn," he repeated. "You drive now."

I gave him the same look my mom gave me when I informed her of my original plans to hike the Mount Huashan Death Trail. "Are you sure about this?"

"Yeah," he said confidently. "Is like riding a bike."

I wondered if Zeman was having a serious lapse in judgement or if he was under the impression I had driven one of these before. Because, had he asked, I would have been honest and informed him that, no, I've never driven a motorbike. And, even if I had, I certainly hadn't driven one on the opposite side of the road as Malaysian streets demanded.

I looked at the bike, and then back at him. "Okay, I'll try it." And after I'd finally stopped pumping the gear instead of the throttle, I was revving my way down the mountain and around the corner, leaving Zeman to follow on foot.

I drove back and forth, leaning the bike into several tight U-turns and teasing Zeman as I threatened to ride off without him. He followed several paces behind, laughing, never able to catch up with me completely. When I stopped to let him take back the bike, he instead climbed on behind me and told me to drive. It was surreal, weaving around the winding roads on a motorbike in Malaysia. As I drove us out of the jungle I began to realize that Zeman was not only a guy worth trusting, but also an incredibly trusting guy. By the time we reached the bottom of the hill I had started to believe I might be in the Southeast Asian remake of *Eat, Pray, Love*.

At the national park we set off on foot for Monkey Beach. Zeman had been fairly quiet up until now - an observer rather than a conversationalist - but while we hiked, he began to share with me pieces of his life. He asked about my travels and I learned of his passion for nature and discovery. I inquired about his jobs on the beach and expressed my envy of his lifestyle.

"I like my jobs," he said matter-of-factly. "My life is good."

I hiked behind him while we both panted in the heat. "Thank you for inviting me to come with you. This is really nice."

I increased my pace just enough to hear his soft-spoken answer, "I'm happy you want to hike. My friends don't come much. Nice to have you here."

I smiled into my shirt as I used it to wipe large beads of sweat from my forehead. It seemed the friendly company was refreshing for both of us.

After we dragged ourselves to the beach and I managed to chug the entire contents of a fresh coconut all by myself, we started the climb to Muka Head Lighthouse. Let me begin by saying, this climb is not for the physically unfit (nor the physically fit who already hiked for an hour under the Southeast Asian sun). This climb was far steeper and lengthier than preferred, but the view from the top was more than worth it. As we rounded the last few stairs at the top of the lighthouse and stepped out onto the platform, the cool breeze embraced my steaming skin. Despite the sweat literally dripping from my eyebrows, I was completely at peace. I caught my breath while looking out at Batu Ferringhi in the distance, the boats waiting off the coast, and the expansive jungle that spread itself before us.

Traveling alone as a female has its moments of fear and discomfort. I grew up in a society that, by default, instills a distrust of strangers and caution towards unfamiliar experiences and people. But the moments in which I find myself happiest and most enjoying my travels are when I can place my trust in others to guide and care for me. No matter where I've gone, I've been fortunate in always finding people I could trust; individuals who invite me into their lives, show me their culture, and quite literally welcome me into their homes. I wish there was a formula for knowing who is trustworthy and who is not, but the only equation I can narrow it down to is:

$$Strangers + (Me \times Mindful\ Intuition) = Calculated\ Risk$$

Do you know how many times my gut has been right and I didn't listen? How many times I've allowed my mind to overpower my heart, only to find that my heart had the best intentions the whole time? When you travel - not just internationally, but through life - you develop an acute sense of intuition. You learn to mindfully read a room, and identify both its faults and its beauties. You begin to recognize the energies that occupy through the space around you when something just isn't quite right. It's not a feeling I can describe accurately with words, but it's a concept with which we are all familiar in one way or another. This is not to say our intuition can't be tricked but, more often than not, our body knows when it's time to change direction. If I knew within a day of working for R that my life was about to get complicated, I knew that my trust in Zeman could be tested.

Trust is not easy to put into practice; it means allowing someone close enough to hurt you, but having confidence that they won't. The primary issue is that we usually view trust as holding someone else responsible for our well-being. Well, that perception is wrong. You see, I think trusting others is more a reflection of how much you trust yourself. Because if all else fails, and your trust is broken, it is still on you to figure it out or turn the situation around. It is not their job to pick up the pieces and make the most of it; it's yours. Blaming someone else for breaking your trust defeats the purpose of having trusted at all. Because if you really trust yourself, then trusting others will come easily. An ability to trust someone else is an ability to trust yourself to handle whatever comes next.

I pondered this while Zeman and I sat overlooking the island.

It was then that he turned to me and said, "Do good and you will receive good. Smile, and people will smile back." I let his words drift into the breeze that encased our sweaty shoulders. There will always be those who disappoint us, but as Zeman so beautifully illustrated in that moment, if someone does not smile back, take it as a sign to redirect your efforts elsewhere and continue moving forward with positivity and good faith. Don't waste a moment on someone who will never smile back, because there are plenty of others who are simply waiting for that extra bit of joy.

We assume that fear sparks action, that perceiving our greatest pitfalls will encourage us to work harder to prevent them from coming true. However, when we calculate a risk and establish specific steps to avoid the outcome, we close off our minds not only to unexpected adversities but also to opportunities for growth. In reality, fear only paralyzes our ability to cope with change. It distances us from the people and places that would bring comfort in our time of need. It prevents us from reaching our full potential because we refuse to see anything else the universe has to offer. It shuts down our intuition by refusing to perceive the world as anything else other than a threat.

"You have to trust, if you cannot trust you cannot be happy." Zeman took the last sip from his water bottle. "Trusting everyone risks heartbreak and disappointment, but trusting no one guarantees loneliness." I looked at Zeman as we momentarily made thoughtful eye contact. I closed my eyes and tilted my face into the sun. Finally, the answer I had been unknowingly looking for had graciously fallen into my open hands. *We should take the risk, not the guarantee.*

I thanked Zeman for the adventure, and expressed gratitude for his selflessness in showing me around Penang. I offered to pay him for gas and food, but he refused to even consider taking my money. To Zeman, the reassurance of a day well spent was more than enough. To him, it was far more about connection than it was personal gain.

He smiled at me and said gently, "If you are good person then you find good people, if you are guilty person then you find guilty people. Good people find good people, with their hearts and their minds. They just know."

Mike & Iyke & Nasi Goreng

Travel is the only thing you buy that makes you richer.

~ Anonymous ~

Penang, Malaysia | October 25 - 28

I was never really a fan of the beloved childhood candy, but when I met Mike and Iyke in Penang, Malaysia, I knew the universe was conspiring to give me a solid laugh I'd never forget. I mean, what are the odds? Mike was one of the few Americans I had met on my journey thus far, and one of the first people to reinforce that I was following the right path. Iyke was a local university student who spent his days driving around the island of Penang, playing soccer, eating Baskin Robbins ice cream, and singing over Bruno Mars while "Uptown Funk" pulsed through his car speakers.

Flashback to shortly after Zeman and I had landed from parasailing, finished our drinks, and exchanged phone numbers so that we could meet up the next day to go hiking. When Zeman turned in for the afternoon, I spent some time at Riverstone Bistro watching the sunset and enjoying a frozen margarita. I know, living the dream! Just when the sun had sunk low enough in the sky to consider it "set," and as soon as I'd decided to head back to the hostel, I was approached by Iyke. Unlike Zeman, Iyke was not a reserved individual; he sat right down at my table and began talking up a storm. But as much as I was enjoying the spontaneous company, I was mentally drained and struggling to make conversation. I was tired from the trip, worn out from the sun, and dreaming of my hostel bed. It's sometimes difficult, however, to tell someone so enthusiastic, that you are sweaty, exhausted, and just want to go to sleep. So I ordered another drink.

Iyke was born in South Africa but came to Malaysia six years ago to attend university and play soccer. He worked hard to support his family who remained back home and was hopeful in pursuing an athletic career. Iyke spoke highly of Batu Ferringhi as he frequently makes trips just to hang out on the sands and see who he would meet. Tonight, of course, it was an American in desperate need of a shower and a four-course dinner. While we sat chatting over drinks I could tell Iyke was a social butterfly, but that he was perhaps longing for a few closer connections.

By the time eight o'clock approached, our conversation had lulled, and the exhaustion began to pull at my eyelids, so I took out my phone and opened Grab to order a ride home. Grab is a mobile app quite similar to Uber or Lyft, but is arguably far better (and cheaper!). With Grab you have several different options:
- Book a trip with a taxi
- Book a trip with a driver who works for Grab (this option is most like Uber)
- Carpool with others who are headed in the same direction (this may make several stops but saves quite a chunk of change)
- Hitch a ride with someone who is headed in the same direction and doesn't mind picking you up along the way (rather than working specifically for Grab, these drivers

typically have full-time jobs elsewhere and are just looking for some extra cash and/or adventure during their regular commute. This option is about half the cost of a regular driver)

Iyke watched curiously and then asked where I was staying.

I replied lazily, "My hostel is in Georgetown, it's not too far."

He practically leaped out of his seat. "Oh! I'm headed to Georgetown. My car is right here. You want a ride?"

This questionable offer was, of course, within a mere few hours of agreeing to hike through a jungle with another stranger I'd just met. I thought for sure this was pushing my luck. *The universe is just waiting for me to say yes to one more iffy thing before it teaches me a very important lesson.* Mom, if you're reading this, just take a deeeeep breath.

I looked at Iyke with hesitancy but answered with confidence, "If you're headed in that direction anyway, that would be great!"

To be fair, this was about the same as getting into a Grab car under the 'Hitch' option anyway. Except this one would be free. Iyke motioned for me to follow and grabbed his keys from the table. I said a silent prayer that my gut was right on this, too....

We navigated through the winding streets of Penang with only the guidance of his headlights. Iyke asked me about my interests, family, and next destination. And at the first pause in conversation he plugged in his phone and cranked up the music. I tilted my head and looked at him curiously as he began to belt along to several songs by Whitney Houston. But to say that was the most surprising turn of events in my time with Iyke, would have been a lie. He asked over the music if I wanted to get food, but in that very moment the stench I could smell from my body was overpowering any hunger pains. I told him I really wanted to change and wash my face (and cake on seven more layers of deodorant) before I went anywhere else. So we drove by the hostel and I ran in to freshen up.

It was in those ten minutes as I changed out of my grungy clothes and doused myself with deodorant, that I met Mike. Since he was one of the few Americans I had met, naturally, I was intrigued.

He started the script rolling, "Where are you from?"

"Columbus, Ohio. What about you?"

He withdrew in surprise. "No way, I grew up there! I still have family in town. I was born at Grant Medical Center, have you heard of it?"

I was about to lose my cool and go total dork mode. "That's 15 minutes from my house! How small can this world really be?!"

It was an instantaneous friendship. We made tentative plans to explore Georgetown together, and I happily agreed to catch up with him when I returned from picking up some dinner.

"My new friend Iyke is going to take me to find some authentic nasi goreng!"

He nodded in enthusiasm. "I can't get enough of that stuff!"

Feeling refreshed, and reenergized by a new connection, I grabbed my backpack and went bounding down the stairs of my hostel.

Over the next few hours Iyke drove me all over Georgetown introducing me to the local night life and showing me his favorite places in the city. Despite my exhaustion I was grateful for the complimentary tour and transportation towards food. And, to top it all off, he made a stop at Baskin Robbins where he introduced me to the staff, who each knew Iyke's order without even having to ask. That kid's obsession with ice cream was nearly on a competing level with my own. Ice cream for dinner was no problemo in my book, but by the time we set out in search of real food, finding a local eatery open that late was proving to be impossible. We meandered through darkened streets attempting to find something, anything, that was appetizing. In the end, I settled for one of the only open restaurants...Subway. And on the drive home I was confronted by yet another surprising turn of events. I began to realize that perhaps our friendship meant something entirely different to Iyke, as his choice in music suddenly evolved from Bruno Mars to twanging country love songs.

Back at the hostel I opened the door to our dorm to find Mike sitting in his top bunk. I set my Subway sandwich and drink on top of the lockers so that I could put away my backpack before finally feeding my now hangry stomach.

"Ah, I see you really enjoyed the local cuisine tonight." He winked at me.

I rolled my eyes but smiled back, and took another sip of my Sprite. After I finally nourished my exhausted body, I showered, crawled into my bunk, and passed out before I could even plug in my phone.

The day after my adventure into the jungle with Zeman, Mike and I went on an endless quest to find the renowned street art of Georgetown. In 2012, Georgetown's streets came to life when Ernest Zacharevic was hired by Penang's municipal council to decorate the city with intricate murals that incorporated physical objects into painted works. The initiative resulted in local streets being filled with culturally significant, one-of-a-kind art, and - depending on how you look at it - an entire map's worth of quality Instagram material.

After a delicious breakfast of roti bakar (the best toast known to mankind), Mike and I meandered through Georgetown neighborhoods under a particularly hot Malaysian sun. We spotted new sights around every corner and wandered into local shops along the way. We allowed our map to make suggestions but ultimately followed our curiosity. It was a scavenger hunt we weren't in any hurry to finish. We chowed down on warm samosas in Little India and sipped on grape Fantas from a corner convenience store to cool down. While we walked, our stories came to the surface, and we realized we were connected by much more than just an American hometown.

Like me, Mike was on a journey of self-discovery. He had been working as a senior research associate at a pharmaceutical company for six years when he began to realize that, despite the job security and pay, his work performance was diminishing. After some time spent analyzing why he wasn't succeeding as well as he had been, Mike realized it was because he was no longer happy. He was missing something. So he quit. And as he recalled the events that led him to Penang, I could tell a weight had been lifted from his shoulders. Despite my parallel experience working for R, understanding what it felt like to be missing something, I was astonished at Mike's dauntlessness. That many years spent building a career only to set it aside and leave it behind....

"Why travel?" I asked. "Didn't it scare you to leave stability?"

Mike didn't hesitate. "Traveling provides a lot of introspection and allows you to actually experience life as an adult. I want to figure out who I really am and what it is that I want." He took another sip of his Fanta.

Well, duh, why didn't I think of that?

We turned down a street draped with string lights and lined with colonial style architecture.

"I have peace of mind," Mike continued. "Mentally and physically I feel better. My job didn't deserve the amount of energy and time I was putting into it."

To Mike, travel was a sort of therapy, and I was beginning to see his point. Despite both of us having nearly $30,000 of student debt each and no specific plan for the future, we still wholeheartedly agreed that travel was a good idea. It was a nerve-wracking yet equally exhilarating lifestyle that had already been proven purposeful in discovering new qualities and relationships in our lives. Mike admitted that although he was initially worried he wasn't making the right decision, within a week he knew the answer.

"I realized for the first time in a while that I was happy." Mike smiled at me. "And I'm proud of myself! I set a goal and I'm doing it."

I knew exactly what he meant; pursuing an adventurous journey and trusting yourself to overcome unexpected adversities was a phenomenal feeling. Travel, if done right, can be one of the few investments that truly pays off.

By late afternoon we had strolled up and down most every street, although the art was far too plentiful to capture all of it. I could have spent every moment of my time in Malaysia locating every unique piece and it still wouldn't have been enough. As Mike and I stood on the sidewalk beneath the hot sun, trying to decide where to go next, I suggested we head to Batu Ferringhi. Our evening winded down as we stuffed ourselves with fresh seafood and fried rice while sitting oceanside in a predominantly empty restaurant. Since tourist season for Penang wouldn't start for another few weeks, the would-be-crowded eateries were blissfully devoid of people. Sufficiently stuffed, we meandered down to Batu Ferringhi where we sat in the sands watching the sunset and tossing back a few drinks with the staff of Riverstone Bistro. By the time we ordered a Grab to head back into the city, it had begun to rain.

Mike and I sat in the back of our car as it slowly inched down a two-lane back road by the beach. A trip that should have lasted twenty-five minutes was quickly turning into forty. I looked out at the rain as it chased itself down the windows.

Turning to Mike I asked, "How did you know this was the right decision?"

"That what was the right decision?" He fiddled with his phone in the dark.

"Quitting your job, traveling, not having a future plan. The general, you know, recklessness of it all."

Although I was still without a career plan myself, at least I knew I would be returning to the United States to take the first job I could land so I could pay off my student loans. Mike didn't have a plan, let alone any idea what the next year would look like. He didn't even have a next destination in mind, but that didn't seem to bother him at all.

He looked up from his phone and declared thoughtfully, "People are raised to think that everything has a certain path. A plus B equals C. It just doesn't have to be like that." Mike looked out the window. "If people think I'm wasting my potential, that's fine. It doesn't affect me."

I stared at Mike, wondering if I, too, would ever discover that kind of confidence. I was still preoccupied by the fear of returning home with nothing to show for my post-graduate career.

"I'm happy," he said thoughtfully. "And that's what matters. I know in the end that I will have lived my life to the fullest. I can't tell you what I hope to walk away with from all this; I want a little bit more clarity, but even if that doesn't happen I know this was well worth the risks I'm taking."

The cars ahead of us slowly started to move as I went back to watching the rain. Mike was right, and I was suddenly at peace.

The next morning Mike and I packed our backpacks and booked a car back into Georgetown. He had a ferry to catch to Langkawi that afternoon and I had a train ticket to Kuala Lumpur, so we headed toward the docks in search of a bite to eat. Hawker centers are massive open-air food courts that offer a variety of different cuisines at more-than-reasonable prices. Popular among locals and visitors alike, these places are hopping with hungry people from all over the world. Mike and I set our backpacks at a large plastic table in the middle and aimlessly wandered the stalls. We watched as locals prepared dishes in giant woks, poured steaming meats onto bowls of rice, and stirred long winding noodles in ginormous pots. After we'd finally agreed upon several dishes to share, we sat down at the oversized table to eat.

"So, Mike, what's your next move? What's the plan?" I took a bite of my noodles.

"Well," he finished chewing. "I'm taking the ferry to Langkawi today where I'll stay for a bit. Then see what happens. I want to end up in Vietnam, I think. There's a lot of teaching opportunities there." He scooped out some rice and mixed it in the sauce on his plate.

Part of me was envious of the way Mike was embracing his adventure. He was truly letting the wind take him as it pleased. He had no plan, no definitive route, and no ultimate goal other than to understand himself. Despite the freedom I had created when I quit my job, I still didn't feel devoid of tethers and time frames. My own trip was far more of a mission than an unscripted adventure.

I booked my trips as I did because I needed to stay on budget while being able to see and do the most that I could with what time I had left in Asia. Most travelers I met were embracing spontaneity and simply seeing where the world led them; they had a one-way ticket into Asia and a one-way ticket out. They enjoyed each day as it came and waited for an opportunity to make their next move. If a cheap flight popped up on their radar they would go there, and if they met friends who were headed another direction then they would join them. My primary setback was my specified timeline and the long list of places I wanted to see. I couldn't afford to get stuck waiting for the next flight, nor did I want to be sitting around when there was so much to see before my paid ticket home.

By the time we finished lunch Iyke had appeared at our table. He had insisted on driving me to the train station that was just across the bay in Butterworth. Mike and I finished our lunches and hugged goodbye. I told him how grateful I was to spend my time in Penang with someone who inspired me to continue on my path; with someone who understood being frustrated with work and needing to escape for a while.

"Mike, I can't wait to see where this adventure takes you. I know you're going to do incredible things."

He smiled back at me. "Likewise. Stay in touch."

And with that, we parted ways.

Iyke and I danced our way over the longest bridge in Malaysia while "Uptown Funk" blasted through his car radio one last time. I watched the city of Georgetown fade further into the distance, taking with it Zeman, Chuah Siew Teng, the beachside sunsets, and unforgettable jungle adventures. As we approached the train station I was overcome with nostalgia for a place I hadn't yet left.

Calls to Prayer
& Cell Phone Plans

Just knowing you don't have the answers is a recipe for humility,
openness, acceptance, forgiveness, and an eagerness to learn - and
those are all good things.
~ *Dick Van Dyke* ~

Kuala Lumpur, Malaysia | October 28 - November 1

When Jenny had first moved in to my Shanghai apartment, I had no idea just how close we would become. Nor could I predict that I would soon be chasing her all over Southeast Asia while her work as the co-founder of InterMore continued to send her to destinations on my list. In September, Jenny headed for Vietnam. But before I could make plans to go visit, she was moved again to Kuala Lumpur, Malaysia. So as I constructed my itinerary from Penang, down the coast to Singapore, I made sure Jenny was on my path. I was playing a fun game of 'Catch Jenny While You Can,' and on this particular adventure it meant heading to the city of the Petronas Towers.

Now, before we get started, I have a short side tangent. First, let me reinforce that I am an American; I grew up in a middle class family in the suburbs of Columbus, Ohio. My family regularly took lengthy road trips to Massachusetts and North Carolina, and along the way we often stopped to eat. We lived in a fast food nation, so nourishment (albeit not necessarily healthy nourishment) was never far from reach. But in my many years of childhood road trips we never ate McDonald's, Dairy Queen, Taco Bell, White Castle, or Burger King. My mom always packed nutritious snacks and PB&Js for the road. And, if for some odd reason we ate fast food, it was always Wendy's or Subway. Because, apparently, 'natural cut fries' solidified the health aspect of Wendy's food. *Insert eye-roll here.*

Throughout high school and college I had fun informing my friends that, no, I hadn't been to some of their favorite late night places. It became a point of pride that I had resisted for so long past the years in which my parents paid for my food. But when my train pulled into Kuala Lumpur that night, I was confronted with a difficult decision. Somewhere along the way my stomach had begun to consume itself out of starvation and the only available options were McDonald's or Burger King.

Yep. You read it here first; it took moving to Asia, quitting my job, and ending up in a train station in Malaysia for this All-American girl to eat Burger King. And it. Was. Delicious.

Jenny and I awoke the next morning to the sound of the Islamic call to prayer as it echoed from the National Mosque below our window. I rolled over and pulled the sheets up over my head in an attempt to block the unwanted 6:30 a.m. wake-up call. Although I'll admit that as aggravating as it was to be awoken so much earlier than intended, the way the vocals reverberated off of the surrounding skyscrapers had a beautifully eerie effect.

In Kuala Lumpur we were living a life of luxury. Two of Jenny's family members had come to visit her in Malaysia just before I arrived, so with the combined efforts of four people's wallets we were able to afford an AirBNB apartment at the Sentral Residences. For the first two nights of my stay we enjoyed a fancy high rise building with pristine accommodations and a private penthouse-style entrance. The 55-story structure included a gymnasium, steam bath, sauna, sky lounge, and several salt water infinity pools that came with a perfect panoramic of the Kuala Lumpur skyline. It was luxury living for $18 a night, and it was certainly a welcomed change from cramped hostels and a severe lack of privacy. I showered beneath a waterfall faucet, made coffee and toast while overlooking the city from large kitchen windows, and watched late-night TV with Jenny while we cuddled up on a cool leather couch. We spent the first portion of our reunion lounging in the sun, working out, eating takeout, and watching fireworks from the pool deck at night. As we sat one evening watching the skyline slowly come to life, I was reminded just how fortunate I was, not only to be in Malaysia, but to be in Malaysia with one of my best friends.

Unfortunately, our high-class living had to come to an end and when it did, Jenny and I moved to a hostel downtown. It was an eight-bed dorm in an apartment complex that featured a small bare-bones gym and an infinity pool. While Jenny went off to work during the day I explored the city on my own. My first stop was Batu Caves, a limestone cliff just north of Kuala Lumpur that is made up of several holy caves and is guarded by the iconic golden statue of the Hindu god of war, Lord Murugan. Inside the caves are multiple temples, collections of Hindu iconography, and hordes of long-tailed macaques. These monkeys are known for their presence in and around Batu Caves, and they certainly made the 272 step climb up to the top quite memorable. As I hiked my way up the steep mountainside I was followed closely by several pesky stalkers that eyed my backpack for trinkets and snacks. At the top I watched while gangs of them dug through garbage bags, bit the lids off plastic milk cartons, and pulled apart wrappers to reveal someone's leftovers. The scavenging and incessant chatter amongst fellow monkeys certainly took the romanticism out of being in such a holy place.

I walked through the caves, past scaffolding and stalactites, and underneath the limestone as it draped itself like curtains over the sides of the cavern. On the walls were intricate paintings of Hindu gods and scenes in ancient storytelling. Moss clustered itself throughout the caves, and tiny trees made attempts to protrude from cracks in the rock. Visitors milled about, taking photos of the cavern filtered with light and shrieking as monkeys threatened to snatch beverages straight from their hands.

After my descent from the caves I booked a car back into the city where I meandered through crowded Kuala Lumpur streets. I walked past shopping malls and hotels, and found myself winding around the corner of an office building where I stumbled upon an event space. Beneath the canopy of several tents were tables littered with vendor samples, reading materials, and colorful decor. I couldn't tell you what kind of event was being hosted, but whatever it was, it wasn't highly trafficked. Vendors stood at their tables flipping through magazines and staring off into space, waiting for prospective clientele. I walked along the inside wall of the venue and followed it straight back to a patio that sat alongside the Klang River.

To the left of the patio was a small restaurant bustling with hungry patrons. Perhaps they had missed the event memo, or were simply refueling before walking the vendor stations. I stopped to look at the fresh foods steaming beneath the glass covers: fried rice, roti canai, stir-fried noodles, fried chicken, samosas, and what appeared to be deep fried hot dogs. After staring at the menu for several minutes and doing another lap around the hot food section, I was approached by a waiter with a writing pad who asked me what I wanted to eat. I pointed at several items before taking an empty seat at one of the nearby tables. While I waited, the family sitting next to me struck up conversation and we chatted about my journey through Malaysia and which countries I was headed to next. By the time my food arrived I was so hungry it hardly took ten minutes to eat.

I was finishing my lunch when the family next to me was getting ready to leave. I watched them walk over to the check-out counter where the restaurant staff looked over at their empty plates and added up their total on a calculator. They eyeballed the amount the family owed based on the foods they knew had been ordered. After the family had left I pulled out my wallet so that I, too, could pay for my meal. While I was standing at the counter patiently awaiting my total, the restaurant worker began to reach for the calculator. But before he could add up my plates, another man - seemingly the manager - shouted to get the cashier's attention and began shaking his head with vigor. He told the man behind the counter to stop what he was doing, and instead took out a pen and wrote a number on a piece of paper. He handed it over to the cashier, who looked confused, but who then handed me the slip with my supposed total.

I should have walked out. I should have shaken my head and insisted they count up my total just as they had the previous customer's. I should have refused to leave until they gave me the proper amount that I owed. But amidst the confusion, I simply handed over a wad of Malaysian currency and left. As I walked back past the vendors I felt an anger boiling inside me. The manager had taken advantage of me knowing I couldn't speak the language and probably didn't know the currency conversion off the top of my head. I stood on the sidewalk and pulled out my phone to see just how much money I had lost in that transaction. My meal should have cost about $5 maximum; for a small local eatery like that I would have been shocked if it were more. But instead, my total came to about $11. An $11 meal in Asia would be about the same as a $20 meal in the States, and I know for a fact that my fried rice and hot dog was not a $20 meal. It was a $6 difference that in the grand scheme of things, wasn't all that much to lose. But what hurt the most was the manager's clear motive and unapologetic attitude. He had taken advantage of someone who had done nothing wrong besides wanting to pay for a hot meal. I had half a mind to turn around and demand my change. But as I stood there on the sidewalk, fuming, I ultimately came to the conclusion that he must need that extra $6 a lot more than I do.

The next day, I headed out to visit the National Mosque. The 13-acre property features a stunning, uniquely-designed structure that is now one of the most prominent symbols of Islam across the country. Its campus, able to accommodate 15,000 people at a time, is a place of worship, tradition, and as I soon came to learn, education.

Knowing I would be traveling through Malaysia for more than a few days, I had purchased a SIM card for my phone as soon as I landed in the airport earlier that week. It was $7 for 5 GB of prepaid, high speed, national data that would be valid for the one week I was there. I hardly went through 4 GB of data back home in a month, let alone one week, so I knew I would have plenty to last me the journey. When I left the hostel that morning, I told Jenny I'd be in touch with her that afternoon and made my way to the metro by heart. I told myself I'd figure out the rest as I went; with cell phone data in my pocket, I had little to no fear of the unknown.

I got off at the closest metro station to the National Mosque and pulled my phone out when I stepped into the sun. As I pulled up a web browser things began to work at quite a slower pace. I stood there squinting into the brightened sky, waiting for the spinning wheel of death to show me something helpful. But, alas, it just kept spinning. I could see the peaks of the mosque's roof over the highway, but besides a long row of busses and a fenced-in park, there was seemingly no way around. As a last resort, I pulled up Maps.Me and thanked myself for pre-downloading a city map of Kuala Lumpur when I still had connection to Internet. From where my blue arrow rested, spinning slowly with my torso as I assessed my surroundings, I could not identify a feasible path. I walked across the street, adjacent to the row of busses, to ask for directions from a metro crew member taking a smoke break.

"Excuse me, I'm trying to get to the National Mosque?" I pointed across the highway at the peaks now barely visible beyond the overpass.

"Yes, is there." He took a long pull from his cigarette, and pointed into the park.

I was not convinced. "Can I get through there?"

He nodded lazily, without an audible response.

"But it is fenced. Is there a walkway?"

"There." He nodded again in the direction of what appeared to be a dead end.

"Okay," I said hesitantly. "Thank you."

He kept his eyes on his cigarette, but nodded one last time as I walked away.

I turned to head into the park, skeptical of his directions. Sure enough, after running into a dead end under a dimly lit highway underpass, littered with graffiti and just out of sight enough to be the perfect place to commit a crime, I began to panic. All I could hear was heavy traffic as it sped over the bridges above, a deafening white noise reminding me that I was lost in a controlled chaos. The trees above were darkening every pathway, and with no one else in sight, I felt both protected and exposed. So I backtracked, and found the first route out of the park that I could. A few moments later, frustrated by my phone not working and anxious to get to my destination, I was playing a Malaysian version of the video game, Frogger. I made my way to the edge of the busy highway as it dipped down off of a bridge and merged into several additional lanes of traffic. With nothing but determination and a dash of stupidity, I bolted across several lanes, walked along the barricade to a median, and then waited for enough of a clearing to finish making my way across the road. If there was ever a time I should have been ticketed for jaywalking, that was it.

Eventually, I found my way around to the front entrance of the mosque where I was handed a long purple robe and shown to a cubby where I peeled off and stowed my sweaty socks and shoes. As I climbed the stairs my feet were met with a cool tile flooring that stretched the entire length of the mosque. I walked along tall archways and columns that repeated one after another, as though someone had copied and pasted the interior design elements. Within the mosque, the white noise morphed from rush hour traffic to an empty hallway. It was peaceful, tranquil, and devoid of crowds or chaos. My bare feet slapped against the tile squares and grounded me as I paced across the compound and back. I meandered into the prayer hall entrance space, where I found a cluster of locals chatting with a handful of other visitors. The doorway to the prayer hall was open and its radiant coloring and expansive walls encapsulated my attention. Despite the red rope blocking the entrance to non-devotees, I could peer into the room and up at the angled ceiling as it folded in and out of the roof.

"Beautiful, isn't it?" I looked over my shoulder to see an older gentlemen smiling at me.

"The architecture is absolutely stunning."

He nodded thoughtfully. "It's like an umbrella, you see?" He pointed at the angular lines that stretched along the ceiling and converged at the top. It was a magnificent view; the triangular stained glass windows resting at the base of each fold in the ceiling illuminated the walls with hues of blue, green, and yellow.

"Men and women pray separate, you see?" He acknowledged the signs scattered throughout the room indicating which areas were intended for each gender. In the male section a man was bent over in prayer while his young son attempted to follow along, but ended up spending more time rolling on the floor and jumping on his father's back.

Outside the prayer hall were several tables lined with books, pamphlets, and photographs. The older gentleman watched as I perused the reading materials, and read over several posters that illustrated the tedious process of preparing to pray. There are cleansing and purification rituals, each one different based on your gender and/or situation in life. There are specific directions to face, times at which to pray, and certain clothing that must be worn.

The gentleman nodded at one of the posters demonstrating dry purification. "Our prayers are very important to us. They are sacred. That is why we treat them in such a way. We must be clean and have good intentions, otherwise it is disrespectful to our religion and others."

I was curious, but fearful of asking the wrong question.

He continued, "We are here to teach others, to educate. We do not want to change your religion, just show you our own. Not many people understand Islam, but it is very beautiful if you see clearly. We are peaceful, kind, and just want others to feel accepted."

I had studied the intricacies of Islam for just under a year back in high school. I attended classes at a local college to learn about Islamic traditions and analyze readings from the Qu'ran. I found it fascinating that a religion so peaceful has been portrayed so violently throughout the world. Just as there are many interpretations of Christianity and Catholicism so, too, exists the possibility for Islam to be misconstrued and manipulated.

"We want people to know that not all Muslims speak for Islam." The older gentleman looked at me with concern. "If you have questions, I want to help you learn."

Here was a man so devoted to his beliefs and religion, that he did not preach or attempt to convert me, but simply wanted me to feel welcome and to make sure I understood. He wanted to teach me about Islam knowing that I could take that knowledge back home and share it with others. He demonstrated several rituals and invited me to join him in the movements. He spoke to me about the history of the religion and how it spread throughout the world.

And then, he handed me a copy of the Qu'ran. "We often ask for donations, but I can see you are a curious girl. You want to learn. You want to spread knowledge. Please, accept this gift. Read it, and you will learn. You will see we are peaceful."

There was a gleam in his eye when he gifted me a copy of a hardback book. It was a deep green color with gold embellishments carved into the front. I ran my hand along the spine that was uncomfortably on the right-hand side. I opened the front cover that swung from left to right, the title page on the left-hand side of the book. Inside it was decorated with Arabic script, light blue and brown borders framing the paragraphs. Along the edges of the pages were English translations and content notes. It wasn't the gift itself that made me smile, but the gesture of sharing knowledge and bettering a global community through patience, acceptance, and tolerance. I was grateful for his time spent educating me and answering my questions, and I was honored that he recognized within me an unbiased and well-intentioned curiosity.

Before I left the National Mosque I tried my cell phone again, pulling up several different web pages and navigation maps to see if my data had somehow come back. I still had no luck accessing the Internet. But shortly after my failed attempt a box popped up offering to connect to nearby WiFi. The National Mosque, my friends, has one of the best WiFi services I've ever used in Asia. The next best thing to having data. So I found a corner of the marble floor, sat down against the railing, and contacted my data provider using the online chat service. To make a long story short, they claimed I was outside the period of my prepaid plan and therefore wasn't eligible for data. Another service representative I talked to said I had used it all, which I knew wasn't true because I had just confirmed I had several gigabytes left before leaving Penang. It wasn't until my third try, when I got in touch with a different representative, that I finally got my service reinstated. I somehow convinced them that I was the CEO of a company whose hundreds of employees travel to Asia quite frequently and that if they didn't resolve the issue for me immediately - an issue that was entirely of their own doing - I would never allow my employees to utilize their business again. Never have I had a problem resolved so quickly. I messaged Jenny to let her know I was okay, and headed back to the metro via a set of bridges and walkways that turned out to be a whole lot safer than Malaysian Frogger.

That night, Jenny and I went for a swim in the hostel pool, doing laps as we discussed her next move to Vietnam and my journey to Singapore. We reflected on how far we'd come since that fateful day in Shanghai when she toured my apartment and it later became our shared home. We talked about travel, culture, and relationships; how different we were because of the experiences we'd survived. With Jenny, I felt stronger. I felt like a more secure version of myself; someone who recognized their abilities and wouldn't sell themselves short. I felt like someone who would always make the most of any situation and never allow the rest of the world to slow me down. Jenny's dauntless character and unwavering determination filled my spirit with a hunger and conviction of my own. That night, as I packed up my bags and headed for the train station, I thought about just how much I would miss Jenny when I headed home in December. She knew me as the person I was in Shanghai; the person who battled through working with R; and the person who came out on the other side of it stronger and more determined to live a purposeful life. Jenny knew the person I was when everyone else back home couldn't. And because of that, there was a part of me that would always remain with her. My train to Singapore pulled out of Terminal KTM Station around one o'clock in the morning. I looked out into the darkness beyond my cozy window seat and wondered what else I might be leaving behind in Asia when I depart.

Kaya Toast & Kopi

Nothing's more charming than someone who doesn't take
herself too seriously.
~ Melissa McCarthy ~

Singapore | November 1 - 4

When I decided to head to Southeast Asia there was no doubt in my mind that Singapore was on my list. Not only because I found it fascinating that chewing gum has been banned since 1992, and eating in public places can get you in trouble with the law, but also because it meant I could spend time with my good friend and previous coworker, Augustine. She had been one of my greatest support systems when I was still working for R, and was eager to share her home with me. So it was only a matter of time before I found myself bound for Singapore on a midnight train from Kuala Lumpur, Malaysia.

The seven-hour journey required two lengthy train rides and one quick shuttle into the city after immigration. The first ride, a three-and-a-half-hour trip from Kuala Lumpur to Gemas, was a comfortable leg of the journey on a fairly new and sleek bullet train. A movie was playing at the front of the car and I was pleased to see charging ports for all of my technological needs. The bathroom was near my seat and, although it didn't have any toilet paper (whoops), I appreciated the "luxury" of a surprisingly well-maintained, Western-style toilet.

When I arrived in Gemas at 3:30 in the morning, I got off the train and checked my cabin assignment for the next trip: seat 4D, superior class. *Superior class? Must be traveler's luck.... I thought my last train ride was comfortable, but this is a step up! I might actually get some decent sleep....* I stood on the platform with a group of other exhausted travelers, looking forward to setting my gear down again. But just as I began to dream of pillows and complimentary beverages, I found myself face to face with my next transport: a rustic train with exposed couplings and semi-fluorescent lighting that screamed, "This vehicle was not designed to feature any kind of 21st century accommodation." If 'superior class' meant I got to sit inside the train instead of on the roof, then I suppose I could have considered this a win.

As I stepped into the car several tiny hitchhikers scurried across the floor, while significantly larger ones whizzed through my peripheral. I'm talking about bugs, guys. Big ones. Roaches and beetles and moths, oh my! I cautiously found my seat and immediately checked for bugs hiding in the cushions. I could practically hear my mom wincing and muttering, "Oh heck no, nope, oh gross. No, no, I can't." But I didn't have any options; it was either sit on this train and continue my journey, or refuse to board and end up stuck in Gemas, Malaysia at 3:30 in the morning. Not that I wasn't up for the adventure, but if bugs were inside the train car, they were most certainly outside, too, and I was not about to be stuck on a railway station bench all night with creepy crawlies. #NoThanks.

I tucked my hiking pack into the overhead luggage racks and piled the rest of my belongings on the chair beside me. I thoroughly searched the rough fabric for hitchhikers again before sitting down and immediately tucking the tips of my shoes into the loose-netted pocket of the seat in front of me. As I reached for my computer, hoping for a distraction, my eyes fell to the yellowing floor where baby cockroaches were dodging in and out of the vents below my seat. I decided that no matter how painful it was, or how frequently my legs fell asleep, my feet would never again touch the floor. Unless, of course, I had to pee. Which, by the way, was another adventure indeed. Inside the small train bathroom was a grimy metal squatty potty accompanied by a sink full of bugs. The toilet paper was placed inconveniently behind me and the toilet, incapable of flushing itself, required the use of a hose hanging from the wall. But hey, there was toilet paper, so maybe I had no reason to complain. Although how I managed to change my tampon on that rickety train while hunched over a metal hole in the floor, I'll never know. I received a new badge in female traveler warriorship that day.

I returned to my seat, walking between the cars just as one of the two men smoking cigarettes was finishing his half-hour shift. He and a friend had apparently decided to split the responsibility and, instead of smoking together to give our lungs a break every once in a while, they just smoked continuously in tandem. *How thoughtful!* The train had already smelled like an abandoned cabin in 90-degree heat, but add an entire carton of chemical-packed cigarettes and you've got yourself an overnight trip to Singapore, my friend.

By the time 5 a.m. rolled around we were still clacking across the tracks, and I had finally accepted that I would not be well-rested (or even slightly-rested) upon arriving in Singapore. But, for just a brief moment, I let my eyes close and merely hoped the cockroaches would leave me alone. My legs were cramped, my back aching, and my stuff poked me in the ribs as I leaned on the only available items I wasn't afraid to touch. Eventually, I felt my tired body give way to sleep deprivation, falling in and out of a conscious state. When the train finally jolted me awake about an hour later, I opened my eyes to see an early morning fog still draped over the trees as the Southeast Asian sun peeked out from behind the clouds. For a few moments, I seemed to forget about the cockroaches doing the cha-cha slide beneath my feet. I felt the cool morning air against the window and listened to the train's rhythmic clacking as it counted the number of modest houses we passed. I so infrequently woke up early enough to watch the sunrise, that to experience it from a train car traveling through Malaysia was the singular reason that temporarily living "Bugs Life: A Horror Story" was worth it.

At the Singapore border I followed the crowd as we passed through security and clumped up (I would say lined up, but that's hardly accurate) at the next boarding gate. Despite all the time I spent in China, I had yet to experience the same level of chaos as when they opened that gate and everyone sprinted to the shuttle. But unlike all the other occasions that I didn't follow suit, this was the one time I wish I had. I sauntered onto the train, suddenly realizing why everyone had been in such a hurry: most tickets (including my own) did not have a seat assignment. It was first-come, first-serve seating with standing room reserved for the rest of us losers. So I crushed myself into a corner and hoped for a smooth ride, because there was nothing to hold onto except the man in front of me, who clearly hadn't planned on sweating so heavily that day.

The race began again when we arrived at immigration; people threw themselves off the shuttle and burst into customs like Black Friday shoppers at Target. Me and my 60L hiking pack had no choice but to speed walk. I felt like a kid on Christmas morning when the immigration officer finally waved me through. Every time I hear that "plunk" on the pages of my passport it sends a burst of joy through my veins, and this time was no exception. It was all I could do not to skip gleefully through the rest of the building. I exited the station and outside the Singapore sun beat down on my shoulders; I instantly began to overheat through my camisole and black jacket. But it wasn't until I had lined up in front of the busses and realized I didn't have any Singaporean currency that I truly began to sweat. Panicking, because I knew nothing of the exchange rate nor whether my bank card would work at the local ATMs, I began pacing the lines showing people my Malaysian currency and asking for an exchange. Finally, someone pointed to a building across the street with a sandwich board out front that boasted, "AUTHORIZED MONEY CHANGER." *Ah, the answer to all my prayers.*

Little did I know the confusion had only just begun. Once I'd exchanged my remaining Malaysian currency for Singaporean dollars, I ventured back to the busses and tried to locate the one I needed. I knew I had to take a bus to the metro where I would then ride for about a half hour before getting off at Bishan Station. But how exactly that was going to happen, I had no idea; I already couldn't seem to locate the line I needed. So I just kept asking for the metro until someone directed me to the proper bus. I climbed on board and kept my eyes on the windows, waiting for signs of a metro stop to come into view. I knew that in the worst case scenario, if I never saw it pass by or didn't recognize it when it did, I could just get off and try again. But I also knew that my lack of Singaporean cell phone data would likely make that difficult. In hindsight, I should have been a lot less worried, because when we finally reached the metro the bus all but cleared of passengers. And in perfect crowd mentality, I exited with them, and was joined on the sidewalk by a horde of hurried locals. I meandered over to a metro map where I proceeded to stare at the interchanging lines until my eyesight was patterned with vein-like streaks. I located Bishan Station, traced my finger along the red of the North South Line, and wandered over to purchase a ticket.

By the time I reached Augustine's house I felt as though I had truly embraced the grunge of backpacking. Here I was, sweaty and exhausted, traipsing down the pristine road of a suburban neighborhood wearing two heavy backpacks and stuffing fruit-flavored Mentos in my mouth. I had picked up two rolls at the train station in Kuala Lumpur and they were the only sustenance I'd had since lunch the previous day. I stood in front of a quaint, gated residence and stared down at the address I had screenshot on my phone, fearing I'd arrived at the wrong house. I rang the bell and caught a glimpse of Augustine waving at me excitedly from a second-story window. A few moments later I was incessantly apologizing to her family for my stench and chattering away about the unforgettable journey.

The first thing Augustine and I did together? Eat. The next thing we did? Eat some more. And the next day? Yup, you guessed it, we ate more food. I jest, but I guarantee at least five of the seven extra pounds I came home with was thanks to Singapore and Augustine's refined ability to track down the most delicious menus. We dined on Kaya toast, soft boiled eggs, chicken satay, waffles doused in chocolate, BBQ stingray, crab, fried carrot cake, spring rolls, roti prata, murtabak, red velvet waffles with custard, and LOTS of kopi (Singapore's signature coffee). I was only there for three days, but who's counting?

Scattered in between our epic meals were adventures to the local heritage centre, Masjid Sultan (otherwise known as Sultan Mosque), the campus of the National University of Singapore, streets filled with boutique shops, and neighborhoods home to expansive works of street art. And while Augustine was in class one day, I traipsed out to Pulau Ubin, an oasis island off the coast of Singapore that is untouched by urban development. Its many bike trails and hiking loops are an open invite to the outdoorsiest of people, and its unused quarries make for some pretty stellar photography sessions. There, I rented a bike and aimlessly pedaled around the island until the humidity had its final laugh at the severe amount of sweat pouring from my body. When the insane temperatures had gotten the best of me, I boarded a ferry and headed back to the mainland where I made my way by metro to meet Augustine in, none other than, Chinatown. What can we say? We just couldn't stay away from China....

While waiting for Augustine I wandered into an expansive building called the "Buddha Tooth Relic Temple and Museum", where it is believed that the tooth on display - originally found in a collapsed Buddhist shrine in Myanmar in 1980 - had once belonged to Buddha. There was much more to see than just the tooth, but the name of the temple and museum certainly had me intrigued. At the door I covered my legs with a long brown cloth wrap and my shoulders with a bright green shawl that clung to my sweaty skin. It was quite the fashion statement, if I do say so myself. As I stepped over the threshold my ears were met with the rhythmic chanting of melodic prayer and my eyes were overwhelmed by the ornate golden elements decorating the architecture. I meandered to the back corner of the temple where columns of tiny, unique Buddha statues extended up the entirety of the wall. Among the collections were a cluster of zodiacs and plaques describing the animals associated with each birth year. Craning my neck, I searched for my zodiac's deity. While taking a photo of Amitabha, The Buddha of Infinite Light, I was approached by an odd elderly man Augustine and I now affectionately refer to as, "Creepy Uncle."

"When is your birthday?" I turned to find an old man looking at me expectantly, as though he'd asked me this question twenty minutes ago and was still anticipating a response.

"January," I replied. "I'm the year of the pig."

He scurried over to the wall of zodiac deities where he pointed to mine proudly and declared, "That is a good one. Very good."

His eyes lit up as though he'd come face to face with Buddha himself.

"My name Bernard," he held out his hand. "I know all about temple. I spend many time here. I can show you."

And with that, Bernard spun around on his heels and headed for the hallway. Before I even had the chance to respond, I was following him up the stairs to the second floor.

Bernard was, by appearance, in his late sixties, but his energy was that of a feisty teenage boy. His kind eyes were accompanied by a widened nose, large ears, and a friendly thin-lipped smile. He wore khaki pants, black tennis shoes, and a blue striped button down with a breast pocket weighted down by an unnecessary number of pens. A pair of large sunglasses sat on top of his head, and he proudly carried an iPhone protected by a purple folio case. Bernard didn't wait for me to ask any questions; he just continued to rattle off facts about the temple, its many Buddha statues, and the relics kept safely within its walls. He taught me about the Vairocana Buddha prayer wheel and together we walked around it three times, a practice of good luck and fortune. He showed me the rooftop gardens that featured thousands upon thousands of tiny Buddha statues, each with an embossed plate displaying the name of its donor. By the time Augustine arrived, Bernard had won me over with his quirky antics, odd jokes, and contagious laughter. I had decided I was adopting him to be my third grandfather. Or, rather, uncle.... After I introduced them, Augustine taught me that in Singaporean culture it is respectful to address elders as "Uncle" or "Auntie". So Bernard quickly became, "Uncle."

Uncle was the neighborhood jokester and Mister Personality. His exuberance radiated in the space around him and it was difficult not to laugh along as he cracked himself up with his own jokes. He showed us the ins and outs of the temple; every room, relic, and model had a story, and he wanted to make sure we understood the significance of each of them. What began as an impromptu tour eventually turned into lunch, which turned into coffee, which turned into a museum trip and an adventure to Marina Bay. Uncle introduced us to every one of his friends across the city, insisted on paying for everything, and shrugged away the idea that we might be taking up his valuable time. He enthusiastically paraded us through the streets of Singapore as we turned corner after corner, following quickly behind his youthful strides.

While waiting for our turn to cross a street, Bernard suddenly slipped his hand into my own as if he were a parent instinctively reaching for its child. He pulled it off so confidently that I didn't even think to consider it a strange gesture. In my mind, he was my adorable Singaporean uncle, watching out for my safety and shamelessly demonstrating his friendly affection.

Later that afternoon, after we'd taken a full tour through the Singapore City Gallery, Augustine departed for her dance class. Knowing where I was headed next, Uncle graciously offered to lead me to the Marina Bay area for the Singaporean light show and to see the Gardens by the Bay. Grateful for a local guide and appreciative of his generosity, I delightedly agreed to share my evening with him. The company was more than welcome until Augustine disappeared into a metro station, leaving Uncle and me to explore on our own. I suddenly began to realize why it was that Uncle insisted on holding my hand, carrying my backpack, and buying me ice cream on more than one occasion (a gesture I certainly didn't mind at the time).

As we sat waiting for the light show to begin he scooted close to my side and said, "Where you want to go? I get you first class ticket to anywhere. You say it."

I turned my head to look at him and that's when he gave me a giant smooch on the cheek and wrapped his arm around my shoulders.

Uhhhhhh. Uncle say what now?

Thinking he had misunderstood my intentions, I thanked him politely for showing me around town and for imparting his knowledge about the city, but told him I wasn't interested in a foreign affair.

After more than a half hour of reinforcing my love for my boyfriend and my disinterest in moving to Singapore, Uncle still hadn't gotten the point.

"You think your boyfriend like me if I come to visit? In the USA?" He wanted reassurance that he would be welcomed there. "You think he punch me? If I visit?"

Guys. I couldn't make up this conversation if I tried. My Singaporean admirer was pretty insistent he was the one for me. He even went so far as to offer to pay off my student debt in full, and I'm not going to lie and say that didn't make me pause for a hot second.

It was a peculiar situation in which to find myself because, while I didn't intend to hurt his feelings and did want to enjoy the evening with him, I felt protective of my space and comfort level. And to those questioning why in the world I didn't just get up and leave, I had a few reasons:

    1. I knew he was harmless. A pushy and idealistic romantic, yes, but incredibly harmless. I never once felt

unsafe - just uncomfy. And that's a feeling I was quite used to by then.

2. I appreciated having someone with the knowledge to guide me through the city and the commitment to make sure I got home in one piece. With no cell phone data, I was happy to have someone I (oddly enough) trusted to get me back safely.

3. He was clearly a little lonely and needed some company for the evening. There was nothing wrong with that. But I wasn't about to smooch him.

By the time we reached Gardens by the Bay I'd managed to place enough physical and conversational distance between us that Uncle began to understand he was being rejected. I could tell I had hurt his feelings, (and there's no worse feeling than making an adorable little old man hopelessly sad), but that was not something I could change unless I agreed to marry him and we all know that was not in the cards for Uncle Bernard. Sometimes, Uncle, you just can't win the girl. By the time I got home that night I had an interesting set of stories for Augustine and her family.

If you haven't yet seen my video of the unconventional adventure to Sentosa, put this down immediately and head over to YouTube (my channel is listed at the back of the book). You won't regret it. It's titled *Lost in Sentosa*. Because, spoiler alert, we got super duper lost. Sentosa is an island resort off the coast of Singapore complete with a Universal Studios and several luxury hotels. It is an oasis of beachside lounges, water sports activities, and local food. After Augustine and I decided to spend my last day in Singapore searching for hidden caves on the nearby island, we came to find that the foolproof directions we'd found online were not so foolproof after all…. The first half hour was spent walking towards the coast line thought to be home to the caves. We took off our shoes and padded across the beaches of Sentosa, taking breaks to tread through the shallow water in the bays. We got distracted by the marina and watching the boats go by, and eventually found ourselves in the front yard of the Shangri-La's Rasa Sentosa Resort & Spa, trying to pretend we blended in with the other luxury vacationers. I can assure you, we did not blend very well. As we wandered the property in search of the secret path that would lead us to our hidden cave, we discovered a walkway that disappeared behind a thick wall of trees. But when we found ourselves standing high above the island on an expansive skywalk, we realized just how far off we were.

Ten minutes later we were standing in a dark museum as a British accent crackled through several loud speakers telling the story of Fort Siloso. What began as a scavenger hunt had quickly turned into a history lesson. We traipsed through the grounds of Singapore's preserved territory still hoping that around one of the bends we might find our hidden cave. But instead, we rounded corners to find ourselves face to face with clusters of lifelike replicas of wax soldiers bearing arms and readying the cannons. My heart skipped one too many beats that day. We never located the caves, and our exhausting walk was supplemented by so many waffles and pieces of kaya toast that the calories we'd burned hardly mattered. But a day spent with Augustine was a day well-spent, and her authentic charm and natural comedy were enough to add definition to my six-pack abs. The abs, of course, that were kept safely behind several protective layers of waffles and toast.

Later that night I sat on the trundle bed in Augustine's room trying to book a car to take me to the airport. I would soon be headed to Indonesia and a 7 a.m. international flight meant I had to be there at four o'clock in the morning. So, in a moment of spontaneity, I decided to embrace my adventurous side and spend the night in the terminal. I would get there far earlier than necessary and just work on videos or take a nap on a bench. Rumor had it, Singapore's airport was one of the few around the world that I wouldn't mind spending a little extra time in anyway. But finding a ride at ten o'clock at night was more difficult than I had anticipated. Grab was a convenient ride-sharing app, I'll give it that, but the people on the other end were much less reliable. Twice someone accepted my request only to cancel ten minutes later. I tossed my phone on the bed, stuffed the remainder of my clothing into the top section of my hiking backpack, and cinched the drawstrings closed.

"Augustine," I decided to distract myself with conversation. "Do you ever feel like travel makes you more connected?"

"What do you mean?" She propped her leg up on a rung of her desk chair.

"I somehow feel like I connect better with others when I'm in a new place with people I've never met."

She thought about this for a moment. "Yeah, I think it's easier to find people you get along with when there's no pressure. You can be yourself, you know?"

"It's just funny." I tried to map out my train of thought for her. "I thought traveling was about seeing the world, you know, taking photos and gaining experiences that you just can't get back home. But I've met more incredible people than I've seen attractions. I've had far more meaningful conversations than I've done tours." And then, after several moments of silence, I finally came to a life-altering conclusion: "I feel like the people are more important than the places altogether. It's as though everyone I meet is intended to help guide me through this journey. It's incredible."

She nodded slowly. "There's a phrase that makes me think of that. It is 'Gui Ren'. Have you heard of it?"

I shook my head.

"It is a written Chinese phrase. It means someone who got you out of a dark period of your life and inspired you. They would be your Gui Ren."

I tilted my head in thought.

She continued, "So, when my cousin was sick and the doctors couldn't diagnose his condition, and my aunt was at her wit's end, somehow she met a lady at the temple that recommended another less conventional doctor and my cousin's condition improved a lot! That lady was her Gui Ren."

Her words ignited my brain. "That's exactly what I've been experiencing throughout this entire trip! People who come into my life to guide or help me without my having to ask for help! They appear before I even realize that I needed guidance and always know just what to say or do." My heart began to flutter and my mind raced with the realization that I finally found a word to define the overwhelming feeling of a connected humanity.

My phone pinged from the bed. I lifted it to reveal a notification that my ride to the airport would be someone named Marc Lim. He would pick me up at one o'clock.

I gathered up the rest of my belongings and dragged my backpack downstairs. Augustine's mom handed me a box of Taiwanese cookies and a tin of pineapple shortbread treats at the door. The Lee family had been so good to me; providing a place to stay, people to laugh with, and delicious meals to enjoy. They had welcomed me into their home not only as a gesture of kindness, but also in friendship and compassion. I could not possibly thank them enough for their generosity. I traipsed out to the car at the end of Augustine's driveway where Marc emerged from the driver's seat, opened the trunk of his SUV, and offered to take my bags. I gave Augustine one last hug before climbing into the car and buckling myself into the passenger seat. As he pulled away I could feel the tears beginning to pool behind my eyes; as frequently as I left places, it never got easier to say goodbye.

Marc was a middle-aged Singaporean. He was dressed professionally and had an approachable spirit. His car was noticeably clean and over my shoulder I spotted a booster seat and several children's toys.

"Do you have kids?"

He pulled his car onto the main road. "I have one, and another coming in a few days."

"Congratulations! That must be exciting."

"Yes," he said. "So what brings you to Singapore if you don't mind me asking?"

I launched into my elevator pitch; the whole, 'graduated college, moved to China for work, boss was a schmuck, and now I was making the most of it' thing.

"Wow, very impressive. Have you enjoyed your time in Singapore?"

Despite my tired eyes his enthusiasm was energizing. "Yes, I have! I visited Pulau Ubin, Sentosa, Chinatown, and ate food from all over the city."

"Did you get to see the colonial houses then?"

I looked out the passenger window, "No, I don't think so. We were too busy eating!"

He laughed. "Well, we have plenty of time to get you to the airport, would you like a quick tour?"

It was 1:30 in the morning and I had nowhere particular to be, so I agreed.

Marc drove past beautiful colonial style housing, elegantly illuminated by rows of street-lamps. I could tell that during the day, their light pastel colors added a bit of charm to the neighborhoods.

Marc turned down another side street. "So, where did you go to school?"

"I went to Butler University, in Indianapolis."

"Ohhh basketball," he smiled at me from across the car. It was the first response I usually received, although I'd never heard it halfway around the world. "What did you study at Butler?"

I told him about my journey from international business to journalism, and my degree in digital media production.

He seemed thrilled. "Good choice of field. I'm actually a news editor for *The Straits Times*."

I had an overwhelming sense I should have recognized this news source, but until that moment I'd never heard of it.

Marc recognized my lack of familiarity by my silence. "It's one of the most widely circulated newspapers in Singapore. Everyone reads it in one form or another."

As headlights drifted across the dashboard of Marc's car we talked in depth about journalism, politics, ethics, and story-telling. I shared my passion for videography and stories of in-fluential people around the world.

That's when Marc told me about one of his most recent projects at work. "Our team has been working on some pretty neat human interest stories." And then, after a moment of thought, he said, "Are you hungry?"

I had started to feel under the weather since earlier that af-ternoon, but I shrugged it off as exhaustion and agreed to get a bite to eat. Marc pulled off at a small family-owned eatery on the side of the highway. I suppose it was one of those places that just never closes. Before we got out of the car Marc picked up his phone and searched through *The Straits Time* YouTube page. I leaned over the arm of my seat to watch human interest stories about an eclectic seventy-year-old Uber Eats delivery driver and a small Hindu shrine that was built and is still deeply valued by workers of a local railway company. They were the types of sto-ries that gave you goosebumps; the types of stories I felt pas-sionate about producing.

"You know," he looked at me with sincerity. "We need more videographers and writers. If these are the types of videos you like producing, you would be a great addition to our team. I can tell you are passionate and I'm sure your abilities speak to that."

Was I just offered a job in Singapore from a guy who is driving me to the airport? Gui Ren indeed.

We sat on the patio beneath a tent outside the restaurant drinking iced kopi and eating roti prata. He asked me about Donald Trump, a topic I couldn't seem to avoid as an American traveling through Asia in 2017. We discussed the complexity of today's media-heavy world and the future of journalism in a time of censorship by media conglomerates. It was a conversation I would have hardly believed if you had told me it would be occurring at two o'clock in the morning outside of a roadside Singaporean cafe with a stranger whose only job was to get me to the airport. When we had finished our meal, he paid for the both of us, and then took me across the street so I could buy throat lozenges for my now-developing cough.

By the time Marc got me to the airport I had his business card in hand and a job offer on the table. He was lifting my luggage from the trunk of his car when I thanked him, and offered the cash I had owed for my trip.

He waved his hands in dismissal. "No, no, you keep that. It was a pleasure spending this time with you. Take care of yourself. Keep telling stories."

And with that, he climbed back into his car, and pulled away. I stood outside Changi airport holding my tin of pineapple shortbread, with an indescribable smile on my face.

$5 Motorbikes & A Water Bottle Full of Gasoline

Love is always complicated. But humans must try to love each other, darling. We must get our hearts broken sometimes. This is a good sign, having a broken heart. It means we have tried for something.

~ Elizabeth Gilbert ~

Labuan Bajo, Indonesia | November 4 - 9

The journey from Singapore was a rough one. After arriving at the airport I checked in and searched for somewhere to rest until my flight. My cough was getting worse by the minute and my body had started to ache. While wandering the quiet terminal hallways I caught my reflection in the windows of a darkened shop. I looked like death, and I was beginning to feel like it, too. Exhaustion was quickly turning into illness. I knew sleep was unlikely; whether it be on planes, trains, busses, or in airport terminals, I've always had difficulty sleeping in public. I have to be completely beyond exhaustion to nod off while surrounded by strangers. Perhaps it's because I want to remain vigilant, or maybe I'm just terrified of people taking pictures of me sleeping. The world may never know. So when I discovered that the doors of the women's bathroom stalls reached all the way to the ground, I dragged my backpack into the corner, locked the door, sat down on the cold tile, and closed my eyes. My gratitude for Changi airport being the cleanest I've ever flown through, was unfathomable.

By the time my flight landed in Bali, I was aching from head to toe, my nose was impossible to breathe through, and my lungs were on fire. My head felt as though it would roll right off my neck and take its rightful place as a boulder on the side of the road. During my layover I hunted through every store in the airport for Emergen-C and orange juice, knowing it was a tad too late for redemption.

At my gate, a local pushed rudely past a young woman in front of me as he fought to be first in line for his already as-signed seat on the plane. You're right, it makes no sense, don't be that guy. The woman rolled her eyes so I leaned over and recommended she try China for a few months.

She chuckled and said, "I couldn't imagine."

While we waited for our turn to board, Laura and I got to know each other. She shared with me that she'd been living in Bali for over three years and had a vast amount of experience traveling through Indonesia. Fortunately for me, it turned out that my seat mate on the plane happened to be the boyfriend of Laura's seat mate. They were more than happy to swap things around so I could continue to pick Laura's brain on things to do in Labuan Bajo. It was a win-win for everyone.

For the next hour I listened to Laura gush over the beauty of Labuan Bajo and the sincerity of its people. I could sense her pride for the island and its inhabitants as she spoke about her friends and the local shop owners she knew. It was helpful to be connected with someone who had lived in Indonesia for so long, knew the local language, and had all the best insider tips.

Considering I had little to no clue what to do when I arrived, Laura quickly became an asset to my next adventure. Despite my throbbing headache and sinus congestion, Laura was inspiring such excitement for the island that I knew nothing would hold me back once I arrived. She told stories of her work as a diving instructor and educated me about the manta rays that occupy Labuan Bajo's surrounding waters. She spoke of hidden swimming caves, rooftop pools, and delicious homemade tempe. By the time our plane landed I was infatuated with her vivacious character and thrilled to have randomly selected Labuan Bajo to be my Indonesian escape.

The moment I stepped off the puddle jumper and into the rain falling from an overcast Indonesian sky, I knew this chapter of my journey was going to be much different from the rest. With a welcoming smile and kind eyes, an airport employee handed each of the passengers a large umbrella already propped open for our trek off the tarmac. Leaving Laura trailing behind, I hurried into the airport, regretting all the water I drank mid-flight. Out front, Laura waited to make sure I had transportation to my hostel. Local men swarmed the sidewalk with lit cigarettes and promises to give us a good deal on ojeks (taxis). Unfortunately, because our flight was delayed, my airport shuttle had given up and left. Laura comically referred to this lackadaisical attitude as, "local time." She graciously allowed me to use her phone so I could call the hostel and confirm someone was on their way. Once she was confident I had it handled and we'd made plans to reconnect the following day, she approached one of the drivers, bartered quickly in a local Indonesian language, hopped on the back of his motorbike, and took off down the dirt road. Her conviction and determination reminded me so much of Jenny.

My evening unfortunately wasn't quite as smooth. As my shuttle teetered up the steepest dirt hill I've ever faced in a van full of luggage and swaying bodies, I thought about going to sleep. My head throbbed and I could feel the pressure building behind my nasal cavities. To be frank, I felt like poop. Fortunately, I hadn't made any plans for the evening so crawling into bed after a nice long shower sounded like an ideal way to recover from the trip. I had booked myself a bed in a beautiful open-air, twelve-bed, rooftop dorm that overlooked the marina. The van parked in front of the building while I dreamed of crawling under the covers protected by a veil of sheer mosquito netting, and watching a movie on my phone while the sun set.

But the hostel had different ideas. I checked in only to discover that their WiFi had been out for days and they had no immediate hope of fixing it. This not only meant my movie plans were ruined, but also, unless I sent smoke signals or communicated via telepathy, my parents would have no idea I made it through the flight. And nothing quite induces panic like a 22-year-old daughter going MIA in Southeast Asia.... So I decided I would at least unpack some things before heading into town to find a cafe with access to the modern world. I began to stash my belongings in the bedside storage locker, looking forward to a quiet evening with which to soothe my pounding migraine. Suddenly, loud music began to thump against the bamboo wall that separated our dorm from the rooftop patio. I waited a few minutes before heading back down to the check-in desk.

"Can I help you?" A young local working at the hostel grinned at me.

"Yeah, um. What's with the loud music up there?"

His smile somehow got wider. "It's our weekly DJ party, you can go!"

I gave him an aggressively blank stare. "How long does it last?" It was only 5 p.m. and I was already regretting some decisions.

"They play until 11!"

We were on two totally different levels; he was bursting with excitement and I was about to collapse on the floor in tears. Six. Hours. Of thumping electronica. Six hours of music blasting directly next to my rooftop dorm with nothing to damper the noise except a thin wall of bamboo and maybe a pillow smashed over my ears. Not even my travel earplugs could prevent that kind of bass from making my skin pulsate. But I figured the least I could do is take a shower and try to relax before reassessing the situation.

I addressed my over-exuberant friend behind the desk. "My booking came with free towels, can I have one?"

"I'm sorry ma'am," he continued grinning at me. "We don't have any towels. They're all wet."

I stared back at him.

He kept grinning. "We washed them but it rained last night so they're not dry. I can give you one but it won't work very well."

I'll admit that in my state of oncoming illness and complete frustration, I gave a lot more snark than intended. After all, I purposefully booked hostels with towels so that I didn't have to tote my own. Now there was no WiFi, nothing to dry myself with, and an EDM party happening right next to my bed. My head was about to explode for multiple reasons. Ten minutes later I had made my voice heard and was moving into a quiet six-bed dorm with air conditioning and the least damp selection of their wet towels.

The next morning, despite my headache and incessant congestion, I joined Laura on an adventure to Rangko Cave, a swimming cave off the coast of Indonesia. I took a shuttle down the hill to meet her at Le Pirate, an all-in-one hybrid of a hotel, juice-shop, rooftop sky-bar, and restaurant. I started my day with a nutrient-dense breakfast before we walked down the street to a small roadside shack where the motorbike Laura had rented for the day awaited our arrival. I handed her my share of the cost; a whopping 35,000 rupiah, *ahem*, $2.50. Yes, that is correct; we rented a motorbike, with gas, for $5 a day. The only thing unreliable about our bike was the gas gauge, so we picked up some extra gasoline sold in water bottles by children at the edge of the road. Welcome to Labuan Bajo.

I held on tightly to Laura's shoulders as we sped down the dirt pathways past tin-roof housing and aimlessly wandering goats. We waved to the kids who walked barefoot along the side of the road, and when Laura had trouble finding the discreet backroad to the cave we stopped to ask for directions. A young local volunteered to guide us all the way to the boat docks himself. We decided he was either highly commissioned or just incredibly bored since the drive would take over an hour one way on extremely rough and unpredictable terrain. He led us off the main road and onto a dirt path that wove in and around boulders and trees. We soon found ourselves in the middle of nowhere, with very little tree coverage from the hot sun, dodging gaps in the road and scatterings of debris. Our bike teetered and tipped as we attempted to follow him through the muddied roads littered with large rocks and fallen tree limbs. The divots in the earth caused our tires to skid and the belly of the bike scraped against the ground with gut-wrenching sounds. Although my adventurous self was loving every second, my anxious self was well aware of the 83.5% chance we would end up stranded out there surrounded by nothing but endless forest and lengthy coastline. By the time we reached the shoreline it was far past noon and the sun was boiling against my skin.

We pulled off the dirt road into a small village of cement brick structures and colorful wooden houses placed precariously around mounds of dirt and chicken coops. Damp clothes lined the fences and we watched in amusement as baby goats pattered around the yards on tiny hooves. We bought two tickets to Gua Rangko from several locals relaxing under a straw-roofed awning. Our friendly guide led us to a Sampan-style riverboat, which appeared to be no more than some wooden slats stacked together and a three-foot-tall tarp canopy under which we could only sit or crouch. I suppose I should have been slightly worried when Laura leaned over and asked me if I knew how to swim…. We crawled to the front of the boat while the driver lifted several wooden pallets to reveal a pull-start motor. As he started it, the overpowering sounds slammed against my skull with the loud clacks of a nearby helicopter. My teeth chattered against each other as the motor shook the wooden slats beneath me. I tried to ignore the pain in my head and focus instead on the translucent teal waters that drifted by.

When we reached Rangko Cave our driver guided us up a dirt path that disappeared into the brush. We eventually came to a sizable hole in the ground accompanied by precariously placed wooden rungs that led down into the earth. I gripped on for dear life as my feet slid against the muddied surfaces. When I lowered myself into the cave, the cool air touched my skin and my eyes adjusted to reveal a stunning landscape of stalactites and stalagmites that framed a blissfully crisp blue pool. Drips of water echoed through the cave and as we made our way towards the water's edge the sunlight dispersed between the rocks. It was a spectacle I'd only ever seen in movies. We took turns diving dramatically into the abyss and capturing photos that would make every Instastar jealous. If it weren't for the spiders hiding among clusters of rocks, I could have lived the rest of my life in that cave, perfectly content.

We dug into the lunches we had brought with us (a meal of rice, tempe, jackfruit, and, my personal favorite, perkedel, each wrapped carefully in a layer of banana leaves). Laura shared with me her dream of capturing the raw beauty of nature and sharing it in a way that reminds others to take care of their planet. A passionate advocate for eliminating the use of plastics and prioritizing the patronage of sustainable businesses and hotels, Laura spends a significant part of her travels promoting eco friendly companies and cleaning up beaches. She strives to lead a zero-footprint lifestyle and works constantly to protect the Earth and its creatures from chemicals found in products like shampoos, soaps, and even sunscreens. As a practicing vegan she lives her life in a way that honors and respects all living things, and she showed me just how easy that lifestyle can be (especially in Asia). It made me question the impact even a small, one-time purchase can make on our planet and the immense footprint I've been leaving behind not only in my own country, but also everywhere I go around the world.

Most of all, I was inspired by Laura's passion for sea life and, more specifically, manta rays. She spoke so highly of their elegant beauty, and the life-changing experience of seeing underwater life up close that I decided to embrace my adventurous side and find a dive shop. I didn't have a scuba diving certification and although it would have been incredible to earn it in Indonesia, I didn't have the time nor the money to get one while I was there. Plus, I certainly didn't feel well enough to breathe through a mask. If I sank too close to the bottom my head surely would have exploded from sinus pressure. So I located a shop that accepted snorkelers, and signed myself up for an all-day boat tour that included several dive locations and a visit to Komodo Island.

The next morning I boarded a double-decker boat complete with rooftop bean bag chairs, complimentary food and beverages, and a group of extraordinarily friendly people. The water was bright blue, the coral making its appearance as the sea floor rose beneath the tides. For the next several hours I swam at the surface, taking in the natural beauty of underwater life and getting one helluva sunburn on my backside. Number one tip for snorkeling: wear clothing over your swim suit or at least layer on the environmentally friendly sunscreen. You'll regret it if you don't. Despite being stuck at the water's surface, by the time we made it to Manta Point, the manta rays were swarming and coming up to greet us. With a hearty kick of my fins I could propel myself down into the water several feet before bobbing back to the surface and into the sun. On more than one occasion I came within an arm's reach of one of Laura's favorite underwater creatures. And she was right: they were one of the sea's most exquisite creatures.

Mid-afternoon the boat docked at Komodo Island where a group of us disembarked and headed inland on foot. I could feel the rocks and sand grinding against the dry ground as we walked through the desert-like terrain to meet our local guide. He showed us our walking trail on an island map and shared with us the rules of observation. Komodo dragons could be large in size and become dangerous when agitated or threatened.

"But don't worry. You see, I have this to protect us." He held up a long whittled stick that split into a V at the top. To say I felt safer would have been a pretty significant overstatement.

While traipsing through the grounds we came into sight of several massive beasts wandering the territory. Their bodies swayed back and forth as they stepped across the dehydrated earth. Snake-like tongues shot out of their disproportionately small heads, and their bellies hung so low they nearly dragged against the dirt. They appeared to be slow and lazy creatures, but when a fresh piece of meat was tossed in their line of sight, my skin crawled at just how quickly they could move. I don't usually run unless something is chasing me, and I sure as hell would be booking it if one of these things mistook me for an afternoon snack. After a unique and thrilling tour of Komodo

Island, we boarded the boat and gorged ourselves on fresh Belgian waffles the entire way home.

Before I left for Taiwan later that week, I spent a day cafe hopping my way through Labuan Bajo while I edited videos and drafted out some blog posts. I was eating brunch on the third floor of Bajo Bakery that morning when life threw me a curveball I couldn't see coming.

I was peering aimlessly out at the Flores Sea when I got a message from my mom on WeChat, "Can u call in 5?"

I texted back, "Yep."

I finished up my sandwich and hit voice call. My parents answered together at the other end. We exchanged dutiful small talk about recent events and I shared my next step of the journey to Taiwan. They asked about my diving trip and I described the manta rays in detail. I told them about Laura and our adventure to Rangko Cave, and at the first lull in conversation, the tone began to change. My chest tightened; I shifted on my barstool and pressed the phone hard against my ear. The mosque below was calling locals to prayer over the loudspeaker and it drowned out my parents' mumbled words that poured through the speaker in my phone. Every momentary pause felt like the world took a deep breath. My eyes welled with tears as my parents took turns reassuring me that not much would change; that this was for the best; that we would still have a home; that we would still be a family.

It was in this small-town bakery in Indonesia that I felt my world start to cave in; the reality that home would never truly be home again had never hit with such force. They shared with me their intention to sell my childhood house, to establish separate living arrangements, and to file for divorce. I knew it would happen eventually, I just hadn't known when. And I knew that going home after six months would feel strange, but I hadn't anticipated everything changing at once.

My parents hadn't been doing well for some time. I can still remember the night my father told me, as we sat in the Walmart parking lot one night, that had it not been for financial stability they would have separated years prior. I then sat quietly in the car while he walked in to buy my mom a last-minute bouquet for Mother's Day. I decided then that the façade was almost worse than the reality of their mismatched marriage. Growing up, I recognized significant differences in their parenting techniques. My mom was the first to encourage me to jump, while my dad was quietly building me a protective parachute. It took me a while to appreciate the balance they had created; they taught me to leap, but to look both ways before I did. But even in my balance I could sense a lack of their own. My dad would disappear in the guest room as soon as he got home from work, and my mom would say with tearful eyes, "I just don't know where we went wrong." The year my parents asked me what I wanted for Christmas, and I found myself responding, "For you to get a divorce," was the year I realized just how far the façade had gone. It was wearing on all of us, and all I wanted was to see the balance restored.

Now let me be clear, I am not in any way ungrateful for the life and the opportunities my parents provided. They fostered a home in which my wildest aspirations were supported, my dream schools budgeted for, and my closest friends welcomed in as family. Despite their differences, my parents raised two kids who recognize the value of putting others first, taking responsibility for mistakes, and seeking opportunities for improvement. They inspired within our own lives a sense of humility, compassion, integrity, and respect. Although I'm taking notes and making some changes to their methods, I have every confidence that my own kids will grow up to understand and appreciate these same values. If it weren't for my parents and their commitment to seeing my brother and me both through college, for the sake of financial stability, we wouldn't have had half the opportunities, nor would we have learned the invaluable life lessons that we did. It was heartbreaking to know that my parents' relationship couldn't last through the friction, but I accepted that it would be for the best; that my relationship with each of them could only grow stronger. But still, that didn't make the thought of going home any easier to process.

I spent the rest of that day in Labuan Bajo trading off between comforting my woes with mocha smoothies from Cafe.In.Hit and mindlessly lounging in the sun at Le Pirate, to chowing down on sushi at Happy Banana while attempting to put my thoughts and feelings into comprehensible words. At Blue Marlin, I learned what a Lassi was (a delicious yogurt-based drink) while I tried to continue focusing on editing my vlogs. And to conclude my tiring day, I watched the sunset from the best view on the island at Paradise Bar. By the time that sun set, I had visited nearly every establishment on the small-town loop that is Labuan Bajo.

Indonesia presented several unique challenges. My start at the hostel certainly wasn't ideal, and my last day on the island was memorable for all the wrong reasons. But out of all of the places I would have wanted to be when hearing the news of my parents' decision to end their 24-year commitment, Indonesia wasn't the worst. In fact, that charming small town gave me just the hug I needed to feel safe and supported. In a town where shoes were optional, animals roamed free, and eating utensils were not a priority, I felt comfortable in allowing my true emotions to surface. As I departed for Taiwan, I was mentally exhausted and physically beaten down. My head was still aching and my cough was getting worse. I longed for the space to mend both my body and spirit. I craved a quiet space with a comfortable bed and several pints of ice cream. But there was still one country left to see on this particular leg of my journey, so rest was going to have to wait.

Pour-Over Coffee
& Combat Boots

If we can share our story with someone who responds with empathy and understanding, shame can't survive.
~ Brené Brown ~

Taipei, Taiwan | November 10 - 14

You know those mornings when your alarm doesn't go off, but your body naturally wakes you up in a panic, so you have just enough time to put on pants and shove some toast in your mouth before running out to the car where you proceed to spill your morning coffee all over your dashboard and your white button down shirt? Then you have to run back inside to change which makes you ten minutes late to the office where your boss is impatiently waiting on the long list of reports you haven't yet started? Well. Taipei was kind of like that....

For having lived in Asia for six months, I was exceedingly lucky. I never got food poisoning, successfully avoided unclean water, and didn't struggle with much more than seasonal allergies on any given day (probably due to the epic pollution and all, but you get my drift). I ate well, stayed hydrated, rested even if I couldn't sleep, and exercised regularly. But by the time I got to Taipei I was physically exhausted, mentally and emotionally drained, and fighting off some strange virus that was unidentifiable by even my wonder-nurse mother back home. I felt feverish, my stomach was constantly churning, and despite consuming gallons of water I still felt dehydrated, perpetually exhausted, and completely detached from reality. It was as though I was suffering the consequences of an unforgettable night, without having actually enjoyed any of the night itself - if ya know what I mean.

The following year, when I came down with similar symptoms, we realized what I'd been fighting in Asia was an untreated case of strep. Whoops!

No matter how hard I tried, Taipei did not have my full attention. In fact, *Stranger Things* from Netflix received more of my attention than I'd like to admit. Oh, and those unbelievably soft bunk bed mattresses; like clouds, I swear. Point is, I spent a majority of my time in Taipei on the horizontal plane. My head was reeling with the news of my parents' divorce, and my body was still recovering from the overexertion I'd forced it through over the last 48 hours. My journey from Labuan Bajo, to Jakarta, to Singapore, to Taipei was lengthy, tearful, and dreadfully lonely. Not to mention terrifying, as our sketchy Tigerair plane quite literally bounced its way through the air to Taiwan. I might have saved quite a chunk of change booking an itinerary that complex, and certainly a good amount on a flight that left me questioning the reliability of physics, but by the time it was over all I wanted to do was go home to Shanghai.

On one of the few occasions in Taiwan in which I'd managed to force myself out of bed, I took refuge in the living room of the apartment-style hostel. There, I sat in silence scrolling through my phone while listening in on the conversations that flowed around me. Young travelers talked of a place called Golden Falls, hiking trails that led to one of the highest hills on the island, a road called Jiu Fen Old Street, and the cable cars of Maokong. Usually, this conversation would have intrigued me, but the weight of my emotional detachment pressed heavily against my heart and I regrettably let my body succumb to the stress. I tried to talk myself out of it.

So what? My parents are getting divorced. A lot of people have divorced parents... I'm no special case. I've seen this coming for years. Maybe I'm just overreacting.

Besides, the thought of losing my childhood home was far more devastating than the predictability of my parents' divorce, so I couldn't understand why pulling myself out from the depths of sadness seemed so impossible. The room suddenly became quiet; the other travelers had departed for an afternoon adventure, without me.

I sat pressed into the couch cushions staring through the windows at several small temples that poked out from the mountainside.

That's it, I thought. *This has to end. I'm voluntarily becoming a waste of space and no amount of feeling sorry for myself is going to change that. What did that kind Chinese mother tell me? Oh, yeah. Cry on the inside.*

I went into my dorm room, put on a pair of more practical pants, grabbed my day pack, and headed for the metro station. I didn't have a plan. In fact, I didn't even really know where I was going, but I knew I had to get away from my safe space. I knew that if I didn't leave in that very moment I would be stuck there forever. Or, at least, for the next three days until my flight back to Shanghai.

I bought a ticket to the end of the metro line and boarded a train. Thanks to my incredibly lengthy ride from the airport the previous day, I knew there was free WiFi onboard (can I get an AMEN?). I tapped on my screen in a lazy attempt to find somewhere to go that was meaningful but incredibly low-key and antisocial. You know, to fit the mood. I scrolled through a few tourist webpages and then switched to browsing on the Maps.me app. As I clicked through the various icons - where to eat, transport, entertainment, and sights - I noticed a station named Longshan Temple.

Temple: quiet, spiritual, serene, calming. Perfect.

I transferred lines and got off.

What I found, however, was not the temple I had assumed would be easy to locate. Instead, in my mindless wandering of the city, I somehow ended up down and around the corner in a 7/11. I realize how ridiculous this sounds, but what's more ridiculous is that it seems like something one would only do after a night of heavy drinking. I was 100% sober, but also 100% mentally checked out. It was as though my spirited adventurous self had fallen asleep inside the frame of an uninspired and uninterested flop. There are times in which we seem to live our lives for someone else; Taiwan was definitely one of these times. I knew I had to keep going. If not for me, then at least for those living vicariously through my international explorations. My friends and family back home were waiting to hear about my grand adventures in Taipei. So after buying a pick-me-up cup of coffee and a disgustingly processed breakfast sandwich, I meandered down the street where I discovered an entrance to Bopiliao Historic Block, an architectural treasure of the Wanhua district.

It might have been the coffee - no, in fact, it had to be the coffee because the breakfast sandwich definitely didn't sit right - but I actually enjoyed walking around the historic district. It was quiet and beautiful, the red brick contrasting the dark wooden beams that supported the frame of each widened alleyway. The noise from the street faded as I submerged myself further into the heart of the district. I watched a couple take their wedding photos, an assistant tossing her veil into the air and jumping elegantly out of frame just before the photographer captured the moment. Locals paced aimlessly through the vicinity on casual afternoon strolls. I sat peacefully beneath a brick archway while I finished my coffee and then made my way back onto the main road.

I soon found myself wandering through a street packed with shops selling the same pairs of embroidered jeans and proud collections of grandma sweatshirts from the '60's. The 'I'm a stay at home knitter with a collection of cacti and cats' vibe, was truly remarkable. It was always so curious to me the fashion trends that plagued Asian countries. How did these mom-and-pop grandma sweater shops stay in business? Where were the hordes of hipsters and wannabe cacti moms who wore this apparel? I must have missed them on the metro. I came across a corner shop that looked promising, bought some harem pants without trying them on, and headed back to the hostel. Along the way I passed by an enclosed metal photobooth outside a convenience store that advertised head shots and passport photos. Knowing I might eventually need one for a visa application, I inserted 100 Taiwanese dollars, put on my best mug shot smile, and collected my less-than-flattering portraits. That was enough spontaneity for one day....

Back at the hostel everyone else boasted about their days: the epic sights, beautiful handicrafts, and delicious food. Their stories were filled with energy, joy, and adventure. Despite being proud for having overcome a desire to stay inside all day, I still felt I had nothing to contribute. I listened as one of the girls described a cafe she had found that afternoon. She was tall and thin, and sat on the couch crosslegged with her combat boots on the floor in front of her. The cuffs of her jeans wrapped around her ankles and the weathered red beanie she wore shifted when she turned her head. Her jean jacket seemed to swallow her as she leaned back against the couch. She was a grade-A hipster. I may have felt older due to sheer exhaustion and my 83-year-old mentality at the time, but I noticed that she looked particularly young. Despite the fact that we shared a bunk, I had yet to meet her. That night, I finally learned that her name was Chase.

The next day, as I worked up the courage to get myself out of the hostel for the afternoon, I decided to ask Chase if she wanted to take the Maokong Gondola up the mountain with me. And before my social anxiety could have a single moment of regret, she responded quickly with a resounding and enthusiastic, "Hell yes!" While walking to the metro I finally got to know my bunkmate. Chase was 18 years old and traveling alone before deciding whether or not to go to college. She talked about her vegan lifestyle and showed me Instagram photos courtesy of her incredibly artistic eye. She told me about her job at a local coffee shop in Maine, her girlfriend back home, and her endless curiosity of Asian culture. I couldn't make up this much hipster if I tried. But I was loving it. Chase embraced her lifestyle wholeheartedly and was proud of her authenticity and honesty. Her energy revitalized my own and made me feel more secure in being myself.

An hour later we were searching for a quick coffee fix at the top of the peak. While walking along the edge of a shaded winding road, Chase spotted a wooden sign pointing into the woods where we wandered in to find a solitary stand serving pour-over coffee underneath a makeshift tent in the clearing of trees. *Of course.*

We stood, now highly caffeinated, looking down over Taipei spread beneath an overcast sky. Picking a random direction, we began to wander down the road. At first it was strange; two so-cially awkward individuals struggling to strike up causal, non-threatening conversation. Normally I was the one to jump in with questions and stories, but I had no energy, and eventually grew self-conscience that she might think I'm straight-up weird and antisocial. So as we began to explore I decided she was owed an explanation. We walked along the side of the road while I told her about my parents' divorce, my fear of the fu-ture, and how I felt drained by mental and emotional stress. I shared stories of growing up in a home that so often felt divided and contradictory. I poured my heart out on that mountainside and Chase calmly took it all in. She empathized with my stories and offered new perspectives on my opinions. She peacefully absorbed my stresses like a sponge and held on so tightly I felt as though they were never mine to begin with. In that moment she was my confidant; a private journal in which to leave my thoughts. And as the night grew darker, my heart felt signifi-cantly lighter.

If I'm being completely authentic, which is a primary goal of this entire book, I don't remember much of what Chase said to me in response. I can't remember the stories she shared of her own life, nor the finite details of her own travel experiences. I wasn't being a good listener. I know we talked about her long-distance relationship and that I gave her advice based on how Josh and I were coping with the thirteen-hour time difference. We talked at length about our travels and personal growth. I know she shared thoughts about her future and we both con-sidered how much we hated the idea of a nine-to-five job. But beyond the overarching subject matters, I can't remember specifics. Sometimes I still feel guilty for this; I was selfish in dumping my word vomit on her and not listening in return. I can only hope that I was able to provide her the same kind of meaningful feedback, despite not being able to recall exactly what it was that I said.

Chase was there when I needed her. She was someone willing to help carry my pain; to lighten my burden if even just for a day. I recognized my adversities, acknowledged them out loud, and she opened her arms. Amidst all of the meaningful conversations I'd had and the phenomenal demonstrations of friendship throughout my time in Asia, this was one of the most selfless and kind gifts I'd been given.

To illustrate, I give you a short story: More than a year after returning from Asia I sat in the bedroom of a dear friend who was fighting through cancer. She asked me to meditate with her and my first reaction was one of fear, insecurity, and self-doubt. *I don't know how to meditate. What if she can tell I'm faking it, or if the experience isn't what she needs because I don't practice enough? Or, worst of all, what if I make her meditation worse?* But I loved her, and wanted what was best for her, so I agreed. I sat in darkness and tranquility, holding her hands, trying as best I could to relate to the visions she was speaking of out loud. She seemed to be on a grand journey of riverbeds and waterfalls, while in the meantime I had a hard time getting out of my head. Forty-five minutes later she lay crumpled on the floor and as I sat beside her in silence she muttered through several tears, "Please leave." My heart sank. I thought I had failed her or, worse, that I had hurt her.

Later that afternoon my friend disclosed her meditation experience. She said that it had been an emotional journey, one that left her feeling both powerless and powerful. She admitted that she began her meditation assuming she would need to feed me energy because I did not know how to channel my own. But, by the end, she said it was not my energy that was lacking; it was her own. She said she was overpowered by my spirit and took from it the positivity, clarity, and strength that she needed in that moment.

"You have so much energy to give." She looked into my eyes with sincerity. "It is energy that I need to help me heal. You are giving me the strength to keep fighting."

I thought it incredible that my perceived failure had, in fact, been a phenomenal success for someone else. My time, patience, and energy alone had added value to her life, despite my inability to understand it. One person's perceived failure could indeed be another person's lifeline.

As the sun disappeared behind the treetops I told Chase about the Chinese phrase I'd learned in Singapore.

"It signifies the people who come into your life to offer help and guidance when you most need it. It's my belief in synchronicity - everything happens for a reason - but with people. And the people I've met in Asia are not just passersby, but rather the individuals I needed in that exact moment in time to teach me about myself and inspire me to achieve even greater things."

Chase nodded in a silent agreement while we waited for our bus back down the mountain.

The people with whom we connect are not always going to be long-lasting relationships. I haven't spoken to Chase since I left Taipei and likely will never see her again. But the impact she made in my life was more meaningful than she could ever realize. Gui Ren isn't just about the people who come in and sweep you off your feet, change your world forever, and become your closest confidant. Sometimes, Gui Ren is the stranger behind you at the supermarket who covers the remaining seventy-two cents you owe for your bill; it's the woman pumping gas next to you who compliments your hair on an otherwise crappy day; it's a bunkmate who lends an ear and unknowingly supports you through one of the hardest weeks of your life. I am still grateful for Chase's generosity; she was a comfort when I needed it most, and offered a place in which I could leave my woes. I confided in her my deepest regrets, frustrations, and sadnesses, and in return she helped me to leave them on the mountain. As we boarded our bus back down the hillside I took one last glance out at the cityscape of Taipei.

"Gui Ren," I let the words sink deep into my heart. "Gui Ren...".

I looked at her through the dark and said, "Chase, I think I'm going to write a book."

Taipei was dreary the next day, a kind of dreary that made you want to pull the down comforter back over your face, roll over, and go back to sleep until the sun decided to come out. The rain and fog were certainly no help to my persisting depressive mood. But I was sick of feeling defeated, and Chase had renewed my hope for an enjoyable experience. So I grabbed my umbrella, wrapped myself in layers, and headed to the metro. I was determined to see Taipei 101 before I left the city for good.

As the train pulled away from the station I noticed an elderly couple sitting on the plastic seats across from me. The man was staring awkwardly at my shirt. We made eye contact for a brief moment, at which point he did something quite odd. He pointed at the Butler bulldog logo on my tank top and smiled with a giddy excitement. He gave me a big thumbs up, much like the one my grandpa gives me when I ask how his day is going. I nodded my head at the man and smiled back. Suddenly, he was digging intently through his bag. *Here we go, just grin and bear it, and hope you don't end up on his Christmas cards.*

Just as I was mentally preparing my signature "stranger taking a photo of me" pose, he pulled out a thin plastic straw. *Huh?*

The old man handed it to me with pride. The straw was bright green, adorned with thin black lines that marked eight tiny feet and two beady eyes; it was a caterpillar. Recognizing my confusion, he motioned for me to hand back the straw. He pulled the two ends of it apart and the caterpillar began to dance. I pointed at the straw and back at him, asking with my eyes if he had made this. He grinned and nodded back at me, handing me my gift. It was the smallest of gestures, and yet, in that one short and silent conversation my whole world changed. It felt as though he had been waiting on that metro all morning just to make me smile. And to think he would never fully know just how impactful that gesture was. I knew right then and there that, no matter how the rest of my day went, it was going to be a good one.

After craning my neck to look up at Taipei 101 from its ground floor, I continued on to find a place called Elephant Mountain. Lisa - my lovely Nanjing companion - had inquired about how my trip to Taiwan was going, and later recommended that I go on a soothing hike that would overlook the city of Taipei. Or, at least, it would have been soothing had it not been for the drizzling rain, swarming mosquitos, and somehow getting lost on a few too many occasions. By the time I finally made it to the top, I was tired, drenched, and incredibly itchy. But as I looked out over the city, now blanketed by a cloud of dense fog, I felt a surprising joy. I was proud of myself; for getting out of bed, for making it across the city, and for hiking up a mountain in the mosquito-infested rain. It no longer mattered that Taipei 101 was hidden behind a row of clouds. All that mattered was that I had done the difficult thing, and got myself out into the world despite never having wanted to get out of bed. I had beat myself at its own game and, for the first time in several days, I finally felt like a winner. At least, I did until I woke up the next morning....

I awoke to itchy rashes and bumps all over my body. Thinking back to the previous day I spent hiking with mosquitos, I was momentarily comforted by the reassurance that a little Tiger Balm would take care of things. But I knew mosquito bites well, and these weren't those. From my wrists to my ankles, I kept finding new clusters of what I could only assume to be... bed bugs. Just when I thought my life couldn't get any more difficult, it did. My heart sank as I reached for my phone and bombarded my mom's WeChat with photos of the backs of my legs, elbows, and forearms. I sat anxiously at the table in the hostel kitchenette waiting for my diagnosis from the States.

My mom responded, "They look like bed bugs! Are they itchy?"

They were itchier than anything I'd ever felt.

So I replied with one simple word of profanity (please feel free to fill in whichever you find suitable). This was the last thing I needed. My mom pelted me with questions about where my backpack and clothes had been kept, the surfaces in which the affected skin came into direct contact, and how quickly the symptoms had appeared. She recommended I tell the hostel receptionist about my bites.

Let me give you some advice. Number one, always always ALWAYS check your mattress for bed bugs before you settle into a room. Even in the swankiest of hotels it's possible to find yourself dealing with bed bugs. Since they are transported on people's clothes and personal belongings, and are not always due to a lack of cleanliness, you never know where you might find them. Number two, know HOW to check for bed bugs. You can't do what the hostel receptionist did and walk into a room, look squarely at the bed, and establish that it's clean. You have to get up under the sheets and inspect the corners and seams of the mattress for tiiiiiiiny little clusters of bugs or egg-like substances. The fact that she didn't even consider using a flashlight immediately made me nervous. My mom and I began strategizing how to sterilize all my clothing. I was stressed, overwhelmed, and embarrassed. I was terrified that I would be blamed for the infestation. So I mustered up the courage and began asking the other girls if they had noticed any weird bumps on their skin. Negative. None of them had any signs of bed bugs nor could we find anything in the mattresses.

After an afternoon of freaking everyone out, scouring the hostel couches and bedding for tiny black dots, and a few tearful phone calls to my ever-so-patient mother, we still couldn't find the infestation. There was nothing that led to a conclusion of bed bugs other than the itchy bumps all over my appendages. I began to think that perhaps I had brushed up against an unfamiliar plant on my precarious hike, or maybe I was just covered in oddly behaving mosquito bites. Or, knowing my luck, I probably had a mean little spider living in my pajamas. Whatever it was, I finally knew what it felt like to be that kid in elementary school that all the other kids' parents told them to stay away from for fear of lice or illness. I had made myself an enemy of the girls' dorm.

And now for the kicker. When I arrived back in Shanghai with plans to locate the nearest laundromat and somehow pull off a winning charades act, explaining in physical movements why they needed to sterilize my belongings with excruciating detail, we came to a new conclusion. Whatever illness I had been fighting off was not behaving as it normally would had I been in the States. My cousin said her kids never got rashes with their viral infections. That is, until they moved to Asia. For whatever reason, whether it was the untreated status of my strep throat or the mere fact that I had been immersed in foreign bacteria for several months, my body communicated its weaknesses with strange bumpy rashes. My hostel meltdown and widespread fear were simply the results of neglecting to understand my symptoms of strep. The rash was a telltale sign that I was fighting something else off beneath the surface.

I wanted to hit snooze far too many times in Taipei. I fought myself to leave the bed, let alone get out into the world. I felt like dirt and took myself on far too many emotional roller coasters to count. But I left Taiwan feeling as though I'd learned a valuable lesson in travel and self-love. Often times we pack our itineraries with one activity or attraction after the other, with disregard for the exhaustion that tends to tag along. A little exhaustion is good - you know, the kind you fight off with adrenaline and thrill. But the kind of exhaustion I had been ignoring was my body's way of begging me to slow down and recuperate. Between my emotional stress and my body's inability to handle such rapid relocations, I had completely worn myself down. I needed to practice a little more patience and a lot more self-love. So instead of feeling guilty for not having spent every second exploring Taipei, I began to understand the value of slowing things down. I understood that travel was not just about learning and growing, but also about healing, both physically and emotionally. Sometimes we need a little downtime, some small wins, and a girl named Chase.

A Trailblazer in
Laos, Cambodia & Vietnam

Life Lessons
& Chocolate Martinis

Don't let the noise of others' opinions drown out your own inner voice. And most important, have the courage to follow your heart and intuition.

~ Steve Jobs ~

Luang Prabang, Laos | November 26 - 30

"Can I borrow your pen?"

It was perhaps the most common phrase exchanged between strangers on an international flight. I looked up to find my seat mate smiling at me as she tucked a stray piece of hair back into the dark cascading braid that curled around her shoulder.

I finished scratching my passport number onto the arrival card and smiled back, "Of course."

In the span of our 85-minute flight, this was the first time we had acknowledged each other. I'd spent the majority of our time in the air thus far feeling intimidated and therefore too afraid of idle chitchat. Her mere presence emitted such confidence and power that no conversation starter I had considered seemed worthy of her attention. Why would she care where I'd been or where I was going? She was the sleek and sexy popular girl every average chubby kid was terrified of in middle school. But now, she had asked for my pen. The power was mine.

We made casual conversation while we began our descent into Laos. She watched in curiosity as I filmed a time-lapse on my phone when our plane ducked beneath the sea of clouds. Come to find out, the popular girl was pretty impressed with this average weirdo's videography skills. A few moments later, at her request, I was adding her contact information to my phone so that I could send her the video when I eventually reached WiFi. She wanted to share it with her friends to let them know she'd landed in Laos. It was then that I learned my seat mate's name was Tamara.

We got off the plane and made our way towards customs, and I was sure that once we left the terminal it would be the last I'd see of Tamara. As we waited in line she inquired about what brought me to Asia, a question frequently used to pass the time in airports. I explained that I was fulfilling my desire to see the world after the conclusion of a particularly challenging work experience in Shanghai. Tamara began sharing that she, too, was on a journey of self-discovery and healing. She confided that she had also experienced an unfortunate work environment and was taking a year-long break to travel the world and rebalance her life.

When we approached the customs desk, Tamara's eyes grew wide and she let out an, "Oh no." In that moment, she had realized that she didn't have any cash for her entry visa.

"Do you think they'll let me run to the ATM? I have the money, I just didn't realize I would need cash."

"I'm really not sure. They might not like that." I glanced at the security walls that separated us from the rest of Laos. You never really know how far you can bend the rules in any given country. Then I thought about the money belt I had tucked away in the middle section of my backpack (because wearing it as an actual belt was uncomfortable and unnecessary). My first reaction was selfish: *I want to do the right thing and help her, but it's not my fault she wasn't prepared. The next two countries on my list require American currency and I can't afford to be the one stuck in customs. Although, if I do run out of cash I can always find a money exchange and just cross my fingers that the rate is fair and they don't give me counterfeit bills.*

I was standing there silently weighing the pros and cons when I suddenly found myself reaching into my backpack and pulling out several $20 bills. I handed them to Tamara with a reassuring smile. I didn't know why, but something told me this was what I had to do. And if there's anything I had learned in my travels thus far, it was that my gut is never wrong.

If I had been paying any attention to recent news, I would have realized that I had just paid for Tamara Holder's entry into Laos. The same Tamara Holder who was a contributor and legal analyst for Fox News when she was sexually assaulted by an executive of the company. The same Tamara Holder who spoke up about her assault despite being paid to keep quiet and who was now an influential part of the Me Too movement. This woman, only in her late thirties, was making enormous strides for women everywhere. As Tamara told me her story I was overcome with fury and awe all rolled into one. No wonder I had been so intimidated by her on the plane; here I was casually waiting for a visa on arrival with a woman who so dauntlessly forged a space in which women all over the country now felt more empowered to speak up about unwanted sexual advances in the workplace. I had been accurate in my recognition of her zero tolerance for bullshit as she recalled the events that led her to standing in the Luang Prabang airport that day. She thanked me sincerely for helping her, and promised to repay me when we found an ATM. She then asked if I wanted to meet up later for dinner and it took less than a second to respond with, "Absolutely." I had a feeling there was so much I had yet to learn from her.

That evening we ate together on the front porch of a small local restaurant in the heart of town. Tamara opened up about her passion for plant-based eating and educated me on how the lifestyle can be healing for both body and mind. I admired the way she scoured over the menu, enthusiastic about the natural ingredients in Laotian cuisine and intrigued to know each of the recipes. I listened as she inquired about the cooking process for sticky rice from our courteous and patient waiter who even brought out the bamboo steamer to demonstrate for us at the table. During dinner she spoke about her recent traumas and the type of therapy she underwent to ease her transition. We discussed women in media, what makes a healthy work environment, and the ridiculousness of patriarchy. *We are women, hear us roar!* Tamara not only encouraged me to embrace my influence as a strong independent woman, but she also so clearly applied it to her everyday life that I believed every bit of advice she gave. She walked the talk, and I was captivated.

The next day Tamara invited me to join her on a private tour of Luang Prabang. I met her in front of her hotel where we climbed into a twelve-seat bus complete with air conditioning, leather seats, and complimentary water; we were traveling in style. As our driver navigated to our first destination, our local guide sat in the passenger seat educating us about Laos's vast history and the many subcultures that occupy various areas of Luang Prabang. We followed our friendly guide through the Royal Palace and Wat Xieng Thong, learned about traditional Laotian foods and cultural ceremonies, and headed into the villages where we were introduced to locals and had the honor of gaining insight into their daily lives. Tamara and I meandered through a small village on the hillside where we browsed through collections of hand-stitched quilts, pillow cases, bracelets, scarves, and cooking aprons. We watched as young children ran through the dry dirt barefoot, chasing after chickens and playing with repurposed rubbish. At the end of a back road we could see the shoulders of a young mother bathing behind a curved piece of corrugated sheet metal. She peered over the top to shout at her kids who were preoccupied by a large plastic bag. Her little girl was laughing at the older son, who was waddling across the dirt with one leg in an oversized bag; a comical gimmick to an audience of three-year-olds.

Our guide introduced us to a woman lingering outside her hut as though she had been awaiting our arrival. The kind-eyed elderly woman nodded with anticipation and escorted us into her home. Her hut was constructed with vertical sticks of bamboo and wooden slats. We stepped across the dirt floor where we noticed stacks of what appeared to be bags of grain, clusters of corn husks hanging from the crossbars in the thatched roof, a wire cot with a thin mattress in the corner, and a small shelf with several worn pots and pans on the adjacent wall. A rusted bicycle was propped up in a shaded corner to our right and a thin straw mat was rolled out along the inner wall. Perhaps what captured our hearts the most was our host's sincerity and joy. She showed us over to a small fire in the middle of her hut where she squatted down before a lidded metal disk. She looked up at us proudly as she took off the lid and stirred a cluster of green vegetables inside. Her face wrinkled when she grinned at us, her eyes searching our own for a response. I smiled down at her, her face beaming with such radiance that I hardly noticed the hut anymore. She was stunning; her greying hair folded into a purple scarf atop her head, a pair of thin earrings dangling from her sagging earlobes, and an over-sized white t-shirt draping over a brown and gold woven skirt. Her toes, covered in dusty dirt, stuck out from a pair of green plastic flip-flops. Here we were, having arrived on a private tour bus with complimentary water, yet the happiest person in the room was the woman cooking dinner in the middle of a dirt floor.

The afternoon sun was beating down as we continued to drive southwest, away from Luang Prabang. We arrived at Kuang Si Falls where the daylight was just beginning to sink below the tree tops. There, Tamara and I changed into our bathing suits and took a refreshing dip in the bright blue waters of the wading pools. It was frigid, but worth every bit of chill as we drifted towards the center and gazed up at the cascading falls. Beneath the surface, tiny fish began to nibble at our toes, causing us to shriek with comical surprise. I watched in awe while the blue waters poured over boulders and wove through the trees to create stunning pools that expanded along the side of the hill. I could have stayed there forever if it weren't for the goosebumps covering every inch of my skin and the fish that were incessantly chomping at my ankles.

Later that evening Tamara and I meandered through the night market together, discussing travel and admiring the rows of embellished crafts and accessories. Tamara spoke to every local as though they were a friend, asking them about their products and making casual conversation as she browsed. Despite only using simplistic English, every interaction left the marketplace sellers with a smile on their faces. She went where her heart led her and she spoke with empathy and compassion. While it was refreshing to be in the company of someone so courageous and spontaneous, it was even more comforting to be with someone who understood what it was like to travel alone as a woman and wasn't afraid to speak her mind.

Over the course of the next few days Tamara and I talked about love, trauma, mental health, change, and purpose. She inspired within me a curiosity for food and holistic healing, and she consistently encouraged a regular practice of self-empowerment and love. And if there were ever a moment in which I expressed self-doubt or fear, she was quick to shut down my negative thoughts and restore a hopeful energy to the space that surrounded us. I was grateful for that day in the Luang Prabang airport when I chose to listen to my gut and truly recognize that everything happens for a reason. Because of that defining moment and the shared experiences that followed, I trusted Tamara with every part of my life. So one evening, while we sat outside a local bar, mojitos in hand, I opened my world to her. Inside the building, groups of travelers watched soccer on TV and played rounds of pool. Outside at our corner patio table, Tamara guided me through the discomfort of my parents' divorce, my worry of finding a steady job, my hesitancy of pursuing my passions, and the unpredictable reality of transitioning home.

I played with the mint leaves that floated at the top of my glass.

"I just can't imagine going home so soon, you know? I feel unsteady and incredibly unprepared to handle so much change at once."

Tamara nodded, but clearly had an opinion to share. "You don't know it now, but the things you're experiencing through your travels, and the adversity you've faced in Asia, is only further preparing you to handle going home." She stated her thoughts with confidence, as though she knew what she said to be undeniably true. "If anything, you needed Asia to cope with this change. Asia has prepared you for any unanticipated pain moving forward."

I sat in silence, considering what she'd said.

She looked at me seriously. "Look, if you can quit a job and travel the world by yourself, you can work through your parents' divorce."

She had a point; if Asia could throw curveballs at me left and right and I could still find the determination to keep going, then my parents' divorce could prove to be nothing more than another hiccup. I realized that I was more ready to face the transition than I thought; after all, the past six months had been slowly preparing me. All of my experiences and the adversities I'd overcome had led to me becoming strong enough to handle this next step. A hiccup it would be, indeed, but a hiccup I could swallow hard and power through.

Amidst an intellectual conversation about creating purpose and using my experiences to create positive change back home, I shared with her my plans for *Gui Ren*. I voiced my concerns about finding a job back home that would be both meaningful and wouldn't impede on my ability to write a book. Ideally, that meant getting an easy front desk job or a position in retail that would pay the bills but wouldn't require me to take work home. I could clock-in and clock-out without any pressure to climb the corporate ladder or give up my hobbies to succeed in a workplace. I shared with Tamara that my friends and family back home had already voiced their concerns about my desire to settle for a mediocre job, even though the extra time would be used to write something meaningful. They had declared quite loudly that I was making a mistake by selling myself short with my career. Pausing even for a moment to work anywhere I was overqualified to work, would set me back in the long run and waste my potential. In their eyes, working in retail or manning a front desk was beneath my abilities. And while they weren't wrong - I was indeed capable of more - they weren't quite grasping the whole picture.

The mediocre job was far more about making sure I had time for the book than it was about my future career. I knew that if I threw myself into a job I was passionate about, the book would never be written. It was less about holding myself back than about ensuring I had the energy left for writing my story.

"First of all," I started, "I'm not ready for a *real* job; I don't have a demo reel let alone a resumé that even closely reflects my work experience. So even if I wanted to pursue a career - instead of just a job - I'm not ready. I would be laughed out of the interview."

Tamara shook her head at me. "You can't wait until you're *ready* to start pursuing the things that make you happy." Tamara set down her drink, ready to get serious. "Erin, if you really want something, you go for it. You don't wait for the right time to come around."

My one-track mind was thinking more about writing *Gui Ren* than it was establishing my future career path. I understood that Tamara was attempting to encourage my passion project while also putting a stop to my lack of career ambition, but it wasn't what I wanted to hear. It wasn't about a lack of career interest; it was making sure I had time for the project that really mattered.

"Honestly, I don't mind the idea of an easy nine-to-five desk job because that would mean the rest of my energy can go into my writing and the things I'm more passionate about. I want a job that pays the bills so that my passions can be fulfilled elsewhere."

She considered my opinion, then nodded her head with confidence as she said, "Fuck up, not down."

I nearly spit out my mojito. "What did you just say?" I laughed uncomfortably.

She repeated herself, "I think you should fuck up, not fuck down."

I tilted my head trying to figure out what this professional woman had just said to me. Surely it hadn't been as explicative as I'd heard. That's when Tamara told me a story about an ex-boyfriend of hers and shared the sound advice given to her by a good friend.

"It's better to fuck up aiming far too high, than to fuck down and sell yourself short." In her story, she was relating this perspective to relationships. But in my world, she was making the comparison to my job applications. According to her friend's logic, it would be more productive to get shot down by *National Geographic* than nail an interview at Bed Bath & Beyond. Why settle for bare minimum when I could be reaching for the stars?

I want to add here that I'm not diminishing anyone who works in the retail industry; we need hard-working individuals like you to keep this crazy consumer culture under control! I'm merely coming from a place in which, at no point in my life have I ever demonstrated interest in the industry, so it's confusing to most people as to why I'd even consider putting in an application. I understood where my friends and family were coming from; they didn't want me take a job just for the money and convenience. They wanted me to pursue something that evoked passion and sincere interest. But the only thing I could focus on was writing that book.

My secondary concern about finding employment back home was acknowledging the fact that my first post-graduate job had been a total flop. I graduated with honors from a private university only to end up traipsing through Asia on a quest of self-discovery instead of returning home to start the traditional climb. To me, that didn't warrant a position on even the lowest rung of the ladder. Everything I learned in school taught me that employers wanted to see commitment, prior success, and intent to achieve greater purposes. And my track record didn't exactly scream post-graduate potential. But, of course, Tamara did as Tamara does and once again had resounding advice as to how to navigate that kind of job interview.

"Highlight the meaningful parts of this adventure rather than the adversities." Tamara sat back against the wooden bench, her eyes bright with reassurance. "Don't tell people you quit because you had a crappy boss; in fact, you don't even have to tell them that it didn't work out. Tell them you were recruited right out of college for an international position that asked you to travel through Asia. They don't need to know it didn't work out; they need to know that you got the job."

Her point made sense in more ways than one:

1. Potential employers want to know that you are skilled, knowledgable, and highly sought after.

2. Pointing to your failures in the same way you point to successes only makes it appear as though your skills are mediocre.

3. However, talking about your failures AS successes not only proves a practice in positive perception but also demonstrates an ability to cope with change.

Boom. You're welcome. Free job interview advice. Now accepting tips at PayPal.me/ItsOnMyList.

Just when I thought Tamara had fulfilled her quota of life advice for the night she began to impart new perspectives on relationships, money, mindfulness, food, yoga, travel, and even coffee. She voiced her opinion on every topic brought to the surface and she did so with sincerity and wholeheartedness. I sat across from her, soaking in every word she said, as though she were the only voice that mattered. If there was ever a time in which I felt the universe had conspired to bring two people together -

people who otherwise likely never would have crossed paths - it was in Luang Prabang. Yet, despite her influence in just the few days we were together, I didn't know how profoundly she would impact my life until the following evening when Tamara looked me dead in the eyes and told me sternly that I was wasting my potential.

It had been an incredible but exhausting day. Earlier that morning Tamara and I had departed by boat for Pak Ou Cave and a stroll through Whiskey Village. A popular tourist destination, Whiskey Village is one of the first recommendations made to visitors so they can learn how Laotian whiskey is produced and purchase unique bottles complete with scorpions, snakes, and insects submerged in the alcohol. While their method of marketing has fallen under quite a bit of controversy due to the indiscriminate killing of the local ecosystem, travelers can still visit simply to learn about the whiskey process and peruse local handmade goods throughout the neighborhood. Tamara and I were joined by a friendly nurse from San Francisco who had an infectious personality (pun intended) and a true sense of adventure. Robert had been staying at Tamara's hotel and, when we met him at breakfast one morning, we immediately decided to invite him on our adventure. Traipsing through Whiskey Village, our trio of laughter lightened the air around us. We were the teenagers who couldn't keep quiet during a school assembly, constantly giggling and whispering amongst ourselves. We purchased a tiny bottle of ecosystem-free whiskey to try later that evening while we relaxed back in town. At lunch our conversation plunged into the depths of societal analysis and critique. We bonded over a shared perplexity toward United States politics and empathized with growing fears of the vast influence of modern day media. To anyone who knows my tendency to drift into deep analytical conversation with strangers, this will come as no surprise.

On the way back to town, when our boat's engine decided to give up and leave us floating aimlessly downstream, we simply started in on the Lao-Lao whisky we'd purchased and continued chatting the time away. While our boat drivers occupied themselves with calling for help, Robert shared stories from back home in San Francisco and spoke boldly about his comfort of being alone in both travel and everyday life. He provided a new perspective to loneliness and aloneness, in which he believed that listening more intently to one's own mind brings a more developed sense of peace and confidence.

Unfortunately, people often assume that if you are alone, you are lonely. Eating alone, traveling alone, shopping alone; for some reason this appears to many as a negative circumstance. It identifies that person as perhaps being unfriendly, boring, antisocial, or just a straight up weirdo. So when we find ourselves alone, we often try to uphold ourselves with different standards and make attempts to convince those around us that we are either alone on purpose or have friends elsewhere (although, I am really sick of people bumping into me because they are too immersed in their Snapchat stories).

Back in Shanghai I'd had a conversation with a co-worker about society's romanticized idea of what it's like to travel the world alone. Because we had both been, at one time or another, immersed in solitude, we had a more realistic expectation of ourselves and the foreign spaces around us. We discussed the massive amounts of energy it takes to figure things out and the occasional discomfort of being completely alone. But we also acknowledged that pure independence is an incredible feeling and overcoming adversity is that much more rewarding when you have no one else to count on. Ultimately, we agreed that while it's not all glamour and stress-free fun, if you want to discover yourself and the world with terrific speed, traveling alone is the best way to do so.

Back when I was working for R, I had spent five days navigating my way around Hong Kong with a craving for adventure and lack of cell phone data. I came to realize something very important about myself in that short week. Three strangers on separate occasions made comments about how optimistic and happy I was, and as I gleefully made my way around the city with my handy-dandy "old-fashioned" map, I came to the conclusion that my new sense of optimism and dauntlessness was the result of one thing in particular: solitude.

In the past I've always traveled with others, which certainly makes things more fun (assuming everything goes as planned). But when things got chaotic, when we got lost or stuck, I always had a tendency to react with stress and shame. I would feel as though it were my fault and become preoccupied by how to resolve the setback; it made me withdrawn and anxious. I got defensive, overanalyzed every little thing, and my optimism vanished faster than a bag of dark chocolate disappears in my possession.

But in Hong Kong, when I took seven wrong turns before heading back to the hotel, only to find out I took the correct turn four moves prior, I didn't shut down. When I couldn't understand where a couple on the ferry were trying to direct me, I didn't feel anxious. And when I ended up spending over an hour walking back and forth between changing gates at the airport, I didn't feel shame. Instead, I calmly asked for clarification or tried another tactic. I used logic instead of emotion; I told myself that I'd figure it out and, if I couldn't, it wouldn't be the end of the world. I happily took another route rather than beat myself up over the one that didn't work.

At first, it felt strange to be so happy when there was no one to share it with. In fact, at times it just felt wrong, as though I were breaking a rule. One of my favorite quotes is from the film *Into The Wild*. It says, "Happiness only real when shared" (that is not a typo, the 'is' is indeed missing). For years I wondered what purpose these beautiful moments serve if they cannot be understood by anyone other than myself. It's one of many reasons I've preferred sharing adventures with others; knowing someone else can share in reminiscence is enough to know the joy was real. But what I felt in Hong Kong, and in each of the countries that followed, was beyond a level of joy I have ever previously felt on my own. I was finally able to understand that the only person who truly needs to validate my happiness, is me.

While Tamara, Robert, and I sat baking in the sun on the Mekong River, I realized that I had never felt so free-spirited and careless in the company of others. Despite the reality that our boat was drifting aimlessly down a river so thick with clay that the water resembled an enormous mud-puddle, I felt no anxiety or distress. I suddenly didn't care if it took another eight hours to return to shore; I was in good company surrounded by a beautiful landscape and was far too busy embracing the present to be worried about mechanical issues. I knew that eventually we would get back, but I hadn't a care for exactly when or how that happened. I turned my face to the sun, closed my eyes, and inhaled deeply. This, was serenity.

When we finally returned to shore we meandered through town together for hours, stopping for fresh coconut cakes and Beerlao, the Laotian equivalent of Bud Light, along the way. We eventually found ourselves in a chic cocktail bar called Icon Klub. It was there that my life was changed by two things:

1. A chocolate martini that, I kid you not, tasted like I'd just stuffed an entire piece of freshly iced chocolate cake into my mouth, and,

2. The moment in which my personal insecurities and Tamara's no-bullshit attitude clashed in one glorious moment of being slapped in the face with a hard truth.

I had just finished informing Robert of my desire to write a book in order to document my experiences in Asia and inspire others to seek travel and moments of authentic human connection. But as I shared my aspirations with him I felt my thoughts being consumed by bubbling insecurities of never being good enough or not having anything unique enough to say. What made my story so special or worthwhile that people across the country would care to listen? So in a moment of self-doubt, I asked Robert if he would read my blog posts and tell me whether or not he thought I could pull off writing a book. That's when Tamara snapped.

She waved her hands aggressively in the air as she swallowed her drink, violently shaking her head back and forth.

"I'm sorry, but no, I need to say something."

She looked at me with a fire behind her eyes unlike anything I'd ever seen. If I thought I was intimidated before she was furious with me, I was 100% more terrified now. I could hear my pulse as the blood began to beat heavily against my ear drums; I had made a huge mistake. My cheeks became hot with embarrassment while Tamara's rigid glare sank deep into my bones.

She leaned into my personal space. "Never, ever, EVER, give anyone permission to tell you whether or not you're worth it. NEVER give someone the power to dictate your abilities. No one has the right to determine your success, so don't even give them the opportunity to do so. You are so much better than that." The air hung still around me until Tamara finally sat back against the wall, her words leaving an empty space where my heart had once been.

I felt my stubborn and fiery nature boil to the surface. I instinctively became angry and defensive. *Who is she to tell me not to ask for advice?! What does she know about success?! Doesn't she know that the opinion of others is what carries your finished work to the top of the charts?! If no one else thinks it's good then why even pursue it?!* But as she continued her lecture on freeing oneself from doubt and embracing a passion for creating meaningful art regardless of anyone else's shallow and uninformed opinion, I realized that perhaps my anger was misguided.

She drilled me. "What would you do if Robert didn't like your writing style or your subject matter? Would you just give up? You couldn't possibly get enough opinions about your work to justify not even trying."

I sat there in a loathing silence.

And then, her final words hit my brain like a load of truth bricks. "You would be robbing the rest of the world of art they didn't even get the chance to see."

I realized that despite my defensive frustration, an instinctual reaction to being criticized, I didn't loathe Tamara as a person. I loathed that she recognized a weakness of mine and didn't hesitate to call me out. Her no-bullshit demeanor had caught me red-handed and, in all honesty, I was ashamed. I loathed her not because she confronted me, but because she exposed the one thing that was holding me back from truly committing to my passions: my fear of rejection. I no longer had an excuse to not follow through on my dream. In that small cocktail bar, my hands still trembling over my chocolate martini, Tamara advised me to stop searching for validation and instead prioritize the opinions of people who already recognize and support my talents and worth; to listen to those who know me well and value me as an individual - with or without a published book.

I looked at Robert, who was nodding enthusiastically in agreement. I could practically see him snapping his fingers and yelling out, "Amen, sister!" And in that moment, my loathing began to turn into love. In fact, I loved Tamara more in that moment than I've ever loved someone I'd only recently met. She so boldly and fearlessly punched the self-doubt out of my head and forced a 180-degree change in perspective. She knew exactly what I needed to hear and had absolutely no qualms about saying it to my face. And as I sat there in a cocktail bar adorned with posters that said, "Nasty Woman," and a bathroom stocked with rolls of Donald Trump toilet paper (yes, the bar owner was a badass), I realized that I'd never felt more empowered and capable of anything in my life. These two individuals whom I'd gotten to know over the past several days somehow already knew me better than I knew myself, and they weren't afraid to say so. Their compassion and sincere investment in my best self left me feeling inspired and filled with hope. Who would have thought that two complete strangers I met halfway around the globe would be so much of the reason that this story is in your hands today.

Asia brought a lot of people into my life who influenced my journey of self-love and confidence, but Luang Prabang proved to be one of the most impactful experiences of my life. Over the next several months while I transitioned home and started writing *Gui Ren*, Robert and Tamara's voices echoed through my mind. Robert reminded me that taking your own path can be just as meaningful, if not more so, than sticking to the script. Tamara reinforced that my greatest aspirations were only that - aspirations - so long as I didn't take action and trust myself to follow through. But above all, I learned that no one should have an opinion loud enough to prevent me from pursuing my passions and making my voice heard. No one has control over whether or not my story should be written.

Rooftop Pools & 75 Cent Beer

If you meet a loner, no matter what they tell you, it's not because
they enjoy solitude. It's because they have tried to blend into the world
before, and people continue to disappoint them.
~ Jodi Picoult ~

Siem Reap, Cambodia | November 30 - December 4

Does anyone else feel like they need a vacation after their vacation? You know, the horrible feeling when you've finished up your relaxing jaunt to the beach where you sipped on cocktails all day while lounging by the waters, not caring what time of day it was, and suddenly you have to function as a normal adult again? Coming home is lovely because you get to shower in your own home and curl up in your own bed, but then you have to wake up to your own obnoxious alarm clock and get back to paying your own bills. And, unfortunately, the longer amount of time you spend away, the harder it gets to fall back into routine.

As I stood mindlessly in the lobby of my Siem Reap hostel, dripping with sweat, suppressing several yawns, pawing at the backpack strapped to my chest in search of my passport, I began to feel overwhelmed with a strange fear. Young Westerners milled about in bathing suits and sat curled up in oversized beanbag chairs eating grilled cheese sandwiches and hamburgers. The hostel staff greeted me with smiles and asked for my name with practiced English. A young Cambodian man led me to the second-floor female dorm where he handed me two papers: the hostel rules and café happy hour pricing. As I nestled my backpack between the wall and my lower bunk, my chest tightened. I no longer wanted to socialize or go outside, or even shower (although I desperately needed to). I wanted to curl up in bed and fall asleep until my next flight. I wanted to avoid all awkward encounters and the, "Where are you froms." I wanted to disappear and pretend I'd never arrived. It felt as though I was observing my life from the outside, as if the walls of my world were paper thin and the people just actors in an otherwise overwhelming and burdening world. And I had no idea why.

The hostel fortunately had a rooftop pool, which is where I sought out comfort by submerging my exhausted shoulders beneath the frigid water, wondering how it had stayed so chilled beneath such an intense Siem Reap sun. The deck was crowded with tanning foreigners chattering away in English, French, and Dutch. I spun slowly within the water, observing the expansive horizon lingering just barely in my line of view, dotted with billboards, palm trees, and red tiled roofs. The breeze was liberating, and the sun blanketed my face with an inviting and gentle warmth.

"But, like, really I haven't even left the hostel all day. There's nothing to see here except Angkor Wat. Like, that was cool and all, but I just feel like it looks like every other temple, you know?" My peaceful serenity was interrupted by 102Basic-WhiteGirl FM.

"Oh, I totally know what you mean."

Another shrill female voice bounced against my ears. "The sunrise was super pretty, but there's just way too much to see for one day and honestly if all I do is work on my tan here that's fine with me. I'm so down for drinks though. Maybe we can find a club?"

I closed my eyes and tilted my head to the sun. If I had rolled my eyes they surely would've fallen out; I was only doing what I needed to protect them. While immersed in the dull glow of sunlight behind my eyelids I reflected on my current state of emotional turmoil. I had been filled with discomfort and anxiety since I arrived in Cambodia just a few hours earlier and, until that moment, I hadn't understood why. But it all started to slowly come together…. The sterile airport with lines of European and American tourists holding guide books and requesting senior citizen discounts for visas on arrival; the tuk tuk that carted me from the airport, its ceiling lined with the names and locations of local Western bars and souvenir shops; the hostel that closely resembled an afternoon on an Indianapolis college campus, complete with ridiculously cheap beer and American music videos streaming on repeat; the hordes of young adults clustering together over laptops and smartphones, making plans to hit the night market in their latest crop-top and jean-short combo. I was drowning in familiarity.

I had been plucked right out of Asia and thrown into a frat house where alcohol, sex, and selfies were everyone's first priority. I could understand the language to the extent of accidentally listening in on conversations to which I would have rather been oblivious. But perhaps most discomforting was the simple fact that I blended in. I became invisible in a sea of white European descendants. At first I thought this was selfish, that perhaps I was disappointed that no one was infatuated with my blonde hair or frighteningly pale skin. But I quickly realized my discomfort was born of a much deeper fear; the fear of having to prove myself in an all-too-familiar environment of judgement and expectations. I worried what people thought about me or what they would say. There was no longer an excuse for not fitting in because it was my own society from which I was estranged.

I had spent six months of my life constantly confused, immersed in cultural and linguistic barriers that challenged my adaptive skills and intuitions. I grew accustomed to an unfamiliar and unpredictable world. 'New' was no longer intimidating or scary because 'new' was all I had. There were no expectations of me; I didn't have to prove myself to anyone because nothing I did made sense anyway. I was the perfect chameleon. I blended in as best I could and assimilated into local culture where I found comfort in not being able to understand the world around me. I had successfully become comfortable with being uncomfortable. And now, Siem Reap was shoving Western familiarities down my throat so quickly it felt as though I might suffocate.

Back in the dorm my roommates asked if I wanted to go out for dinner with them, a courtesy often extended to new arrivals. Despite my deep desire to bury myself in blankets and disappear from the world, I forced myself to say yes. I needed dinner but, most of all, I needed some kind of distraction, even if it were an uncomfortable one. *Yes, I will walk through the night market with you and pretend to be interested in your life. Yes, I will curiously peruse menus as if I actually have an opinion on our choice of cuisine. Yes, I will laugh at your jokes and participate in your banter as though I'm far more energized than I actually feel. Yes, I will assume the supporting role of fellow traveler and social butterfly extreme. But I will not enjoy it. I would rather be in bed.* I felt bitter, anxious, and prone to self-sabotaging. I didn't want to be a part of the crowd; I wanted to be back in a place where being alone was socially acceptable and my language barrier could be a safety blanket from superficial socialization.

I regretfully clung to this sour attitude until twenty-four hours later when I found myself sitting crossed-legged with another traveler on the roof of a river boat as it floated down the Tonlé Sap River. I had met my rooftop companion, Nanne, a few hours earlier while our van bounced along a dirt road in southern Siem Reap. We had set out for an evening of sunsets and boat tours when we found ourselves squished together in the first row of seats, listening to our fellow tour mates as they spent their time planning to find a place that served happy pizza (a food I later learned involved marijuana) and get trashed at the pubs. Nanne and I were the only ones not participating and, seeing as we bumped elbows every time the road dipped, we decided to overcome the severe lack of personal space and start a conversation.

I learned Nanne was originally from Amsterdam and traveling on holiday from school in Hong Kong where she was studying business administration. She shared with me that her mom works for an airline so she has traveled quite a bit throughout the world. We talked about Amsterdam and my brief experience biking the canals with my friends during a study abroad program in college. She told me about her passion for clothing design and upcycling, a creative process by which people produce items from recycled goods by making something new or improving its sustainable quality. I was fascinated by her unique interests and seriously extensive travels. But it wasn't until later that evening as our boat drifted down the Tonlé Sap and the Cambodian sun set lower in the sky, that I realized just how powerful our friendship would be.

Nanne and I spent the afternoon observing local life in the floating villages from the rooftop of our tour boat. We found ourselves separated from the rest of the group, free from chatter about partying and getting high. We watched groups of young kids playing in the river, sitting on wooden planks, and floating by in plastic tubs. Some of the locals living on the river drifted by on houseboats while others lived in houses that stood tall from the surface of the water, their seemingly heavy structures supported by thin tree trunks and pieces of lumber. Nanne and I talked about what life might be like in the villages, wondering if our abundant lifestyle would leave us feeling limited or if we would feel relieved by a lack of material desire. As we drifted down the river our boat was approached by a woman selling concessions from her canoe. She extended a fishing net high into the air so that we could toss in a few bills. I leaned over the railing when she hoisted our package of Oreos into the sky.

I began to feel overwhelmed with apprehension as the sun finally began to set behind the thick clouds that layered the skies. It was the same feeling I had during childhood when my parents would drop me off at a sleepover. And, nine times out of ten it ended with them driving across town and picking me up at three o'clock in the morning. It was a feeling of isolation; of being stranded and alone. It meant the future was unpredictable, and the chaos far too close for comfort.

Nanne broke the silence from her rooftop perch. "Sometimes I feel this is just too extraordinary to be real."

I looked at her curiously. "What do you mean?"

"I don't know," she paused. "It's just hard to believe I'm here sometimes."

She now had my full attention. "I know exactly what you mean. I've been feeling that way since I got here. Although I can't really be sure why."

"I have these nightmares where I wake up back home in my bed, but it's not in a good way." Nanne looked at me as she leaned back against the boat railing. "In my dream, everything feels cold and dark; it's as though none of this really happened and all these adventures were just made up in my head. The worst part is, even in my dream, I'm already sad that I can't share these experiences with anyone. Because no one will understand. And when I actually wake up, I feel this great relief that I'm still here, and it's not over yet."

For the first time since arriving in Siem Reap, I finally felt a connection to something, to someone. I looked at Nanne as though unsure whether to run away terrified or leap for joy.

I stumbled over my thoughts. "Do you sometimes feel like you're not really here? Like you're awake but it's all just a dream?"

She barely let me finish my question before lunging forward with an exclamatory, "Yes! All the time! It's like what is happening to me is so surreal I can't comprehend how this is possible. To travel like this and see the world; it's so unreal."

Either I had finally found someone who understood, or simply found someone strong enough to admit it.

I opened up to her about my hesitation going home. "I feel like over the past six months I've gotten used to being on the outside. I'm so comfortable with not understanding that the thought of being able to comprehend everything again is actually overwhelming. Even being in Siem Reap has been a complete shock."

She ran a hand through her thick, curly blonde hair. "Oh man, I know exactly what you mean. Everyone here is so…I don't know. I can't describe it."

Without exchanging any other words, we knew exactly what was said. I looked back to the open waters, the moon beginning to rise over Siem Reap. Suddenly it felt like I could breathe again.

On our way back to the hostel Nanne and I decided to book a sunrise tour of Angkor Wat for the following morning. What better way to start a day than to watch the sunrise of a sunset you'd watched the night before? Poetic, if I do say so myself! The tour was certainly not cheap, but after a van-wide conversation about the value in booking a tour versus visiting on your own, Nanne and I decided it was worth the expense to have a guide who could help us understand the historical significance of this global wonder. There were a couple options when it came to booking tours. You could do the budget-friendly version and join a potentially larger group, or you could book a private tuk tuk with a few of your select friends. Several members of the party-hardy crowd attempted to sway Nanne and me into paying for part of a private tuk tuk tour with them, rather than go with a larger group. But we confidently declined the offer. If we decided to chip in and they didn't show, Nanne and I would be responsible for paying the entire fare. And if I was going to wake up at four o'clock in the morning for a sunrise tour, I needed to know I could count on my ride. Sure enough, the next morning, as Nanne and I climbed into our oversized van out front, there was no sign of the happy pizza people - just one disheartened tuk tuk driver waiting for his appointment to show. Always trust your gut.

The sunrise tour was awe-inspiring. We arrived in front of Angkor Wat in complete darkness, and as the sky began to lighten only then did its magnificent shape and expansive size come to realization. I've always felt there is a bit of magic in watching a sun rise and being embraced by the refreshing chill of a subtle blue morning. You know, the crisp air of a new morning that is the slow transition between night and day. Perhaps it has something to do with my nostalgia for Concepción, Chile, when I would wake up at the crack of dawn to go to school with my host sister. Or perhaps it is the numerous early trips to the airport at the start of a new international adventure. It is the daybreak at summer camp, the commencement of a long day of dress rehearsals, or the anticipation of a big day on campus. It is either a poetic nod to new beginnings, or a testament to the fact that if I'm waking up before the sun, it'd better be for something spectacular. And Angkor Wat was certainly worth the wake-up call. As the sun rose higher in the sky we traipsed through the temple grounds listening to our guide speak of Vishnu, the

Hindu God to which Angkor Wat was dedicated. We learned of the thousands of temples that made up the city of Angkor, and of the religious site's transition from Hindu to Buddhism.

Walking through the ancient city, my mind wandered to what it must have looked like before it began to deteriorate. Darkened patches of time marked the edges of the stone while the intricacies of what had once been carefully crafted slowly began to fade. Etchings of religious symbolism were interlaced with ornate carvings of detailed embellishments, the edges seemingly less prominent than they once were. There were places along the corridors and reaching up onto columns where - in an act of selfishness - tourists had left their mark in the forms of initials or childish depictions of self-portraits. I walked with caution along the uneven stone, unsure how much longer it would be until it crumbled away, leaving another gap in what had once been an architectural masterpiece. I stood looking out over the relic empire and wondered if, years from now, I would be able to fathom that I had really been here; that I had walked within the walls of such a foundational piece of Cambodia's history.

An afternoon at the hotel pool was well deserved; my body was exhausted and my eyes refused to stay open long enough to edit videos. So I patiently waited for a deck chair to open up, claimed my territory, and proceeded to drift in and out of a restless sleep. Siem Reap was bustling in the streets below, but at that very moment in time I felt no pressure to be out exploring. I had finally learned that there were more important qualities to life than rushing through to see it all; sometimes taking it slow and embracing the moment was in fact the way to make the most of a journey. Late that afternoon, Nanne and I took our time exploring several handicraft markets and outdoor shopping centers before getting a bite to eat and heading back to the hostel.

The next morning, while I sat in the hostel cafe sipping on a banana and pineapple smoothie, Nanne proposed we rent a tuk tuk and make the trip out to the lotus farms. Nanne knew me better than most people do within such a short time, but she couldn't possibly have known how thrilled I would be at that particular suggestion. Now, I have never been a tattoo person. Ever since I was little I have been terrified of needles and therefore uninterested in having myself repeatedly stabbed with one for the sake of art. But with my high school and college careers came a profound number of unique challenges that tested my resiliency and ability to face adversity. In addition to being bullied in high school, I spent several years fighting chronic headaches and survived two abusive relationships. I was dealt a lot of pain, both physically and emotionally, but I carried myself through and refused to let it win. Shortly after my chronic pain subsided, and I started at Butler University, I began reading about mindfulness. It was in those studies that I learned about the lotus flower.

If you've ever come across one you may have noticed the layers of beautifully reaching petals unfolding from the core of the flower. What you may not have noticed was the foundation from which it grew. Lotus flowers bloom on the stems of long roots that sink beneath the muddy waters of rivers and ponds. They protrude from murky waters and provide beauty where there otherwise may be none. Because of this, they are a treasure to many cultures around the world and are considered to be a symbol of purity and enlightenment. The lotus flower thrives as a token of radiant color despite its murky surroundings. From this flower I learned that despite my hardships and the adversities that pulled me down, I could still flourish into something beautiful.

I began drawing the outline of a lotus flower accompanied by a long and winding stem on my left wrist. Every morning I would wake up, get ready for class, and trace over the design with a thin-tipped Sharpie. And as I drew that flower on my skin I was reminded that, no matter what I faced that day, it would only help me grow. When people began asking me about it, I began to realize that I had a story to tell. I had the opportunity to share with them words of encouragement and hope; I created a space with which to use my own journey to influence the journey of others. Several months later I had my lotus flower design permanently tattooed on my wrist. The discomfort of getting a tattoo was suddenly far less important than my desire to make this symbol a part of my story for the rest of my life. I made a vow that when my kids, and their kids, ask for the story about my tattoo, that I would take the opportunity to remind them that with every struggle comes strength, wisdom, and beauty.

What's poetic to me now is that when I got that tattoo back in 2013, I could not have possibly anticipated that four years later my life would be changed forever within the borders of multiple Asian countries that consider the lotus to be a sacred flower. I had no idea that the flower I had permanently planted on my wrist would continue to serve as a comfort and reminder when my waters got murky once again. So when Nanne asked if I wanted to visit the lotus farms, my answer was a heartfelt and resounding, "Yes."

Our tuk tuk drove down the narrow dirt road alongside the Siem Reap River while Nanne and I watched the locals buzz about their everyday lives. Motorbikes sped noisily past and the markets were bustling as merchants set up shop for the day. Farm animals roamed aimlessly along the berm and children ran by barefoot, shouting and waving. By the time we arrived at the farm we had been completely removed from the land of tourism. There were no other Westerners in sight, and no accommodations that would have encouraged them. Nanne meandered out onto the rickety wooden bridges that extended into the lotus farm and across the murky waters consumed by clusters of tall green stems. Despite it not being the season for lotus blooms, the mere expanse of the territory and the way its horizon was dotted with thatched huts and bridges was truly an extraordinary sight. As we stood in the sun looking out across the farm, we were approached by a young girl who said nothing to us, but handed Nanne a piece of folded notebook paper. We looked at each other in confusion. Nanne unfolded it to reveal a crayon drawing depicting a girl holding a lotus and we both smiled.

"For me?" Nanne pointed at herself and smiled at the girl. The little girl nodded, smiled bashfully, and ran back across the wooden bridge to a nearby hut.

We climbed back into the tuk tuk energized by the sights and the friendliness of a young stranger. A few moments later our driver parked across the street from a village where he encouraged us to go and experience local life. We began to walk towards a cluster of homes that were divided by a single dirt road that stretched down the middle. The houses were perched above shallow water on the same stilts we saw in the floating village, and between them the man-made mound of dirt created a walking path that served in tandem as a barricade to rising waters. As we approached the small village several groups of children milled about, watching us with caution. Nanne and I smiled and waved with reservation, not wishing to invade their space or appear threatening. But the kids took to us quickly; as we walked we morphed into a human version of the game, Snake. Several young girls approached and held our hands, and several other children followed in suit. For every house we passed there were a handful of children attaching themselves to our train. By the time we reached the end of the lane we stretched the entire width of the road and beyond.

We stood in a group at the end of the road, the kids flitting anxiously around us. A little girl wanted to hold my backpack while another counted out loud in English the number of pineapples on Nanne's shorts. They played with our phones and Nanne's camera, wanting to see photos of themselves as they struck flashy poses and made silly faces. I opened Snapchat and let them play with the filters that exaggerated their features or turned them into dogs. When I crouched down to their level, I was tackled by kids wanting to climb on my back or wrap their arms around my shoulders. Nanne and I were swallowed whole by a horde of adorable local children and we certainly weren't upset about it. When Nanne and I decided to start heading back, the kids skipped with us, singing songs and yanking at our hands. Their smiles and laughter was every bit of joy the world needed in that moment.

Just as we were beginning to feel as though the grins would never disappear from our faces, we made it to the middle of the lane where the parents of the children were waiting. They approached us with vigor, handing us packages of food, paperback books, and pencil cases.

"Please buy food for my children."

"Ma'am, please, school books for my kids."

"Miss, they need food, you see?"

"Please can you spare, they are hungry?"

I was overwhelmed and suddenly drained of my energy. We were encircled by overenthusiastic children and desperate adults. Nanne and I both looked at each other, unsure of what to do. There were several thoughts that tore through my brain in that moment but the most prominent one was: *they know we have a few dollars to spare. Our clothes, our phones, even our hair gives that away. If we were to tell them 'no,' they'd know we were lying.* Perhaps I felt guilty for having so much more than they did. Maybe I felt it was my duty, considering that to give so little of myself would be giving so much to those kids. Or perhaps I was proud that I could make a difference. Whatever the reason, I still to this day regret doing what I did next.

I hesitantly pulled out enough cash from my backpack to pay for a bag of individually wrapped snacks. In my mind, this made sense; I could be there to make sure that the kids actually received and consumed their gifts. If they were hungry I could make sure they were fed. A father handed me the bag in exchange for my cash and I opened it to begin handing out food.

But suddenly there were far more kids in front of me than a few minutes prior. Groups of children started emerging from the woodworks; they were running down the lane, leaping out of houses, and arriving in the arms of their older siblings. The more snacks I handed out, the more children appeared. I could no longer keep track of who I'd given food to and, in the chaos, I handed out the last package with at least ten sets of empty hands remaining in the air. I had reached the bottom of the bag and it seemed there were just as many kids as before. My stomach churned, the adults offered us more things to buy, but all I could do was shake my head and turn away. I began to feel as though I could have stood there all day, handing over cash and distributing items. Yet, somewhere deep down I knew that when all was said and done, the gesture wouldn't make much of a difference. I would be broke by the time any of it truly mattered.

Nanne and I made our way out of the village in a hurry, knowing that we couldn't possibly feed everyone and feeling at odds with the chain of events. What had begun as such a cheerful experience ended with regret. My heart tried to justify my actions by focusing on the joy and laughter of the kids we spent time with, but my head was distraught, trying to figure out what I had done to feel so disgusted with my decisions.

It wasn't until months later when I discovered an article discussing "voluntourism" and the "white savior complex," that I understood why my experience had felt so unforgiving. What I had done only reinforced the narrative that white Westerners will come swooping in at random to slap a heroic bandaid over a much deeper cut, without attributing the underlying societal issues. Now, I'm sure there are many sides to this debate; some may feel my actions were harmless while some may feel I had made the worst mistake a traveler could make. But here are some considerations to account for when taking your stance:

1. It is not uncommon for locals to make a business out of requesting visitors buy schoolbooks or food for their children, only to turn around and continue to resell the same products to the next buyer. In this case, the child rarely sees the benefit and the parents may or may not use those funds for the right purpose.

2. Those young kids are growing up under the impression that foreigners will provide for them without actually having to exchange services. This means raising a new generation of socially acceptable begging practices. It has been proven time and time again that begging, rather than working, does not effectively fix poverty.

3. By offering bandaids you're allowing the country as a whole to overlook the deeper issues at hand. Just because you put Duct Tape over a hole, doesn't mean it won't spring another leak with time. But if there's a temporary fix, governments may overlook the leak altogether.

4. Perhaps most importantly, if children are successful enough at bringing in funds for their family - either by conscious or unconscious begging - their parents are less likely to send them to school.

I don't think I will ever feel good about what I did that afternoon in the village. Although I try my best to focus on the exchange of smiles and laughter, I will never forget the valuable lesson I learned through the experience. It made me realize just how important it is to support local non-profits and organizations that know exactly where to apply funding to help make progress towards reaching a larger goal. Resolving issues of poverty is not as simple as we'd like to think, and although it may feel good in the moment to give a small child a "treat," at the end of the day, it's not what they need most.

When Nanne and I made our way back into Siem Reap we headed to the Night Market to find some dinner. On our way, we passed by a frozen yogurt shop named Project Y where we were offered a sample by a young local holding a tray and dancing energetically to a global top hits playlist. She asked us if we wanted to buy some but, although my appreciation for ice cream and froyo is quite profound, I was on the hunt for something more substantial.

When we passed, I shouted back in her direction, "I promise we'll be back later!" It was a promise I knew with confidence that I could keep.

Sure enough, traipsing back to the hostel from a delicious dinner, we fulfilled our promise and stopped for some frozen yogurt. I loaded my cup full of chocolate and Nutella swirl while a young man began telling us about Project Y's marketing manager.

Sompeas was just one of the many leaders of the Cambodia Rural Students Trust whose story was featured on the walls of Project Y. She was almost exactly one year older than me and grew up in rural Cambodia. When she was three years old her father passed away from complications with an illness, and she was taken to live in another province with her grandmother where she started her primary school education. In third grade, when her grandmother passed, she was taken back to her family where she had to repeat her academic year. Sompeas's oldest sister began working at eighteen years old, and her other sister at age seventeen. But the sole income of her mother and sisters was not enough to support the family, nor pay off the outstanding loan from her father's medical treatments. By the time Sompeas was fifteen she was taking care of the house and cooking for her family. In tenth grade she began working as a waitress; it seemed as though her education would no longer be a priority.

Such a story is not uncommon in Siem Reap; students of rural areas often find themselves deciding between their education and supporting their family. Founded by an Australian in 2011, the Cambodia Rural Students Trust aspired to provide opportunities for rural Cambodians to not only gain the education they need to be successful, but also to alleviate the burden of familial financial debt. They redefined the dynamic of volunteerism and charity in Cambodia; their NGO operates with complete transparency of funding and accountability of services as they provide educational opportunities and leadership development to children in need. Students are utilizing their scholarships to the full potential as they support their family financially while receiving the education they need to be independent.

The frozen yogurt shop, Project Y, was started in 2015 with the goal of not only providing a workplace for students to earn a livable wage, but also to expose them to leadership positions and experiences in business management. This shop is run entirely by university and high school students in an effort to support themselves through school while gaining valuable academic and life skills. One look around the shop illustrated just how motivated and sincere these students were in creating a viable future for themselves and others in need. Their energy was infectious, their passion invigorating, and their frozen yogurt delightfully delicious. Nanne and I hardly anticipated such a story coming from an unsuspecting frozen yogurt shop in the Siem Reap Night Market.

The next day, before a tuk tuk took me to the airport for my flight to Vietnam, Nanne and I returned to Project Y to capture interviews on camera and get to know more of the story behind the efforts of the Cambodia Rural Students Trust and the young leaders involved. We learned that, in between skills development and classes, these students build homes for impoverished families in rural Cambodia and foster working relationships between disadvantaged local groups to fund basic necessities. The heart of every student we spoke to radiated with generosity, unconditional love, and gratitude. They recognize the opportunity they had been given, and work diligently every day to ensure they can give the same chances to generations after them. As my plane lifted off the tarmac at the Siem Reap International Airport, I couldn't help but feel a sense of honor, having learned the lessons I did and having witnessed the phenomenal power of what a group of devoted and loving students can do to change the world.

Heineken & Sunsets

Sometimes, home doesn't need to be more than a single 60L backpack and a friendly smile.

~ Erin O'Neil ~

Ho Chi Minh, Vietnam | December 4 - 9

I spent my last week in Asia in the company of my dear friend and previous roommate, Jenny. When she moved from Malaysia to Vietnam, I knew I would have to continue the chase to spend time with her in as many countries as I could before heading back to the United States. And in the same fashion with which I arrived in Laos and Cambodia, I landed in Vietnam with no particular plan in mind. At the tail end of my adventures, I wanted nothing more than to simply embrace what came my way and focus on enjoying every unanticipated moment. Fortunately, this mentality worked to my advantage as I unexpectedly spent more than my fair share of the first afternoon in Vietnam in a crowded customs waiting area at the airport, nervously anticipating my visa-on-arrival. Those mug shots from Taiwan had come in handy after all.

Just over an hour went by before I grew uncomfortable from the sweat that was beginning to make my back itch. My name was finally called and my patience was rewarded with the satisfying 'thud' of a passport stamp. I enthusiastically headed towards baggage claim, eager to see my friend again. Outside the airport terminal, I stood in what remaining WiFi I had and ordered a car to Jenny's apartment. It was the cheapest option considering a bus would have taken three times longer and a motorbike would not have been able to sustain the combined weight of my 60L hiking pack, backpack, and the body that spent several months consuming nothing but dumplings and noodles. Plus, by the time I decided to book the car it had begun to rain, and as much as I embraced a spontaneous adventure, motorbiking through the rain was not something I would have enjoyed. So I happily gave my bags to the driver and climbed into a small four-door car where I watched Ho Chi Minh come to life outside my window.

I had heard the rumors about Vietnam traffic, but nothing quite compared to actually being stuck in it. To make matters worse, the rain quickly flooded the streets and prevented any-one from going over seven miles per hour. Motorbikes weaved haphazardly through the traffic jam, narrowly missing the side mirrors of idling cars, and wading through deep puddles as they walked their bikes forward. It reminded me of my first ex-perience riding in a car during rush hour in Concepción, Chile back in high school. I had been watching from the back seat when my host mom pulled up next to another car within a mere inch of its back bumper, turned the wheel hard to the right, and narrowly pulled herself up along the right side of the vehicle. When the turn got too tight, she merely leaned out the window, folded in her side mirror, and kept going. She was dauntless, and it had terrified me. Now, the weaving motorbikes and aim-less driving oddly put me at peace. I had become accustomed to chaos and feeling overwhelmed, so much so that in the heat of the moment I just sat back, took a deep breath, and trusted the driver to get me there safely. Somehow, the unpredictable chaos was far more comforting than a promise of stability; when everything is unpredictable it makes it much easier to cope if something goes awry.

My driver pulled into the parking lot of a sky rise apartment complex off of a narrow backroad. The rain had subsided but the streets were now rapidly flowing rivers, threatening to sweep away any stray motorbikes or debris. Jenny's apartment building was now protected by a murky moat. My shoes became soaked as I traipsed over the puddled ground to where Jenny was waiting for me at the elevator. Despite having lived with her for several months in Shanghai, and having spent a week with her in Kuala Lumpur, we still squealed like girls when we finally saw each other. Traveling the world is a fulfilling adventure, there is no question about that. But the prolonged solitude can sometimes grow old, and there was nothing more relieving than being with someone who understood that feeling.

Over the next five days Jenny and I embraced the momentary pause in our otherwise chaotic lives. We laid out at her apartment pool, watched movies while curled up in bed, and drank more Vietnamese coffee than my body could physically handle. I followed her through the winding streets of Ho Chi Minh while we ventured to the Notre Dame Cathedral of Saigon, the Central Post Office, and City Hall. We stopped to admire the rustic exterior structure of 42 Nguyen Hue, an apartment mall featuring a variety of innovative and eclectic pop-up shops. And later that evening we ventured into the Bitexco Financial Tower to watch the sunset from the Saigon Skydeck. Jenny and I sat side by side on the 49th floor of the tower, watching the Vietnam traffic swarm below us like ants. I thought about how far I'd come, how many cities I'd seen, and how much I'd learned about myself and the world around me. I leaned over and put my head on her shoulder, suddenly preoccupied with the thought of going home.

Asia was not my first international adventure. In fact, by the time I found myself in Vietnam I had twenty-two countries under my belt; one country for every year of my life. Each country was unique and every travel experience offered a new lesson in adventure, purpose, and connection. But the one thing that never altered, regardless of which part of the world I was visiting, was the uncomfortable sense of closure. Despite my intentional lackadaisical attitude towards "seeing and doing it all," I always felt as though I hadn't had enough time. There was always something more that I could experience or see. There were always people I hadn't yet met, and topics I hadn't yet discussed. And as I sat there on the 49th floor of the Bitexco Financial Tower, I felt that same sense of longing. For more time; more money; more countries; more conversations; more stories. It just wasn't possible that in merely one week I would be headed home. And this time, home didn't mean Shanghai.

I have seen sunsets all over the world; against the sands of the Gobi Desert, between the skyscrapers in Shanghai, from a beachside bar in Malaysia, and the top of a tour boat as it drifted down the Tonlé Sap in Cambodia. While I watched the sun set amongst a row of boats in an Indonesian marina, I mourned the loss of my childhood home. When the sun sank behind the tea farms that marked the horizon, I practiced gratitude for the stories and life lessons imparted by strangers in Leshan. And as I sat there in Ho Chi Minh, with Jenny by my side, I said good-bye to an incredible adventure and hello to a new unpredictable world; a world full of opportunity and willingness to become whatever I dreamed it to be.

The night that my flight left Vietnam, Jenny was at a work event and I was headed out to get tacos. Priorities, am I right? Because my flight didn't leave until two o'clock in the morning I knew I had time to spare and that I certainly wasn't going to waste a moment of it. Mike and I had kept in touch ever since we hugged goodbye at the hawker center in Penang, and he happened to now be in Ho Chi Minh while he pursued his interest in teaching English to students in Vietnam. So I took the opportunity to connect with an "old" friend and we went to get Mexican food at a local place called District Federal. There, Mike updated me about his adventures, sharing how fulfilled he felt traveling through Asia and challenging himself with new experiences. He didn't know how long he wanted to stay, but he certainly didn't have any intentions of going home soon.

After we had gorged ourselves on platefuls of delicious tacos, we meandered down the street in search of dessert. We were slowly making our way down the small, two-lane road, and out towards the busier main road. We stumbled into Osterberg Ice Cream where I definitely ordered too much for one person, and then we continued walking down the street. By the time we reached a local gastropub called BiaCraft we were somehow, miraculously, ready for a drink. While we were busy trying local beers we met another friendly American who later invited us to head to Pasteur Street Filling Station for wings and more craft beer. If I had been working with a personal trainer at that time, I would have been doing quite a few burpees to make up for the mass amount of carbohydrates I had consumed in just a few hours. But it was the perfect way to end an adventure; good drinks, great food, and even better company. When Jenny messaged me that she was heading home from her event, I booked myself a ride back to the apartment. But this time, I opted for a motorbike.

Not a thing in the world could wipe the smile from my face as my driver wove through the backroads of the Thao Dien district, my legs lazily draped over the edges of the seat. I thought about the first time I'd been on a motorbike in Asia, my hands tightly grasping the shoulders of the driver in Bangkok. I had been enthralled, but terrified, my thighs clinging to the sides and my body fighting gravity with every turn. But now, as the cool evening air braced itself against my skin, I felt grounded and weightless all at once. My weight shifted with the bike in a coordinated dance. I leaned into the corners and allowed myself to give in to the pull of gravity. I closed my eyes and breathed in the crisp night under a beautiful Vietnam sky. It was a ride I never wanted to end, for more reasons than one.

I cried on the way to the airport that night, the tears unapologetically falling from my cheeks. It was going on midnight and my last day in Vietnam was coming to a close. Jenny and I had said a heartfelt goodbye when she helped me down to the car, but there was so much I felt hadn't been said. If you know me well, or even at all, you will know I am a complete and total sap. I'm the kind of person who has to write it all down and hand it to you in a letter, because if I try to tell you face-to-face you will get nothing but tears. I am fortunate to feel such deep connections with the people and places in my life, but because I do it makes it that much harder to leave them behind. If I would have been able to speak my mind without turning into a puddle of bittersweet tears, I would have told Jenny how honored I was to have a friend like her; how proud I am to know someone so headstrong and confident; how everything she does serves as a reminder to embrace every moment and make it your own. I would have told her how much I would miss her and all of the small moments that made our friendship memorable: cooking stir fry together in our tiny apartment kitchen; biking to the grocery store under the hot Shanghai sun; eating cheesecake in bed and talking about guys; and the way she would so boldly tell me exactly what I needed to hear.

Saying goodbye to Asia was not easy, but saying goodbye to the people I left behind was far more difficult. The night before I flew back to the States, I met up with Lisa in Tianzifang, one of my favorite shopping centers in Shanghai. We walked through the narrow passageways lined with one-of-a-kind boutiques and craft shops, talking non-stop. They were conversations I would very quickly miss upon leaving Shanghai. Before we said goodbye I handed her a letter, knowing that whatever would come out while we hugged, would not be the full story. I wanted to tell her how grateful I was for her patience and empathy; how much I valued our time together and would miss our conversations. Lisa and Jenny had been my yin and yang, each of them offering unique perspectives that made my world feel whole. When I ran into a problem, Jenny was there to fight for me and Lisa was there to listen. When I had a decision to make,

Lisa drew out my opinions and Jenny gave me her own. They were the perfect balance of dauntlessness and reservation; one helped me process and strategize, and the other was standing by my side, fists raised.

Asia helped me realize that there is no perfect friendship, but rather a network of people who inspire you in their own way. Gui Ren means the right people coming into your life with synchronicity to help guide you. It doesn't mean you'll be best of friends with everyone you meet, but rather that each of them has the chance to teach you something worthwhile. Jenny and Lisa were the exception to the short-term connections, but there wasn't a single person who didn't leave some kind of imprint on my life. Mike reminded me about the spirit of adventure and purposeful travel. Laura taught me to be mindful about my environmental impact as I go. Fay and Yok reinforced that being someone's friend doesn't mean you have to speak the same language, so long as your intentions are authentic and supportive. Zeman demonstrated unconditional trust and inspired an ability to recognize the good in those around me. Chuah Siew Teng brought art to life as he reiterated how important it is to appreciate natural beauty and love. Chase reminded me that, sometimes, listening is all I need to do for someone. Tamara and Robert encouraged me to forge ahead and make my own path, to embrace the unknown and trust myself to turn my dreams into reality. Nanne was the breath of fresh air in an otherwise overwhelming and chaotic destination; she was the living proof of always having a place to belong. Augustine brought an unwavering sense of joy and wonder to my adventures. Henry reminded me that art exists both within the act of creation and the interpretation - neither can be incorrect or misunderstood. Niu was my Rafiki from *The Lion King*, bopping me on the head with her vacuum-sealed snacks to help me realize that, underneath it all, we are human, and that is the only thing that matters when it comes to caring for and loving our neighbors. The storytellers of Leshan illustrated how valuable our stories are, and how important it is that we continue to share them.

I didn't know it then, but I recognize now the kind of spark I had created in the world around me when I decided to take an alternate path. I had unknowingly started traveling through Asia with the same spark for which I had been searching before graduating from Butler University. I met people along my journey who only encouraged that spark to become larger, and to ultimately grow into what is now a flame of passion for adventure and meaningful human connection.

But perhaps what I learned most of all, from everyone that I met along the way, is that the stories we tell of our own lives and of others, are stories that don't have to be extraordinary themselves. It is the people in those stories who make them worth telling. The places we go wouldn't be the same without the people who inhabit them, and you don't have to book an international plane ticket to recognize that gift.

Everywhere we turn there are ordinary people doing extraordinary things, and they may not even know it. To some, the ability to get out of bed in the morning is extraordinary. To others, it's watching someone make their dream a reality. In the eyes of someone else, somewhere around the world, you are doing something every day that puts a smile on their face and makes them say, "Wow." We're all searching for that certain someone to help us change, grow, and learn. And for most of us, we won't need to look very far. But while you're waiting for your Gui Ren to make themselves known, remember to never sell yourself short or doubt your ability to make a positive impact in someone's life. Never underestimate the possibility that you could be someone else's Gui Ren, too.

EPILOGUE

Dear Erin

I thought about writing my own epilogue, one that would tell you in great detail about how I came home from Asia, began working at Life Time Fitness, and started the adventure of writing my first book. I was going to tell you about the relationships I discovered within the boundaries of my own home town, much like those I discovered abroad. It was going to be a testament to how easy it is to find Gui Ren everywhere you go. But then I realized that there was one voice in particular, a voice that was consistent throughout my entire journey in Asia, that hasn't yet been heard.

Columbus, Ohio | June 13, 2019

Dear Erin,

Today marks the two-year anniversary since you left on a journey that changed your life forever. I am happy to say, in hindsight, that the unfortunate situation you were put it might have been the best thing to ever happen to you. It always sucks to see someone you love be hurt in the moment; it sucks to know there is little you can do to help. However, I am so proud that you were able to turn it not only into a life lesson, but also into an adventure that can be used as a foundation to help inspire others. This is one of the many things I love most about you; you are kind, selfless, and have a desire to change the world and help those in need. There are few other people I know who have the desire to grow and evolve as you do, and there are even fewer still who have the power of mind to be able to even think about taking on such an adventure.

I was scared when you left two years ago. I know you couldn't tell, because I tried very hard to hide it, but I was. Having your girlfriend travel alone halfway across the globe can be stressful, even though I know you are tough and have all the know-how. Not to mention, new relationships are hard work, let alone ones that endure such a far distance so soon after it starts. But before you came along, I had never met another person who could take their whole life and go to the other side of the world with such confidence. I could not believe that we had only been dating for two months before you left. As hard as it was to let you go, I knew you would return, and I truly believe that, in the end, we both needed the adventure.

You needed to travel; I will forever love your passion for the unknown, the desire to go to new places and to experience things very few others have. You needed to learn these lessons and grow from the adversities you faced. You needed to meet new people and hear their stories, to help write your own. I needed the practice in trust; I needed to take this time to mature in our relationship and establish a life that involved you, whether halfway around the world or right beside me. I needed to get to know you as the passionate and engaged person you are, without being distracted by the routine of our lives back home. I needed to see you, and watching you travel gave me just that.

This book you are writing (the one that you, the reader, is currently enjoying) is so much more than a retelling of the stories and people you met along your journey. It is a conversation starter, a voice for the voiceless, and a way of taking the struggles you went through and helping those who seek meaningful change in their lives. You have grown both as an individual and a storyteller within these past two years. I was so proud of you during your first event series at a local library, and I am even more proud of how poised, professional, and caring your message has become since.

It's so clear to me, and to anyone that has had the opportunity to hear your message, that you have embodied a life of Gui Ren. This is so much more than just a book; it's a way of perceiving life and the people around you. Everyone has a story, and every story is important. Your subtitle, "The Extraordinary Stories of Ordinary People," says it all. You don't need to travel to Asia to find these life lessons. You don't need to spend three months and a few thousand dollars to get the experiences that you did. All you need is a shift in perspective and an ability to see the extraordinary in what is so mundane or ordinary to the rest of us.

I believe that this book has changed you in more ways than one. First was your ability to resolve conflict. You were put in a tough spot in which you had to reevaluate your place and purpose in life. It's not easy to say, "I'm not happy," and actually do something about it. How many people around the world feel stuck in a dead-end job, a toxic relationship, or simply aren't happy with their lives? I would argue most everyone has been there. But you learned the critical piece of knowledge that you have the power to change. Now, I know it's not easy in any way; sometimes it's hard to even identify that you are in a bad place to begin with. But this trip has shown you both how to identify a negative situation as well as how to move forward even when it's hard.

Second, this has helped you find your voice. After what you went through, and as you have been writing *Gui Ren*, you have celebrated the fact that everyone has a story to tell. Some are deeper than others, some take time to find their meaning, and some will come into your life but won't be understood completely until the time is right. But there is always a story to be told. And you've learned first and foremost how to tell your own, and how to empower others to tell theirs.

Finally, you have become more grounded. I've seen you grow in your message and who you are as a person. Your morals and your beliefs are stronger than ever. Not only have you discovered who you are and who you want to be, but you also have developed a way with words that help others navigate their own inner journeys. They see the impact of Gui Ren, but they also see that you are a haven of support, someone who can be accountable and reliable in life. You have matured in ways you won't fully see until you reflect on this experience in many years. And I can't wait to reminisce with you when you do.

I am truly in awe of the person you have become. I know it didn't end as you had pictured when you left, but I think you made the right choice. It wasn't easy to see you struggle; it wasn't fun knowing there was little to nothing I could do to help. But I knew, after everything was said and done, that you would make a great adventure out of the journey. And what you did deserves to be expressed in so much more than just a blog. Your experiences have created something of meaning and self-empowerment, both lessons we all can learn from.

This has been one heck of an adventure. Not only for you, but for all of your friends, family members, and everyone who has been following along the way. You have shown us all that anything is possible, that time is valuable, and that we should respect our own stories and the stories of others. And most importantly, you have shown us that it is possible to find truly extraordinary stories in some very ordinary places. I love you, Erin.

Love,
Josh L.

Gui Ren

/ Gui Rɛn/

Gui Ren is a written Chinese phrase that encompasses the synchronicity of people entering your life with purposeful timing to help guide you through difficult challenges.

In Deepest Gratitude…

…to each and every individual who has supported my adventures, comforted my losses, celebrated my successes, and contributed to the creation of *Gui Ren*. This book would not have been possible without the enthusiasm of friends and family, and the selfless support from so many.

To my family: my mother CarolLynne, my father David, and my little brother Ryan. Thank you for staying calm when I informed you of my questionable decisions. Your faith in me is truly out of this world, and I hope I didn't cause too many spikes in your blood pressure. To Dagan and Bree for your generosity and kindness in helping to make Shanghai a home. Your mentorship and love made all the difference. To my grandparents, great-grandparent, aunts, uncles, cousins, and relatives by love, for your continued support throughout this journey and for sending Starbucks gift cards my way in times of need. I am truly blessed.

To my friends: Hayley G., I likely would not have ended up in this whole mess without you. So, thank you. Truly. You always know what I need to hear. Gabi R., I'm sorry I never got to try that brownie on the airplane. Thank you for loving my weirdness. Kim R., for your unconditional friendship and all those notes you snuck into my luggage before I left. It meant the world to have pieces of home in a place so far away. Cat T., for reminding me that Gui Ren is never far from home (or work), and that the strongest of people are those who know how to love deeply. Jennifer A., for encouraging my passions and knowing all the right words to say. Dee M., for always being there to talk things through, wrap me in a hug, and remind me what truly matters. Jake Z., for buying the first copy of my book before it was even written (or priced, for that matter). You are good people, my friend, and for that I am grateful. To everyone I met through Life Time (Dub Club and Team Beaston) who graciously supported my work-life balance and provided a family away from my own. You all are awesome and I love you.

To my Patreon subscribers/investors: Judy C., Lauren C., Emma E., Amy I., Joshua L., Renee L., CarolLynne O., David O., Meredith S., Cat T., and Matt T.. Thank you for your continued support and for believing not only in the future of *Gui Ren*, but also for believing in me. This truly would not have been possible without you. *(visit patreon.com/guiren)*

To my editor: Susanne J., for connecting with me and my writing in an unprecedented way. Your perception and understanding of my journey, and the message I aspired to share with others, allowed this piece to reach its full potential. I can't thank you enough for your time, effort, and devotion to making *Gui Ren* all that it is. Plus, your spunk and unapologetic sass made my editing process so unbelievably amusing and memorable. I am so thankful for you.

To my fellow storytellers: members and leaders of the Storytellers of Central Ohio, the Northlands Storytelling Network, and the National Storytelling Network. Thank you for recognizing in me an ability to perform, share, and inspire. But most of all, thank you for providing me the opportunity to learn from and engage with professional tellers from all over the world. Your generosity will be remembered for years to come.

To the ordinary people of *Gui Ren*: thank you for making me a part of your journey, for guiding me when I needed it the most, and for honoring me with your stories. Your influence in my life has been truly profound, and I cannot express enough gratitude for your generosity, unconditional kindness, and patience. Language barrier or not, you positively impacted my perception of the world and helped me to see the underlying qualities that connect us all: vulnerability, empathy, and love. This story would not exist without your meaningful contribution to my life. I am forever grateful.

To the love of my life: if you have would have told me years ago that this would be where my life lead to, I would not have believed it. I would not have believed that it was possible to meet a man so grounded and faithful that I could leave the country for six months only to come home to an even stronger, more secure relationship. I wouldn't have believed that someone could love me the way that you do. You see me for all that I am, and all that I can be. Thank you for being my rock, my greatest supporter, and my emotional stability. This would not have been possible without you and your late-night Kroger runs for the dark chocolate that I needed to keep writing. You get me. I love you.

www.OnMyList.Org
guirenbook@onmylist.org
Instagram: *@_itsonmylist*
Facebook: *www.facebook.com/CollectingStampsInAsia*
YouTube: *Erin O'Neil Productions*

Who is your Gui Ren?
Submit your story on Instagram *@GuiRenBook,*
or on Facebook at *www.Facebook.com/GuiRenBook*

69764117R00209

Made in the USA
Columbia, SC
19 August 2019